LAWYER, JAILER, ALLY, FOE

LAWYER, JAILER, ALLY, FOE

Complicity and Conscience in America's

World War II Concentration Camps

ERIC L. MULLER

THE UNIVERSITY OF NORTH CAROLINA PRESS
CHAPEL HILL

This book was published with the assistance of the H. Eugene and Lillian Lehman Fund of the University of North Carolina Press.

Set in Minion by Copperline Book Services, Inc.

Manufactured in the United States of America

Cover illustration: guard tower © shutterstock.com/Dn Br;
silhouette of man © iStock.com/PhotoEuphoria;
barbed wire © iStock.com/Maravic.

Library of Congress Cataloging-in-Publication Data
Names: Muller, Eric L., author.
Title: Lawyer, jailer, ally, foe : complicity and conscience in
America's World War II concentration camps / Eric L. Muller.
Description: Chapel Hill : The University of North Carolina Press, [2023] |
Includes bibliographical references.
Identifiers: LCCN 2022042584 | ISBN 9781469673974 (cloth ; alkaline paper) |
ISBN 9781469673981 (ebook)
Subjects: LCSH: United States. War Relocation Authority—Officials and employees. |
Government attorneys—United States—History—20th century. | Government
attorneys—Psychology. | Japanese Americans—Forced removal and internment,
1942–1945. | Japanese Americans—Legal status, laws, etc.—History—20th century. |
World War, 1939–1945—Concentration camps—United States. | Role conflict.
Classification: LCC D769.8.A6 M86 2023 |
DDC 940.53/1773089956—dc23/eng/20220920
LC record available at https://lccn.loc.gov/2022042584

for Leslie,
forever

It may seem a paradox, but it is nonetheless the simple truth, to say that . . . the decisive historical events take place among us, the anonymous masses. The most powerful dictators, ministers, and generals are powerless against the simultaneous mass decisions taken individually and almost unconsciously by the population at large. It is characteristic of these decisions that they do not manifest themselves as mass movements or demonstrations. . . . Decisions that influence the course of history arise out of the individual experiences of thousands or millions of individuals.

—Sebastian Haffner, *Defying Hitler*

CONTENTS

ILLUSTRATIONS

The thin old lawyer in the loose-fitting suit and bolo tie inched toward me on the arm of his son. Jerry Housel was in Laramie to receive some sort of recognition from the Wyoming Bar Association or the University of Wyoming; I can't recall which. It was the sort of award that institutions like to confer on their elders, especially their generous ones, for achieving success or for making it into their eighties. In Jerry Housel's case, it was for both.

I was there to interview him about a job he'd briefly held five decades earlier, at the outset of his career.

It was 1997, and I was at the outset of my own career. I had just begun studying the Japanese American concentration camps of World War II, a subject that would become my life's work. My dean mentioned to me that Housel would be coming to town. "Did you know that Housel was the lawyer at the camp up in northwest Wyoming, the Heart Mountain Relocation Center?" I remember him asking me.

And I remember my response: "There were *lawyers* at those camps?"

To my way of thinking at the time, a lawyer at one of these camps was like a rescue squad at an execution. The camps were sites of injustice, stains on American history. The only role for a lawyer was to fight them, not run them.

I knew so little about the camps at that time that I didn't ask many good questions of Jerry Housel during our brief conversation under the watchful eye of his son. I still have my notes, though, and I must have asked him something that surfaced some regret, because he told me he reached a point in the work where he "wanted out," and that was why he joined the navy. "But I probably should've just quit," he said.

Damn right, I thought. *Damn right you should've quit.*

It is now 2022—several books and many articles and two museum exhibits and a podcast later—and I am even surer than I was twenty-five years ago that the camps were sites of injustice, stains on American history.

But should Jerry Housel have quit? Of that I am less certain.

When we think about professionals as perpetrators, our minds tend to go to the extreme cases—the "desk murderers" of Nazi Germany, men who put on

ties each morning and rode trams to Berlin ministries where they planned
the murders of millions. This book is about perpetrators of a less brutal and
extreme injustice: men who put on ties each morning and walked to desks
in the desert to oversee the detention of some 120,000 Japanese Americans
forced by the U.S. Army from their West Coast homes after the Japanese attack at Pearl Harbor.

The lawyers in this book worked for the War Relocation Authority (WRA),
the civilian agency charged with the mission of housing and, in the termi-
nology of the time, "rehabilitating" those prisoners. They neither hatched the
idea for the camps nor set their major policies nor defended their legality in
the courts. Higher-ranking lawyers working for the WRA and the U.S. Justice
Department handled such matters in Washington, D.C. These were lawyers in
the field, working in offices behind the barbed-wire fences.

Their job title was "project attorney." The position placed them in an am-
biguous space. One of their two main functions was to advise their camp's
chief executive, the "project director," and others on his staff. The other was
to run a legal aid office for their camp's prisoners. In a day's work, a project
attorney might just as easily fight to protect a prisoner's farm back in California as advise the camp director on quelling a labor strike. Most days included
tasks of both sorts.

It was a job riddled with uncertainties, conflicts, and possibilities. Although
the lawyers in this book worked at three different camps—Gila River and
Poston in Arizona and Heart Mountain in Wyoming—they all confronted
similar challenges. They arrived knowing nothing about Japanese Americans.
They had no clear idea of what they were supposed to do on the job, because
nothing like the job of a concentration camp lawyer had ever existed before.
They could never be sure who their client was supposed to be—the agency
employing them or the prisoners they were employed to assist. They were
tasked with sifting the prisoners into "loyal" and "disloyal" categories whose
meanings and boundaries were unknown and frankly unknowable. And they
confronted all of this in isolation, with little more supervision from headquarters than could arrive by letter in the U.S. mails.

In the context of their time, these project attorneys were progressives. The
WRA, created in March 1942, was a late addition to the alphabet soup of New
Deal agencies, but it shared some of the liberal outlook of its predecessors.
Most of the WRA's senior leaders transferred to the agency from the Department of Agriculture and the Office of Indian Affairs under their respective
reformist leaders, Claude Wickard and John Collier. The WRA was enlightened in its dealings with Japanese Americans, at least by comparison to other
federal agencies and the state and local governments where the camps were

located. The WRA saw its mission as protecting its charges, helping them weather a challenging time while preparing them eventually to assimilate in a postwar America. Japanese Americans naturally saw the WRA differently from how it saw itself. Their views were generally far less admiring, and with good reason. The WRA was, after all, their jailer. But they would have been unable to point to a government body more interested in their well-being than the WRA.

The lawyers in this book held few illusions about the system of mass racial incarceration they were administering. They were sure that most Japanese Americans posed no security threat to the United States. They had little but contempt for the politicians and military officials who instigated the mass removal of innocent people from their West Coast homes and the military police who patrolled the camps' boundaries. They harbored serious doubts about the constitutionality of confining loyal American citizens without due process.

And yet they picked up their briefcases and went to the office, day in and day out, helping to operate a system of which they disapproved.

Why?

Eighty years later, this might seem an impossible question to answer. These were ordinary men doing mundane things in all-but-forgotten places. They were not prominent in their careers before the war, and none of them achieved anything approaching celebrity afterward. Historians never sat them down for oral histories. No publishers clamored for their memoirs.

Yet it is possible to reconstruct a great deal of what they did and what they thought and felt about what they did. Their boss at WRA headquarters in Washington, a seasoned New Deal lawyer-administrator named Philip M. Glick, required his field attorneys to write him biweekly letters throughout their time on the job. He made clear he didn't want just statistical reports— the numbers of wills drafted and loyalty hearings convened—but full accounts of the broad range of problems the lawyers were confronting. He told them he wanted to learn about "new developments, the more important or significant conferences, significant developments or prospects at the relocation center, and significant news items." He encouraged his lawyers not to treat the letters as "a routine matter, or as a burdensome nuisance," but as a "regular, frequent, two-way avenue of communication" with the home office. He wanted reports that were "clear, interesting, [and] human."

That is what the project attorneys gave him. They canvassed the legal work coming across their desks, including the advice they gave the camp administration and the legal aid work they rendered to the prisoners and their community organizations. But they also shared details about their own lives—their offices, their living quarters, their families, their relationships with the Japanese Americans who worked for them as attorneys and accountants and secretaries. They reported on relations between the camps and the towns and states around them. They shared vignettes of camp life that struck them as funny or poignant. Because they copied each other on every letter, they came to know each other across the hundreds of miles separating them and sometimes laced their letters with playful jabs at each other. Phil Glick told them to be clear, interesting, and human, and that's what they were.

They were also loquacious. Their orders were to write to headquarters biweekly. Some did a better job of keeping up that pace than others. But their output was, by any measure, prodigious. For example, during the nine months in 1942 and 1943 when Jerry Housel served as project attorney at the Heart Mountain Relocation Center in Wyoming, he regaled the home office with 243 single-spaced pages of typed correspondence about his experiences. From his outpost at the Gila River Relocation Center in southern Arizona, James Hendrick Terry pounded out 479 pages over three years. Theodore H. Haas produced 647 single-spaced pages during his roughly fifteen months at the Poston Relocation Center in western Arizona. Add to these letters a smattering of surviving memoranda and notes, and we have an extraordinary trove of the lawyers' own words about their work and themselves.

The project attorneys were also observed by others. Two of the three concentration camps in this book, Poston and Gila River, were research sites for teams of white and Japanese American anthropologists and sociologists. The social scientists were there chiefly to study the imprisoned community, not the WRA staff, but it was inevitable that the researchers would cross paths with the camps' lawyers and record their own, and the prisoners', impressions. Local journalists also wrote about the lawyers from time to time when they made news in the communities surrounding the camps. So the historical record leaves us at least some evidence of how the lawyers were seen, as a supplement to their own voluminous words about themselves.

What the historical record lacks is evidence of the project attorneys from the prisoners who were their "clients" and sometimes their victims. It is difficult to know why. Perhaps the lawyers' work did not touch their lives deeply enough to make an enduring imprint. Perhaps the lawyers encountered Japanese Americans in moments they later preferred not to talk about—divorce, crime, loss. In any event, the historical record offers little basis even to speculate about how Japanese Americans saw the project attorneys.

If this were a book about the camps themselves, the absence of those voices would be fatal. But it isn't about the camps, even though its stories unfold within them. It is about the complicity of the white men who helped them function. The book centers these men's perspectives not because they were reliable narrators of the incarceration experience or of the prisoners' lives but because they were unreliable narrators. Their blind spots and prejudices can help us understand how they were able to continue lending their energies to a system they thought unjust. Perhaps they can also help us see how, in our own lives and systems, we might fall into doing the same.

Early in the life of this project I discussed it with a group of colleagues at my university. One, a distinguished historian, voiced admiration for the topic but reservations about my approach. "You're going to have to walk a very fine line if you don't want to end up humanizing these men," the professor said. I understood where the comment was coming from, but I do not worry about the fine line. These men were human. That is what makes their stories relevant to us. Unjust systems are mostly run not by moral monsters but by ordinary people like us, people with plausible, self-comforting stories to tell about tempering evil.

Jerry Housel did bad. And he did good. That is why I am sure his story matters—and unsure whether he should have quit.

A NOTE ON STYLE, SOURCES, AND TERMINOLOGY

I present three contemporaneous narratives in this volume that begin in the early fall of 1942 and end in the late fall of 1943. All are about the real project attorneys at three of the WRA's ten concentration camps. Book 1 follows the work of Jerry Housel at the Heart Mountain Relocation Center in northwest Wyoming; book 2, the work of Ted Haas at the Poston Relocation Center in far western Arizona; and book 3, the work of Jim Terry at the Gila River Relocation Center south of Phoenix, Arizona. Book 2 also features a Japanese American lawyer, Thomas Masuda, who worked in the Poston Project Attorney's Office with Ted Haas and substituted for him during a lengthy period when Haas was hospitalized.

Why these camps and these lawyers? They represent nicely the broader system of which they were parts. There are camps on American Indian reservation land (Gila River and Poston) and a camp not on such land (Heart Mountain). There is a camp organized under the influence of the Office of Indian Affairs (Poston) and a camp wholly outside that influence (Heart Mountain). There is a lawyer who served from a camp's earliest days to its last (Jim Terry at Gila River) and one who fled without lasting a year (Jerry Housel at Heart Mountain). There are two displaced men in the middle of their careers—a wealthy former New York prosecutor and Wall Street lawyer (Terry) and a liberal Jewish champion of the rights of minorities (Ted Haas)—and a young man with deep ties to his local western community (Housel). There are three markedly different personalities on display—that of a muted technocrat (Housel), an anxious empath (Haas), and an aggressive curmudgeon (Terry). And there is, in Thomas Masuda, a Japanese American prisoner-lawyer trying to negotiate the space between the jailers and the jailed.

If this were a novel, I would take the liberty of creating a character who travels from camp to camp interacting with and connecting these men, involving them in projects and conflicts that would set their differences in sharp relief. Through the thoughts and impressions of such a character we might learn incisive lessons about the nature of complicity.

But in reality there was no such person—or at least none who left behind any written record. This is not surprising, since one defining aspect of the lives of the project attorneys was their isolation, including from one another.

This means that you and I have to be that person.

I have the advantage of having read all the many words these lawyers wrote during their time as project attorneys as well as the words that others wrote about them. I use these words to support the liberties I take within each of the three narratives to animate the things these men did and the decisions they made, liberties I explain more fully in the author's note at the end of the book. I invent dialogue that is as consistent with their voices as I can achieve, as well as little events—an encounter in a hallway, an evening at the movies—to bring more significant real events to life. I do this in service of guiding you through these men's lives during the roughly yearlong period the book presents.

Of course, like any guide, I have my own viewpoint. The historical record is voluminous, and some things were more interesting to me than others. Some things stood out to me as encapsulating the nature of the project attorneys' jobs, the dilemmas they faced, the solutions they crafted. Some aspects of their histories and their temperaments suggested themselves as explanations for what they did and why.

Any guide has a reason, conscious or subconscious, for walking visitors to one wing of a museum but not another, for highlighting one painting in a gallery out of many. That is true here too. I wrote a few paragraphs earlier that one thing that makes these lawyers interesting is that they are unreliable narrators of the history of the camps where they worked. I like to think I may be a bit more reliable than they, given my vantage point, my years of study, and especially the benefit of hindsight. I explain a bit more about the reliability of the narrative and its relationship to its sources in the author's note at the book's end. But I encourage you to read these stories with the same discernment you would bring to a guided tour of a museum. Pay attention to what your guide shows you but wonder, too, about what might be off the tour.

In keeping with its storytelling approach, the book uses the language of its time. For example, the lawyers speak of "evacuation" and refer to Japanese Americans as "evacuees"; the sites of confinement are "relocation centers," "centers," or "projects." Today we recognize all of these words as euphemisms. "Evacuation" was really a mass uprooting and internal exile. "Evacuees" were prisoners. "Relocation centers" were concentration camps (though certainly not Nazi-style ones). When I write in my own voice—here and in the introduction, epilogue, and author's note—I avoid the euphemisms. When the book's characters speak, they use the language of their moment, including upsetting racial epithets. In using these words, I intend no endorsement, and I encourage readers interested in today's accurate language to consult the excellent online resource Densho (densho.org/terminology).

THE WRA AND JAPANESE AMERICA

The stories in this book begin in the fall of 1942, with Japanese Americans already uprooted from their homes and confined in the War Relocation Authority's ten concentration camps. This introduction offers the reader a very brief account of the events that led to that moment.

The War Relocation Authority (WRA) came into being on March 18, 1942, with Milton S. Eisenhower, Dwight's youngest brother, at its helm. Eisenhower was doing important work at the U.S. Department of Agriculture (USDA), but the president thought him the right man to run the WRA. He faced a daunting task: to receive around 110,000 uprooted people of Japanese ancestry from army custody and figure out what to do with them.

He lasted all of three months. On June 18, 1942, he resigned to take a job elsewhere in the federal government. He simply couldn't tolerate the job at the WRA. He was exhausted and beset by worries. He said he lost a year's sleep in those ninety days.

Eisenhower doesn't figure in this book, but I mention his departure because of the shadow it must have cast over the WRA lawyers who are its subject. They were arriving just as the boss was leaving. Eisenhower didn't advertise his misery as an explanation, but the fact of his exit made national news. It's impossible to believe the agency's staff didn't know he was unhappy in his position. As we explore the choices the project attorneys made in their jobs—about how to do them and about whether to stay in them—we should remember that quitting was in the air at the WRA from the very start.

The WRA was an exercise in improvisation.

Before the Japanese attacked the American naval fleet at Pearl Harbor, no government official would have imagined planning for an archipelago of concentration camps for every person of Japanese ancestry along the West Coast. Intelligence agencies had their eyes on a much smaller group: hundreds of

Japanese aliens they thought they had some articulable reason for surveilling and arresting if war broke out. But well over 100,000 Japanese aliens and American citizens of Japanese ancestry lived along the coastal strip between Seattle and San Diego. No government filing cabinet held even remote contingency plans for uprooting and confining them all.

This remained true even after the shock of the December 7 attack in Hawaii. Jitters afflicted blacked-out cities and towns all along the coast, exacerbated by false reports of Japanese planes in the air and true ones of Japanese submarines in the sea. Some employers began firing Japanese employees, but the federal government's response was to try to squelch such hysterical reactions rather than support them. "War threatens all civil rights," Attorney General Francis Biddle declared on December 28, and "if we care about democracy, we must care about it as a reality for others as well as for ourselves" lest we slip into "the whole Gestapo method as a way of handling human beings."

A less civil libertarian air circulated at the Presidio in San Francisco, headquarters of the Western Defense Command, where Lieutenant General John DeWitt presided over the army's efforts to secure the coast. Several times in the month of December he sought authority from the War Department to set up zones from which he might exclude people he deemed dangerous in the event of a Japanese invasion. He drew the line at U.S. citizens, though. On December 26, he dismissed the idea of removing them not just because of the overwhelming logistical difficulty of such an operation but because "an American citizen is, after all, an American citizen."

The landscape began to shift in January 1942. Public fears, however ungrounded, of an imminent Japanese assault on the coast mixed with longstanding anti-Japanese prejudice into a toxic stew. Individuals and organizations began appealing to their representatives and the president to take action against the Japanese living among them. Newspaper columnists amplified these appeals in increasingly strident opinion pieces. And perhaps most influential, white commercial and farming interests along the coast saw an opportunity to capitalize on the hysteria to attain a goal they'd long sought: the elimination of the Japanese as business competitors. Legislators were listening carefully. In the middle of January, Leland Ford, the congressman representing the Santa Monica area in Southern California, sent a letter to the Justice and War Departments demanding that "all Japanese, whether citizens or not, be placed in inland concentration camps." Attorney General Biddle demurred, noting that he knew of no way to intern an American citizen of Japanese ancestry without suspending the writ of habeas corpus. The War Department replied more favorably, though. Removing all people of Japanese ancestry from the coast would "involve many complex considerations," but the army was "prepared to provide internment facilities in the interior to the extent necessary." The idea of mass removal got a further boost at the end of January when an investigative commission headed by Supreme Court associate justice Owen Roberts announced, without documentation, that the Pearl Harbor attack had been aided by Japanese Hawaiian spies.

This pile of pressures pushed Lieutenant General DeWitt into accepting that all people of Japanese ancestry along the coast needed to go, aliens and citizens alike. He formally proposed this in a memorandum to the secretary of war in mid-February. "The Japanese race is an enemy race," he explained, and "while many second and third generation Japanese born on United States soil, possessed of United States citizenship, have become 'Americanized,' the racial strains are undiluted." It followed from this that "along the vital Pacific Coast over 112,000 potential enemies, of Japanese extraction, are at large today." DeWitt was not troubled by the fact that no person of Japanese ancestry had been charged with any wrongdoing. Getting a jump on George Orwell, he argued that "the very fact that no sabotage has taken place to date is a disturbing and confirming indication that such action will be taken."

Justice Department officials had spent the latter part of January and the first days of February fighting to prevent a roundup of citizens, believing such a step unnecessary and unwise. They tussled with their War Department counterparts until the middle of February. But in the end, it was the secretary of war, Henry Stimson, who captured President Roosevelt's ear. On February 19, Roosevelt put his signature to Executive Order 9066. It conferred on Stimson, and by extension DeWitt, the authority to declare military zones along the West Coast "from which any or all persons may be excluded." "Be as reasonable as you can," the president told Stimson as he gave the go-ahead. The executive order didn't specify anything about this group of "any or all persons" who might be uprooted en masse, but it was understood that they would be Japanese persons, not German or Italian.

From that moment on, the Justice Department's role receded. The attorney general was willing to help secure legislation to enforce any orders the army might issue under Executive Order 9066 and to defend the system against court challenges to the removal and detention of citizens that were sure to follow. But the Justice Department wanted no part in administering any system of removal and detention; the War Department had pressed for this system, and the War Department could run it.

Lieutenant General DeWitt and his staff at the Western Defense Command threw themselves into that task right away. On March 2, 1942, DeWitt designated as "military areas" two contiguous wide strips of land from the Canadian border south and east through Washington, Oregon, California, and the southern portion of Arizona and stated vaguely that "such persons or classes of persons as the situation may require" would be excluded from those areas at some unstated moment in the future. He didn't specify who those "persons or classes of persons" might be, but his proclamation elsewhere referenced German aliens, Italian aliens, and people "of Japanese ancestry," so there was little question that the only U.S. citizens for whom the army was hatching plans were the ethnically Japanese ones. He put a finer point on it in a statement to the press the same day. "Eventually," he said, "orders will be issued requiring all Japanese, including those who are American-born, to vacate" the area. But he also dropped a hint: "Those Japanese . . . who move into the interior out of this area now will gain considerable advantage and in all probability will not again be disturbed." In plainer terms: leave now on your own or we will force you out later.

Later came sooner than expected. The Western Defense Command did nothing to prepare the states to the east of the coastal strip for a wave of migrants from the coast—migrants the government deemed too big a security threat to stay where they were. A relatively small number of Japanese families took DeWitt's hint and left, but they encountered hostility, chaos, and even violence. DeWitt realized that voluntary departure was not going to work, so he did a quick about-face and forbade people of Japanese ancestry to do what he had earlier encouraged them to do and leave on their own. Instead, the army would move them out, and to do that, it would have to find or build places to put them.

The plan envisioned two steps: a first forced movement of all 110,000 people of Japanese ancestry from their homes to temporary holding facilities and a second movement from those temporary spaces to . . . somewhere. The first step was an army function, to be carried out by a civilian arm of the Western Defense Command called the Wartime Civil Control Administration (WCCA) that DeWitt created on March 11, 1942. The second step—the one that involved figuring out where those 110,000 people would go next and what they'd do when they got there—was to be executed by another brand-new agency, civilian rather than military, created a week later.

That was the WRA. It was a civilian agency, situated within the Office of Emergency Management in the Executive Office of the President. Its task was enormous, ill-defined, and essentially unprecedented. Director Milton Eisenhower, transitioning over from the land use section of the USDA, hired trusted colleagues to staff the new agency. The assistant to the director, executive officer, director of information, and chiefs of the Community Management, Employment, Agricultural, and Industrial Divisions were all USDA men. So was the WRA's new solicitor, Philip M. Glick, who would become the boss of the project attorneys in the various camps once created. These men brought with them more than just a USDA line on their résumés; they brought their New Deal outlook. These were administrators who believed that problems could be solved through public-private cooperation, voluntarism, and self-government by the administered.

With the task of planning for the relocation of 110,000 people before them, these farm bureaucrats unsurprisingly saw possibilities in farming. The food production needs of a country at war were higher than normal, but its man-power levels were lower. With foreign sources of sugar cut off, the country was going to have to generate its sugar supply at home, mostly through the vast fields of sugar beets across the western states. A potentially record crop lay in the ground without nearly enough hands to harvest it. The Japanese of the West Coast were widely known to be skilled farmers. The opportunity struck Milton Eisenhower and his USDA colleagues as heaven-sent. They began to scratch out plans to relocate Japanese Americans to new, open communities dedicated to agricultural production and, to a lesser extent, manufacture of camouflage netting and other high-demand military equipment. The com-munities would be self-supporting. The residents, not the federal government, would run them.

In early April, Milton Eisenhower took these fledgling plans to a meeting in Salt Lake City with the governors of the western states in which the WRA hoped to establish these communities. What greeted him was not an embrace but a buzz saw. They hated the idea. Why, they asked, if Japanese Americans were dangerous in California, would they be any less dangerous in Idaho or Montana or Wyoming? Why should the mountain states become California's "dumping ground"? The governor of Wyoming predicted that there would be "Japs hanging from every pine tree" if the WRA tried to let them move around his state freely. Grudgingly they agreed to allow land in their states to be considered for these communities, but only if the federal government designed them as "concentration camps" under army patrol and guaranteed that the prisoners would be gone when the war ended.

Here began Milton Eisenhower's misery. He'd walked into the meeting already convinced that one day Americans would come to "regret the un-avoidable injustices" of uprooting people of Japanese ancestry en masse. He walked out of the meeting shaken, seeing "no alternative to the unhappy one of creating evacuation camps where the people could live in modest comfort, do useful work, have schools for their small children, and thus retain as much self-respect as the horrible circumstances permitted." The only relief from this alternative he and solicitor Philip Glick came to see was to conceive of the camps as way stations rather than terminal points. The WRA could try to "Americanize" as many of its captives as were educable (even though the majority of them were already U.S. citizens) and then "relocate" them to new jobs and lives in states off the West Coast. Quickly Glick began sketching out plans for a system of "leaves"—furloughs that would let Japanese Americans spend months laboring in the beet fields or attending college.

"Camps as way stations" made sense to the USDA-dominated leadership of the WRA, but that model clashed with the vision of another federal agency with which the WRA had to cooperate. This was the Office of Indian Affairs (OIA), an agency within the Department of the Interior. One of the first sites chosen for a camp was in far western Arizona, just a stone's throw from the Colorado River and, across the river, California. Its official name was the Colorado River Relocation Center, but people called it Poston after Charles Debrille Poston, the first superintendent of Indian Affairs. The Poston camp was sited on the Colorado River Indian Reservation (over the objections of the reservation's tribal council), and that gave the OIA jurisdiction over the camp. The OIA and the WRA reached an early agreement that the OIA would administer the camp using the WRA's rules and regulations.

At one level it was sensible to turn to the OIA for expertise on administering an enclave housing an ethnic group; the Indian reservation was the closest thing to a model for the WRA's confinement sites in existence. But at this moment in the OIA's history, the two agencies could hardly have worked from more different premises. This was the time of the "Indian New Deal"— a bold reorientation of the agency's posture toward the American Indian tribes that OIA commissioner John Collier had launched in 1933. After decades of suppressing Native languages and cultures, undermining tribal governments, and destroying Native Americans' collective ownership of land and assets, the OIA was now working to restore and support those languages and cultures, bolster tribal governments, and protect collective ownership of land and assets. Where once the agency was forcing assimilation on Native Americans and trying to eliminate their reservations, now the agency was celebrating Native identities and working to assure the longevity of their reservations.

It was inevitable that the OIA would bring its Indian New Deal perspective to Poston. So coadministration at Poston was destined to fail, with one agency, the OIA, envisioning it as a place to build an enduring, self-sustaining, Japanese community and the other, the WRA, conceiving of it as a stopping point on an eastward path to American assimilation. By the end of 1943, the OIA-WRA marriage would prove unsustainable and the OIA would walk away from the project, leaving it entirely in the hands of the WRA.

After the Salt Lake City smackdown from the western governors in

April 1942, Milton Eisenhower had no choice but to abandon plans for open communities and reorient the WRA toward out-and-out confinement. The logistical challenges were staggering. First, the agency had to secure and prepare the land for camps to house well over 100,000 people. They settled on ten camps. Two of them, Manzanar in California's Owens Valley and Poston in Arizona, were already under development as temporary WCCA "reception centers"; these would be transferred to WRA control (and, for Poston, OIA management) by June. The other eight would have to be built from scratch: Tule Lake in far northern California; Rohwer and Jerome near the Mississippi River in Arkansas; Granada (also called Amache) in eastern Colorado; Minidoka in southern Idaho; Central Utah (also called Topaz), about 150 miles southwest of Salt Lake City; Heart Mountain, just east of Yellowstone National Park in northwest Wyoming; and Rivers (also called Gila River), on the Gila River Indian Reservation south of Phoenix, Arizona.

With sites secured, the WRA turned its attention to construction. Squadrons of contractors were called upon to turn millions of board feet of lumber, tons of gravel, and countless spools of barbed wire into thousands of barracks, administrative buildings, mess halls, latrines, laundry buildings, and recreation halls and countless miles of roads and fences across half a dozen states. And that was just to build up the camps' physical footprints; then came the planning for electricity, heat, sewage, food production, K–12 education, internal security and fire protection, recreational facilities and equipment, and dozens and dozens of other needs. Calling these facilities "camps" is in many ways a misnomer; they were really small cities. They required every type of service for daily living as any municipality of comparable size.

That included legal services. This is where the project attorneys entered the picture. Recruited from private practice and other government agencies, they played three distinct roles at the WRA. First, they were responsible for legal advice to the "project directors," the chief WRA officers at each of the camps, and to their staffs. Second, the project attorneys were responsible for advising the camps' community organizations—their governance bodies and their business and recreational enterprises. And third, the lawyers were expected to offer counsel to the Japanese American prisoners on their personal legal problems. "Broadly speaking," said the WRA in its own account of the position of project attorney, "his was the combined role of government lawyer, city attorney, and private attorney to [a population] of from 5,000 to 17,000 persons," depending on the size of the camp. The position description might easily have added "prison administrator" to the list of roles. These were vast, difficult, and at best vaguely defined positions that demanded loyalties to both the jailers and the jailed.

It was in the midst of this frenzy of planning and construction that Milton Eisenhower left the WRA. Replacing him was Dillon S. Myer, a friend and former colleague of Eisenhower's at the USDA. Eisenhower warned Myer to take the job of director only if he was confident he could do it and sleep at night. Later Myer recalled that "the antagonisms on the part of much of the country against Japanese Americans" had proved more than Eisenhower could bear. That would only get worse. Throughout its existence the WRA would be derided for what many saw as a dangerously compassionate stance toward its wards—"too much social theorizing at the expense of a realistic and safe disposal of the evacuees," as the *Los Angeles Times* once put it. Myer, however, was able to take in stride what Eisenhower could not. "I never have been bothered when it comes to carrying on a job that I feel I am responsible for," he later said. "With a very few exceptions," he recalled, "I went to bed at night and slept soundly until time to get up the next morning."

However poorly any WRA official was sleeping in the summer of 1942, Japanese Americans along the West Coast were sleeping worse. The last ordinary day any of them knew was December 6, 1941. Pearl Harbor upended their lives in countless ways.

They were mostly of two generations. The first, or Issei, generation was the immigrant group. They had left Japan in the late nineteenth and early twentieth centuries and settled along the West Coast, many of them directly, some after a stint in the territory of Hawaii. They were mostly laborers, groundskeepers, shopkeepers, housewives, domestics, and farmers. The successes of Issei farmers in the first few decades of the twentieth century are legendary, as are the resentments of the white farmers with whom they competed. They came to harvest a vastly outsized percentage of fruits and vegetables from an undersized fraction of the land of the coastal states—undersized because of racist laws that made it illegal for them to own land. Most of these immigrants intended to remain permanently in the United States, but they could not expect to naturalize as U.S. citizens because the law didn't allow that. Citizenship by naturalization was available only to white people and people of African descent at that time. After 1924, immigration itself became impossible due to the passage of the Asian Exclusion Act.

When members of the Issei generation had children on American soil, those Nisei (second-generation) children were U.S. citizens by birthright. (So were the Sansei, the children of the Nisei, though there were relatively few of them by 1941.) Some parents chose to send their Nisei children to Japan for part of their education, which made them Kibei (in the Japanese vernacular) when they returned to the United States. Naturally, the Kibei were more comfortable with Japanese language and culture than the rest of the Nisei generation, who grew up attending American public schools, speaking English outside (and sometimes inside) the home, and absorbing the popular American culture of the day.

The first blow after Pearl Harbor came to hundreds of Issei men. Before the war, U.S. intelligence agencies had drawn up lists of Japanese aliens they deemed suspicious, and not long after the attack, FBI agents swept through Japanese communities to make arrests. "Suspicion" could arise from nothing shadier than the wholly innocent fact of leadership of a Japanese religious, cultural, or business organization. The Justice Department held these men as "enemy aliens" for periods of weeks or months, sometimes even years, and paroled them back to their families in the WCCA and WRA camps only if they were able to clear their names at cursory hearings. Their absence in the weeks and months after Pearl Harbor forced communities and families to confront all the challenges lying ahead without their usual authority figures and breadwinners in place. Nisei children—especially eldest sons—were thrust into unaccustomed positions of responsibility.

The challenges lying ahead were many. In March of 1942, all people of Japanese ancestry within Lieutenant General DeWitt's military zones were confined to their homes from dusk to dawn except with a permit. By month's end they were required to register with the WCCA—for what reason they did not know—and surrender a variety of items to the police, including cameras, weapons, binoculars, and shortwave radios. Shortly thereafter they began seeing notices requiring them to report for "evacuation" on a certain date, often weeks but sometimes only days away. The WCCA supplied little information about where they would be going or what they would need when they got there, but packing up most of their belongings was not an option because they were permitted only what they could carry. The contents of homes and the stock and equipment of businesses had to be packaged up and stored or else sold—or abandoned. Seeing the Japanese community over a barrel, white bargain hunters swept in and offered pennies on the dollar at hastily convened "evacuation sales" for everything from cars and furniture to dishware and toys. The economic losses were huge.

On their appointed day in the spring of 1942, individuals and families reported to WCCA control stations under the watchful eyes of army sentries. They either drove themselves or were taken by bus, truck, or train to the two "reception centers," Manzanar and Poston, and fifteen temporary "assembly centers" operated by the WCCA in large open spaces such as racetracks and fairgrounds. "Assembly center" was a euphemism for a hastily constructed prison camp, with carefully patrolled fencing all around and observation towers from which armed guards swept the beams of searchlights. Family units and groups of unrelated single individuals lived in cramped spaces for which "spartan" was too kind a word. Living quarters at a couple of the installations included stables that had held racehorses weeks or even just days before. Days were spent either in idleness or in long lines for meals and latrines. Food ranged from passable to inedible. Medical care was rudimentary.

In the late summer and fall of 1942, Japanese Americans were placed on trains and shipped off to the various WRA camps that, if not yet actually occupation ready, were close enough to accept incoming prisoners. That is where the newly hired project attorneys first encountered their charges-cum-clients. To the lawyers, this was all a brand-new experience. But to Japanese Americans, it was just a new chapter in a story of suffering that was already many months old.

BOOK ONE

JERRY HOUSEL
AT HEART MOUNTAIN
IN WYOMING

I find no provision in the memoranda of understanding
between the WRA and the War Department specifying
that a barb wire fence be built around the center. Can
you advise me whether it is necessary?

—Jerry Housel to WRA solicitor Philip M. Glick,

November 17, 1942

CHAPTER ONE

LATE OCTOBER 1942

HEART MOUNTAIN, WYOMING

Jerry Housel thought he'd set the radio quiet enough, but when Mary Elaine mumbled in her sleep in the next room, he jumped up to turn it lower. She was a trooper, putting up with his late nights. The least he could do was not wake her.

KOA out of Denver really carried at this hour. Must be 400 miles as the crow flies from Denver up to the northwest corner of Wyoming, and Fred Waring's show was every bit as crisp as if it were coming from tiny little KPOW right here in town. *Pleasure Time* was what Waring was calling his show these days, and tonight, like every night, he was kicking it off with "Sleep," his signature tune.

Housel turned his weary eyes to the stack of files and his loose-leaf book of War Relocation Authority regulations open on the kitchen table.

Pleasure. Sleep. He'd welcome a bit more of either.

He'd have to settle for another Dr Pepper.

Bottle in hand, Housel returned to his chair and reached for the next file, an insanity case. An evacuee was having some kind of episode the center's infirmary couldn't handle and needed treatment at the state asylum in Evanston. But the hospital was demanding to know who'd be paying the bills, and it wasn't clear if this was a cost the WRA should absorb. Housel's job as project attorney was to figure that out.

A half hour later he had his answer and made a note to include it in his biweekly report to headquarters. Grabbing the Dr Pepper for a celebratory swig, he spotted a ring on the table and quickly reached for one of the coasters they'd gotten as a wedding present from some relative or other. The last thing he needed was for Mary Elaine to wake up in the morning to a permanent mark on their new table.

For the next task on his list, Housel pulled over the regulations. Although the book was thick, it was still a work in progress. New rules seemed to come down weekly. Heart Mountain and the other relocation centers were little cities when you came right down to it, and every day brought a new challenge, an unforeseen hitch. A problem at one of the projects would eventually present itself at all of them. Might as well get out ahead of it with a regulation.

The rules were the work of the legal staff back in Washington. A few months ago, he'd been one of them. From there, the regulations seemed so detailed and comprehensive, like tightly woven mesh. Now, from his kitchen table in Powell, Wyoming, they looked different—gossamer strands across huge gaps. Being a project attorney in the field meant confronting a dozen decisions a day, none of them quite covered by a rule and none of them with a clear right answer. Or a clear wrong one. This rule book could be a foot thick, and it still wouldn't settle things. Every day would bring Housel to unexplored terrain, and he would be on his own to navigate it. The best he could usually do was to find a perch on the nearest rule, look both ways, and jump.

The topics flitted by on the pages under Housel's thumb. Community Activities. Industry. Fire Protection. Education. Internal Security. About two-thirds of the way in, Housel reached the section he needed, Project Employment. Now he slowed down, running a finger across each paragraph. Here it was: "The development of private enterprise other than by the WRA is not permitted within WRA Centers."

Housel's mouth tightened in frustration. Someone in Washington no doubt thought this a model of clarity. But what did it really mean in a specific case? What did it mean for these Montgomery Ward girls at Heart Mountain that he had to figure out what to do with?

They weren't quite sales-counter girls, they weren't quite office girls, and they weren't quite ad girls; they were a mix of all three. Montgomery Ward recruited them to hand around catalogs, answer evacuees' questions, and help them with order forms, especially the older ones who didn't speak much English. The catalog companies were already doing a brisk business in the centers, and it could only help to have some bright young Japanese faces out in the mess halls and the residential blocks talking up the merchandise. For the girls, it meant extra income—a small monthly wage and a slender commission on top.

Was this forbidden "private enterprise"? That was Housel's problem.

It seemed foolish to put these girls out of business. Not only were they showing admirable pluck in a tough situation, but Americanizing the Japanese was one of the WRA's key goals. What better way to help young people learn the ways of American retail than by letting them do it?

But Housel worried that it could come back to haunt him. It was an open secret that little businesses were thriving here and there in barrack apartments. Clearly against the rules. Most were harmless, but not all. Housel had a rival in Kiyoichi Doi, a Nisei lawyer running a law office right under Housel's nose. It irked Housel, the brazenness of it. If he let the Montgomery Ward girls keep selling, would he have a tougher time shutting down Doi?

Housel finished off his Dr Pepper and rose in slow motion so as not to disturb Mary Elaine. Pacing gently around the small kitchen, he turned the question over and over in his mind, and an idea took shape. Maybe it was just a question of definitions. Private *enterprise* in the centers was forbidden. But private *employment* was not. If hawking catalog merchandise was employment rather than enterprise, the girls could carry on.

Housel stopped pacing and allowed himself a little smile. He liked this solution. It was clever. A line he could defend.

Just then, Mary Elaine appeared in the doorway, hair flat and nightgown askew. "Jerry?" she mumbled, squinting into the brightness of the kitchen. "It's one in the morning. That's enough for one day. Come to bed."

He glanced at his watch. She was right. The hour had gotten away from him. "Coming," he said. "I'm at a good stopping point anyway." He switched off the radio, placed his empty Dr Pepper bottle on the counter with the others to return, and turned off the kitchen light.

Mary Elaine was back asleep in an instant, but it took a few minutes for Housel to settle in. Just as he began to drift off, a thought jolted his eyes back open. Subsistence. The Montgomery Ward girls would have to pay room and board to the WRA if what they were doing was private employment. Those were the rules. Twenty dollars a month for their barrack apartment and three meals at the mess hall. That seemed awfully steep—maybe more than the girls were even bringing in.

Housel flipped to his stomach, exasperated. How would the WRA even collect the girls' money? They had no WRA paycheck to deduct it from, which left only one option he could think of: bill the girls, hope they'd pay it, and deny them food in the mess halls if they didn't.

The hands on the night table clock now glowed 1:30. Housel sighed into his pillow. He'd write to Washington in the morning. Let them figure it out.

Jerry Housel turned off Douglas onto Coulter for his drive to the office after a decidedly short night. Coulter was the main drag through Powell, Wyoming, population 1,948. It ran along the tracks of the Chicago, Burlington, and Quincy Railroad, two iron lines slashing through the little rectangular town in the northwest corner of the big rectangular state. The railroad was there first. The town came later, near the end of the first decade of the twentieth century, when the government was trying to lure people to the area to help irrigate the Big Horn Valley. The street grid should have been platted to align with the tracks, but the town's planners did it the hard way, twisting the streets across the tracks at an oblique angle. The one straight street across was, of all things, Bent Street. It was named for some forgotten explorer, but Housel often wondered if the choice reflected an understated western sense of humor.

The twelve-mile drive southwest from Powell to the Heart Mountain Relocation Center took Housel past the Coffee Cup Café and Roulette's Service Station and then through a whole lot of nothing until he got to Ralston, which was really just a post office and a few railroad buildings, and then a few more miles of nothing until the center. Off to the west loomed Heart Mountain itself, an odd, isolated summit of bald stone that resembled a heart only to those with a better imagination than his.

Housel hadn't expected to move back to Wyoming, at least not this early in his career. Just barely thirty, six years out of the University of Wyoming's law school, he imagined he'd eventually make a career in the state, but there were things he wanted to do first. Like so many other young Democrats with law degrees, he'd felt the pull of the New Deal and moved to Washington in 1937 after a brief stint at a Laramie law firm. Things were going well for him as a staff attorney at the Federal Trade Commission when the war came. By early summer of 1942, Housel had shifted to the staff of the new WRA in Washington, under Phil Glick, an old New Deal hand from the Department of Agriculture who was the WRA's solicitor.

Housel had hoped to stay with Glick's team at headquarters, but when the agency set up a regional office in Denver, Housel felt all eyes on him. Who better than he, the man of the West, to staff that office? And who better than he, the man of Wyoming, to handle the legal affairs of the Heart Mountain project from his Denver outpost? It all made sense on paper—unless the paper was a map. The road from Denver to Heart Mountain was 500 desolate miles of arid high desert and twisting mountain passes. Housel soon found himself spending endless days on pointless commutes across these vast open spaces. Before long he wasn't sure which was wearing thinner, the tread on his Firestones or his patience.

Housel came to sense that the arrangement wasn't working for the project director at Heart Mountain either. Chris Rachford took every opportunity to insist the center needed its own project attorney, right there on-site, not least because an evacuee lawyer had set up a legal aid office on the sly and was charging fees in violation of WRA rules. Rachford made Doi out to be the project's Svengali, a smooth-talking Nisei in his early forties, bilingual, who could command respect from young and old alike. One of the very few attorneys among the evacuees, Doi took every chance to regale whoever would listen with stories of trials won and deals brokered over fifteen years in the trenches.

Rachford insisted that someone needed to bring Doi to heel, and he seemed to think Housel was the man to do it. Housel wasn't so sure. Doi was ten years his senior, and he knew his clientele at Heart Mountain better than Housel could ever hope to.

By October, headquarters agreed to Rachford's request and tapped Housel for the job. He understood why; as a Wyomingite and the son-in-law of a local mayor, he knew the law and the players. But he also knew he was still pretty green, and that concerned him. Nothing in his law school education prepared him for managing the legal affairs of a federal agency while also giving advice to a community of 10,000 Japanese Americans. But he was convinced he could do some good up there, maybe smoothing the WRA's relationships with Wyoming officials and making the lives of the evacuees a little easier. And there was a personal plus, too—a happy homecoming for Mary Elaine. He expected some late nights at the office, and it was a comfort to know she'd have her parents and some childhood friends nearby to keep her company. So off they went, and now here he was.

Housel rumbled along the Powell Highway toward the center at a pace not much faster than a horse's trot. It had been snowing off and on for several days—a classic early-season storm—and the wind was relentless. That damned Wyoming wind. When he told people back east where he was from they always asked how he could stand the cold, but anyone from out this way knew the real enemy was the wind. Locals liked to joke about the Wyoming Wind Festival—January 1 through December 31!—and that had it about right. The wind whipped the night's accumulation of powder into shimmering layers that hid the road and left him feeling like he was piloting his car through clouds. If the road wasn't so utterly straight, he might have driven right off into a gully or a drift.

Housel turned off the Powell Highway when he reached Burlington's little depot at Vocation, a cluster of wooden buildings beside the tracks that no one had ever paid much mind until just recently, when thousands of Japanese disembarked there. From the trains they'd walked or been carried in trucks up a little hill to find row upon row of freshly built barracks stretching off to a vanishing point on the wide prairie bench. Heart Mountain, Wyoming: the state's newest city and its third-largest, with more than double the population of Powell and the nearby county seat of Cody combined. "Ten Thousand Is a Lot of Japanese" was how the *Powell Tribune* had put it, and for rural Wyoming it sure was. The project had people on edge. Housel heard it over Sunday dinners in the voice of his father-in-law Ora Bever, the mayor of Powell. He saw it in the eyes of the regulars at the Coffee Cup Café, where he sometimes stopped for breakfast. Nobody knew what to make of the evacuees or of Housel for working with them.

At his office in the administration building he found Phil Barber waiting for him. "Konnichiwa!" Housel said with a wink, clapping the community services director on the shoulder as he rounded his desk. Barber was a fish out of water at Heart Mountain, a New York intellectual and former Yale theater professor who signed up with the WRA when he saw what was happening to Japanese Americans. Now he filled his days helping the community stage plays and organize scouting troops and athletic leagues. Housel liked him. Admired him for pitching in.

Barber grinned at Housel's greeting and responded in kind. "Ohayō gozaimasu!" he said.

"Huh?"

"Ohayō gozaimasu. It's what you say at this hour. 'Good morning.'"

Housel looked at Barber blankly.

"What you said to me was 'hello,' but in the morning they say 'ohayō gozaimasu.'"

Housel tried out the unfamiliar sounds, turning them over a few times on his tongue to Barber's amusement. The lawyer had wanted the evacuees to see he was interested in their culture, so he had signed up for a few Japanese lessons. But he hadn't yet gotten very far—not even past "hello" to "good morning." He had a lot to learn.

Barber wanted to talk about the first big problem to crop up in the WRA's relationship with local officials. The center doubled the county's population pretty much overnight, and with it, the demands on county services—birth certificates, death certificates, marriage licenses. The county wanted reimbursement, but it was already getting it and then some. You didn't need an accounting degree to see the center was bringing Park County a windfall that could be measured in dollars and cents. Cheap labor in the sugar beet fields. Thousands of young mouths for milk from the dairies and, at the other end of life, more corpses for the mortuaries. Big tax dollars on sales in the center's stores and hair salons and shoe repair shops. The local economy was making out handsomely. But Barber said that the county officials seemed blind to the boon; all they wanted to talk about was their outlays. It was a thorny problem that Housel suspected was going to fall to him to solve.

A rap at the office door startled both men. A young woman stepped halfway into the office. Housel sized her up as early twenties, short, professional looking.

"Excuse me, Mr. Housel, do you have a moment? My name is Sadie Tanabe. I saw in the *Sentinel* that your office needs a stenographer?"

Perfect English, Housel noted. He stood up and made sure he had Barber's attention. "O-MAY-o goo-ma-ZAS!" he exclaimed, bowing stiffly.

The young woman cocked her head to listen more carefully.

Housel's confidence drained and he turned to Barber for help.

"I think Mr. Housel means to say ohayō gozaimasu, Miss Tanabe."

Her shoulders slumped. "English works just fine, Mr. Housel. I'm from San Jose."

"Ah," said Housel quietly.

"It's the official language out there, you know," she added.

That was more sass than Housel was expecting. "Yes, of course, Miss Tanabe. My apologies. Just trying to be friendly."

They exchanged a few perfunctory words about the position, but the job interview was over before it started. With an awkward curtsy Sadie Tanabe slipped back out the door.

"High marks for effort, Jerry, but that wasn't quite right," Barber said after her heels clicked away.

The lawyer shrugged. "I was never much for languages."

"It's not your diction, Jerry. She's a Nisei. No need to address her in Japanese. An Issei might appreciate the effort. But with a Nisei it can be more than a little awkward, as you probably noticed. Some of these kids aren't able to say a whole lot more in Japanese than 'pass the salt.'"

"You mean the soy sauce," Housel said with a wink.

Barber looked back flatly.

Touchy, touchy, Housel thought. All he'd done was say "good morning" in Japanese. Or tried to. No good deed, it seemed, went unpunished.

Later that morning Barber invited Housel to walk over to the center's courtroom, where the evacuee-run judicial commission was hearing its first case. "You'll get to see Kiyoichi Doi in action, Jerry," said Barber.

"Doi is on the judicial commission?"

Barber stopped short. "Doi basically *is* the judicial commission! Come on. You'll see what I mean."

The men put on their topcoats for the walk to the courtroom. As they walked, Barber told Housel about the case the commission was trying. Twenty-year-old William Hada was charged with assaulting twenty-one-year-old Seiji Ito and breaking his glasses. "Sad case," said Barber. "Hada's a loner. Mostly stays in his room. The mother's in a mental institution back in California. The father's here but he works all the time and basically never sees his son. Looks like the kid snapped during judo class. He and Ito started fighting there, and they took it outside. Ito ended up on the ground with his glasses in two pieces."

"Judo class?" Housel raised an eyebrow.

"Yes, judo class."

"We are letting these people do Japanese wrestling?"

"That's sumo, Jerry, not judo, but yes, my department has worked with them to organize judo classes for the young people. Keeps them out of trouble."

Housel shook his head. "I'll be damned," he said.

"By the way, they do sumo wrestling here too. Just so you know."

"I'll be damned," Housel repeated. "Are we sure this is wise?"

"Sure *what* is wise, Jerry?"

"Sumo. Judo. Japanese stuff. The papers could have a field day, couldn't they? You know, 'WRA Schools Japs in Martial Arts,' headlines like that?"

"I suppose so. But they have to stay busy, especially the kids. Or we'll be looking at a different kind of trouble."

Housel weighed Barber's words.

"Plus, the regulations allow it. As long as we're not doing it in the schools."

Ah, thought Housel. *It's not against the rules. So be it.*

By now the men had arrived at the barrack building that housed the court-room. Court proceedings were a break in the boredom for the evacuees and tended to draw a crowd. This morning small groups clustered at the windows despite the cold, peering in for a glimpse of the action even though the windows were closed and all that could be heard was what filtered through the gaps between the green wallboards. Barber held the outer door for Housel, and the men paused before entering the interior door to the courtroom.

"There will be no mistaking Kiyoichi Doi, Jerry. He'll be the one talking, I can pretty much guarantee it."

The men quietly entered the courtroom. Housel was startled by what he saw. He'd been expecting a bare room with a few tables pushed together for the commissioners and some chairs for onlookers, but that was way off the mark. The room was impressive—solemn, almost stately. A big American flag, tacked taut to the wall, dominated the space. An attractive bench seating seven commissioners and two alternates had been fashioned from leftover plywood, and an empty witness's chair stood just beside it. Two evacuee sec-retaries worked at a small table directly in front of the bench at its midpoint. Desks for litigants and their representatives stood on either side of the room, and behind them were more little desks for a clerk, another secretary, and the courtroom marshal. Most surprising were the spectator benches, carefully crafted and big enough to accommodate a sizable audience. Housel scanned the crowd and estimated around forty onlookers, all of them comfortably seated with some room in the back to spare.

"Wow, Phil," Housel whispered to Barber. "These are some fancy digs. How'd you pull it off?"

"I didn't pull off anything," said Barber. He nodded toward the Nisei in the front of the room. "*They* pulled it off."

A middle-aged man of just-under-average height, right at the edge of stocky, held the courtroom's attention from his spot at the center of the bench. "Doi?" Housel asked. Barber nodded.

Housel and Barber watched the proceedings from the back of the spectator section for about an hour. The session was chaotic. The trial of William Hada hadn't yet begun because the commission was stuck on procedural points. Hada's representative kept urging the commission to dismiss the assault charge. This was a matter for the Community Welfare Division, not the courts, he argued. Who was going to benefit from convicting his client of assault? These arguments weren't pulling weight with a couple of the commissioners, who insisted that the boy had been caught red-handed and they should dispense with a trial and get on with imposing sentence. After each of these skirmishes, Doi would remind the room that they couldn't take any action at all until they had heard from witnesses. That was what due process demanded, Doi insisted. Housel knew Doi was right, but they weren't asking his opinion and he was new enough that he didn't feel comfortable volunteering it.

Housel felt some sympathy for the Nisei lawyer. It was a challenge to be the only one in the room with a law degree. The room fell silent when Doi spoke and everyone listened carefully, but after he finished, the conversation would quickly spin back into the same confusion. Voices rose and nerves were frayed as the morning grew long. At the first sound of a mess hall lunch bell, Doi gaveled the room into silence and adjourned the hearing until the midafternoon.

Jerry Housel snaked through the milling spectators and extended his hand to Doi across the bench.

"Ah, Mr. Housel, welcome," said the Nisei lawyer before Housel had a chance to introduce himself. "Your fine reputation precedes you."

"You've obviously been talking to people who don't know me very well," said Housel to deflect the compliment, and the men chuckled. Doi gathered the papers in front of him, straightening the stack with two sharp raps on the bench, and Housel continued. "When you have a free moment, Mr. Doi, I'd love to get your perspective on the legal needs of the evacuees."

"I believe those needs are quite well met," clipped Doi.

"Even so . . ." said Housel, trailing off.

Doi broke the silence. "Might I walk you back to your office?" He rounded the bench to Housel's side and ushered him toward the exit with a light hand on the shoulder. The two left the courtroom, donned their coats, and stepped back out into the cold.

Housel wanted to talk about the organization of the Project Attorney's Office, but Doi seemed to want to steer the conversation in a different direction. "Please don't judge me by the mess you just witnessed in our courtroom, Mr. Housel. You know how it can be, trying to talk reason into people who lack our training and experience."

"Do I ever," said Housel.

"Now, if you'd seen me handling the Yamatoda case back in Los Angeles, you would have quite a different impression. What a case that was. Perhaps you've heard of it?"

Housel hadn't heard of it and shook his head.

"Surprising. It made national headlines."

Housel opened his mouth to try to nudge the exchange back to Heart Mountain, but Doi carried on, narrating a sensational story featuring rival gambling gangs in Little Tokyo, an unpaid debt, the murder of the debtor with a sawed-off billiard cue, the disappearance of the corpse, and a kidnapping across the Mexican border. There were complexities over jury instructions, debates about prosecution without a corpus delicti, convictions and acquittals, reversals on appeal, and retrials. Housel couldn't quite figure out what Doi's role in the cases had been, or even whom he'd represented. Perhaps he wasn't meant to.

"But let me get to my point, Mr. Housel. There are several divorces ongoing here in camp."

Housel knew this, because other project attorneys had been circulating memos about whether the courts of the states where the centers stood had the power to dissolve California marriages. Housel had already looked into the question under Wyoming law and concluded that a judge in Cody could grant a divorce to Heart Mountain evacuees that would stick back in California.

"Yes, I'm aware of those," Housel said.

"I wanted to speak to you about representing the parties to these divorces here in the Wyoming courts."

"I wish I could do that, Mr. Doi, but I can't. WRA rules don't allow it. Most I can do is put people in touch with capable attorneys in Powell and Cody, fellows I know and trust."

"No, no, Mr. Housel, you're misunderstanding me. What I'd like is your advice on what *I* need to do in order to appear in the local courts."

"Y-*you*?" stammered Housel.

"I am licensed to practice in both California and Utah. Surely there is some provision in Wyoming law that allows for the appearance of out-of-state attorneys."

Housel walked along in silence for a few moments, trying to picture Kiyoichi Doi in a Cody courtroom, thinking about his father-in-law, about the regulars at the Coffee Cup Café, about the judges who had undoubtedly never even met a Japanese American let alone seen one stand up and speak in a courtroom. "That won't be possible, Mr. Doi, I'm sorry to say. WRA policy requires evacuees to get representation from lawyers who are licensed to practice in the local jurisdiction." He didn't say "Caucasian lawyers," but he didn't need to.

They hadn't yet reached the administration building, but Doi thrust out his hand. "It was a pleasure, Mr. Housel. I am sure your office and my office will have occasion to be in touch about matters from time to time. I look forward to it."

Startled, Housel shook Doi's outstretched hand. "Uh, yes. Why, yes, of course."

Doi wheeled and began tracing his footsteps in the snow back toward the courthouse. Housel watched him walk off, unsettled. It wasn't until he reached the administration building that Doi's words sank all the way in.

"His" office? Did Doi actually believe he was in charge of the legal aid office here?

That would have to change. There would be only one law office at Heart Mountain, and it most certainly would not be Kiyoichi Doi's.

CHAPTER TWO

NOVEMBER 1942

HEART MOUNTAIN, WYOMING

The last time Jerry Housel lunched at the Irma Hotel had been in October, on a visit to Heart Mountain while he was still stationed at the WRA's regional office in Denver. He'd had a tough time getting a seat in the dining room then. Some electricians and linemen were lingering in town to put finishing touches on the center, long after the summertime frenzy of construction had ended and most of the workers had pocketed their last paychecks and headed home. Between the tradesmen and the season's last wave of Yellowstone tourists grabbing a fancy meal in Cody before heading up to the park, the place had been packed. Now, in November, it was a different story. A few men were eating lunch at the bar, or maybe drinking it, and a ladies' group was holding some sort of event at two big round tables in the corner. Other than that, the place was empty. Housel chose a table facing the bar and asked the waitress for a Coke while he waited for his guest to arrive.

The Irma always made Housel smile. Buffalo Bill had been dead for twenty-five years, but his spirit haunted the hotel he'd opened in 1902 and named for his daughter. Like Bill himself, the hotel and its dining room lived in a space between reality and fantasy, just genuine enough not to put off the locals but just Hollywood enough to let tourists feel they were on the set of a Western. The thin, dark bentwood chairs were the sort you'd expect to see a gunslinger spin around and straddle. Light from frosted fixtures reflected dully off the squares of the patterned tin ceiling. Waitresses stacked dishes and cloth napkins on the massive, ornate cherrywood backbar, a gift from Queen Victoria to thank Bill for bringing his *Wild West* show to London. Nearly matching trophy elk heads stared each other down from either edge of the bar's huge central mirror. Western landscapes by minor artists dotted the walls, along with a couple of portraits of Buffalo Bill himself. Housel's eye was always drawn to the centerpiece of the room, a huge turn-of-the-century painting of an enraged, arrow-riddled bison dominating the broken body of his Indian hunter. The artist, Henry Cross, titled the painting *The Victor*. Housel liked the irony in the name. Out here the bison proved no more victorious than the Indian when all was said and done.

Gop Goppert called out a hello to Housel as he strode into the dining room, and the young WRA lawyer jumped up to greet him. Just shy of fifty years old, Goppert—officially Ernest, but everyone called him Gop—was a Cody old-timer. Shorter and squatter than Housel, Goppert had a round face perched atop a vest and bolo tie. He was the dean of the local bar, with decades of experience and a hand in just about every aspect of legal and civic life. Housel was going to need the cooperation of Gop Goppert and the rest of the ruling class if the Heart Mountain project was going to have a shot at an amicable relationship with its neighbors. It helped that Housel's father-in-law was the mayor of Powell, the smaller town just north of the center. But Cody, the bigger town just to its south, was the county seat and the heart of local power. It was Gop Goppert's town, and that was why Housel had invited him to lunch.

Goppert asked Housel how he was settling in up at the "Jap camp." Housel still clenched up a little inside at that phrase, even after hearing it for weeks on end. Back at WRA headquarters in Washington, the young lawyer had learned to be careful about the words the agency used to describe its facilities. But out here pretty much everyone called it the "Jap camp," and Housel was learning that it didn't mean exactly the same thing coming out of every mouth. Nobody meant it as a term of honor, of course, but not everyone meant it viciously. Goppert, for example, was showing himself to be more reasonable about things, accepting the necessity of the center and offering to help out where he could, such as letting Housel use his law library for legal research and offering to give presentations to evacuee community groups. Sometimes Housel made a point of correcting the term "Jap camp," but with Goppert, he let it slide.

Housel filled Goppert in on some of the details: the partition he'd had installed to create some private office space, the help he was getting from a few evacuees with accounting and business experience, the intricacies of some of the evacuees' legal problems. Housel told Goppert about an elderly man who'd died without a will or any known heirs but with some valuable items tucked away in his barrack. What to do with them was anyone's guess. The lawyers batted around a few ideas for how to handle the problem until Goppert seemed to get bored and launched into a story about a Japanese acrobat who'd been part of Buffalo Bill's entourage. Goppert had been on the board of the Buffalo Bill Memorial Association since 1928 and knew his trivia about as well as anybody in town.

Housel hadn't come to the Irma with specific agenda items in mind; it was more of a social and diplomatic mission. But he did need help with one problem. The issue was divorces, he explained between bites of burger. Every week it seemed there were two or three couples ready to throw in the towel. "It's not surprising, given what these people have been through," Housel said. "I'm not sure how my marriage would fare if Mary Elaine and I were cooped up in one of these barracks. But anyway, we've got to deal with these situations, and some of them are pretty urgent."

Housel told Goppert about one difficult case where a husband had brutally beaten his wife and then left the center to work in the sugar beet fields in Montana for a while. It was rumored he'd be back soon, and the wife wanted to get moving on the divorce before he returned. In another situation, a husband and wife worked out a property settlement, but the husband was walking around camp bragging to his friends about how he was going to withdraw all of the money from their bank account so that his wife couldn't get her hands on it. "Gop," Housel said, "you know we need to be able to move fast in a case like that—get a restraining order against the husband and keep him from touching those funds."

"Sure, Jerry, I get it, but what's the problem? Go get the order. The courts are open."

Housel explained that he wasn't allowed to personally represent any of the evacuees in court, file divorce papers for them, that sort of thing. WRA regulations forbade it. "We need help from the local bar, Gop. We need lawyers to step up and handle these cases."

Goppert still didn't see where the problem lay. Cody and Powell were small towns with small-town lawyers who handled divorce cases as a matter of course. Sure, some of the less enlightened ones might not be eager to take on a "Jap" as a client, but as long as the client was paying in greenbacks rather than yen, Goppert supposed they'd hold their noses and take the work.

"Oh, they'll take the work. For one hundred and fifty bucks a pop."

Goppert's eyes widened. "Holy smokes, that's highway robbery. I never ask more than seventy-five dollars for an uncontested divorce."

"And you're the cream of the crop, counselor; I'm told the riffraff charge just fifty." Housel smiled and winked.

The waitress swept their plates away and told them about the Irma's apple pie, which the men declined.

"I'll talk to some people, Jerry. I'll see what I can do."

"Thanks, Gop. I really appreciate it."

Their conversation then turned to politics. Lester Hunt, a Democrat, had just turned the Republican incumbent Nels Smith out of the governor's office down in Cheyenne, and everyone was curious to see the differences the change would bring. Housel told Goppert he'd already taken the long drive to Cheyenne a couple of times on Heart Mountain business and was running into some deep suspicions among lawmakers about the center. "They seem happy to let the evacuees harvest sugar beets," Housel explained, "but beyond that, nothing. Keep them locked up and move them out as soon as possible—that's the attitude."

"And get a load of this, Gop," Housel said, shifting forward in his chair. "I tried to talk to Carl Sackett about a bunch of things—travel passes for evacuees, some criminal cases, those sorts of things." Carl Sackett was the U.S. attorney for the District of Wyoming, the top federal law enforcement official in the state and a Wyoming legend. Everyone had heard Sackett brag of being born before the Battle of the Little Big Horn and fighting Indians and hunting buffalo and growing up on a dirt floor in a trapper's cabin. "The old bird didn't want to talk about anything except his ranch. It was the ranch, the ranch, the ranch—he needs hands, and with the war on he's having trouble finding anyone reliable. He made clear that things would go better for us up here at the center if we could see our way clear to getting a few young able-bodied Japanese out and down to his ranch to work."

Goppert shrugged. "So? If they can head north to the beet fields, they can just as easily head south to Sackett's ranch."

"But he won't say what he'll pay them, Gop. We've asked him a couple of times. Won't quote a figure. The only thing he'll say is we won't get to other center business until we settle the ranch issue."

Sackett was trying to drive a bargain, and it had Housel riled up.

Goppert sighed, leaned back, and dropped his shoulders. "What are you doing?" he asked, a note of fatherly concern in his voice.

"Hmm?" The question caught Housel off guard. "Doing . . . about what?"

"I mean, what are you doing with all this, Jerry?" He threw a hand vaguely in the direction of Heart Mountain. "This Japanese business?"

"Well, I suppose I'm . . . doing my part, Gop. Toward the war. Aren't we all doing what we can for the war?"

Goppert's eyes bored into Housel's like searchlights. "Is this really what you want?"

Housel was silent.

"You're a young man. You've got talent. You're smarter than most of us here in town put together, and you know it. You've been doing everything right, working for the Arnold firm down in Laramie, your fancy government jobs in Washington. Now you're back and you've got a bright future. Is this really what you want? To be going toe-to-toe with the U.S. attorney over a few nickels for some Japanese ranch hands?"

Housel wanted to respond but found no words. It was a good question.

By the time Housel finished lunch and returned to his car, the morning's snow had ended. The sky was blue over Cedar Mountain to the west and the clouds were slipping eastward over town and toward the striped McCullough Peaks low on the eastern horizon. It had been a pretty big dump, close to a foot, Housel guessed as he brushed away the couple of inches that had settled on his windshield while he was lunching with Goppert. The snow was a little heavier than usual, he noticed, a little wetter than what was normal for December in this part of Wyoming. Traffic had already started to compact the snow on Sheridan Avenue through town, and once he got out of town on the Powell Highway up toward the center, he was able to keep his tires in the tracks laid down by other drivers, so it was a quick trip back to the office.

Snow was a fact of life for anyone from this part of the world, mostly an annoyance except when it made it a little easier to spot a pheasant or a rabbit through the sight of your Winchester. But for the evacuees at Heart Mountain it sometimes seemed nothing short of miraculous. Housel, who'd grown up knee-deep in the stuff, enjoyed the chance to see it anew through the eyes of Californians. Most of these people were from Southern California, Los Angeles and thereabouts, where the only frozen water they were likely to encounter was in a glass of soda pop. The kids went nuts when it snowed, running up and down the streets of their blocks and throwing themselves into drifts. Housel noticed that even the old folks, the Issei, allowed themselves smiles at a fresh blanket in the morning so long as it wasn't deep enough to make it hard to get around. As Housel crested the rise up to where the administration building stood, he spotted a swarm of small figures on the hill out by guard tower 5. It looked like the kids had managed to fashion something like sleds for themselves and were sliding downward toward a ravine.

Good, Housel thought. *Let them have a little fun.* Juvenile delinquency cases were starting to cross his desk from time to time. Too many youngsters in too close a space with too little to do: it was a recipe for mischief. Let them sled and have their snowball fights. It'll keep them out of trouble.

The parking spaces at the administration area looked to be full, so Housel took a right and parked by the hospital complex. As he walked past the fire station, he heard laughter coming from around the corner. Poking his head around out of curiosity, he found himself face-to-face with Adolf Hitler—an enormous bust of Hitler, that is, made entirely out of snow. Young people were heaving snowballs at it and hooting and hollering. A Nisei woman who looked to be in her twenties explained that the evacuee firefighters had spent the morning piling up the snow and shaping it into a bust of the Führer, complete with ears and shoulders.

Housel laughed. It was an amazing likeness. Big chunks of coal sat in the hollows of eye sockets and smaller ones marked his two nostrils. Just below them, a piece of sandpaper, probably left over from the construction of the barracks, formed the famous rectangle of his moustache. Hunks of tar paper topped this snow Führer's pate, jutting across the forehead just like the real Führer's Brylcreem comb-over. The young woman bounced away, grabbed the end of a dangling rope, and began making a big show of tugging downward. Housel's eye followed the rope to something he'd not noticed at first, a makeshift gallows made of a wooden pole and sticks. The other end of the rope circled Hitler's neck. "Heave ho! Heave ho!" the little crowd shouted as snowballs started flying again.

This is what people on the outside need to see and hear, Housel thought as he walked along to his office in the administration building. Sledding, snowball fights, young people laughing and playing—in English. Patriotism. Support for the war effort.

Nobody made those young people build that frozen Führer and hang him in snowy effigy. That came from them.

"Mr. Doi is in your office waiting for you, Mr. Housel."

Housel's mood, brightened by the shenanigans in the snow, now darkened. This was not on his schedule and not what he wanted. He had yet to have a single interaction with the Nisei attorney that he enjoyed. And it was getting harder, not easier. Doi was feeling his oats these days, having just been elected chair of the Heart Mountain Charter Commission, the evacuee body that would draft a plan for self-government. And this was on top of the position he already held as chair of the judicial commission. The man had a knack for getting out ahead among the evacuees.

Housel thanked his secretary and walked into his office. Kiyoichi Doi sat in a chair by Housel's desk reading the *Heart Mountain Sentinel*, the evacuee newspaper. As Housel walked around his desk to sit down, he had the impression that Doi repositioned himself so that the front page was staring Housel in the face.

"Have you seen today's *Sentinel*, Mr. Housel?" asked Doi, continuing to make as if he were reading.

Housel allowed that he hadn't, but he could plainly see the bold headline: "Protest Petition Sent to WRA Director."

The fence. That's why Doi was here.

Things had taken a turn for the worse at Heart Mountain in the last few days because of this blasted inner fence. From the very start a fence had run around the remote perimeter of the huge tract of land the WRA managed. Closer in, nearer the residential area, guard towers marked a line the evacuees weren't supposed to cross from dusk to dawn. It was a line—not a fence. But last week the army had surprised everyone—evacuees and WRA staff alike—by announcing a plan to plant posts along that line and string them with barbed wire. In some spots the fence was to stand within yards of the residential blocks.

The fence was proving a real irritant. The evacuees had been living there for several months without incident, playing by the rules. Not a soul had strayed outside the center's boundaries. No one had left without a pass. Now they simply couldn't understand what a fence could be for, other than to insult them. And Housel tended to agree. The army seemed incapable of anything but mistrust. They broke their own rules, patrolling the inner boundary in broad daylight when they were only supposed to be there at night. Housel had alerted Phil Glick in Washington, but the solicitor wasn't inclined to press the matter.

Kiyoichi Doi shook the newspaper in front of Housel. "Three thousand of us signed a petition to Mr. Myer in Washington," he said. "We're going straight to the top, straight to the director."

"That's certainly the community's right, Mr. Doi, I imagine Director Myer—"

Doi interrupted. "May I read you a few words from the article?"

Housel told the Nisei lawyer that he understood the situation well and would make a point of reading the paper later that afternoon.

"Just a few words, Mr. Housel." Doi turned to the front page and swiveled in his chair to face him. "We, the undersigned residents of Heart Mountain, comprised of American citizens of Japanese ancestry, and Japanese nationals, individually and jointly as a group, hereby respectfully represent in the above-entitled subject matter as follows, to wit"—he paused to make sure Housel was paying attention—"that a barbed wire fence is now being erected to surround the entire said camp above mentioned; and that the watch towers now situated about the camp are unnecessary and conducive to ill-feeling since the residents here are not prisoners of war; and—"

Housel cut in. "I'll read it carefully later, Mr. Doi."

Doi cleared his throat and continued. "That said fence and guard towers are devoid of all humanitarian principles, understanding, and principles of democracy; and that if the WRA sanctions and approves such erection of fence and maintenance of towers, it seems that our status will become similar to that of prisoners of war in a concentration camp; and that the citizens have cooperated in every respect with the asserted good intentions of the WRA, in the assumption that, wherever duties and obligations are required of one, there also exists one's rights and privileges; and—"

"Mr. Doi . . ."

"—that the said fence and the towers are ridiculous in every respect, an insult to any free human being, a barrier to a full understanding between the administration and the residents."

Housel found himself wondering whether perhaps Doi himself had drafted the petition. Given his prominence, it would stand to reason.

"Now therefore, we the undersigned, request that you, as the director of the WRA, exert every effort to eliminate the said barbed wire fence enclosure and the watch towers."

"That is a powerful statement, Mr. Doi, and a credit to the eloquent men who drafted it, whoever they are."

Doi flushed and smiled. "Three thousand signatories, Mr. Housel."

"Yes, Mr. Doi."

"That's more than half of the residents of this camp who have attained the age of majority, Mr. Housel."

"Yes, Mr. Doi."

The Nisei lawyer paused, waiting for more of a response. Housel just returned his gaze, so he pressed on. "What are you prepared to do about this, Mr. Housel? You are an attorney. You are a student of the Constitution and of the common law. Would you not agree that this fence presents prima facie evidence of the tort of false imprisonment?"

Housel breathed in deeply, trying not to let on what he thought of Doi's grandiloquence. The community evidently admired Doi, but Housel had a hard time seeing just why.

"Mr. Doi, you know that I share the community's concern about the fence."

"Do you?"

"Certainly. There's already a fence out around the boundary of our land. One fence is plenty."

"It's not just that this is a second fence, Mr. Housel, it's that this is a second fence right up in our faces, right along where we all live. You can imagine how this makes the community feel."

"I believe I can, Mr. Doi, but you know better than I."

"It makes them feel they are prisoners of war."

"Well, they may feel that way, but that doesn't make it so. You're an attorney, Mr. Doi; you know that the evacuees do not have war prisoner status under the Geneva Convention."

Doi paused and seemed to recalibrate. "It makes us feel like prisoners. Like internees. Like detainees. You choose the word."

"But you're none of those things. You are not prisoners. You are not internees." Hyperbole irritated Jerry Housel, and that's what this was. The evacuees' situation was certainly not enviable, but no good would come from exaggerating. "You are *evacuees*, Mr. Doi. Evacuees."

"We have none of our rights as citizens here, do we?"

"I suppose you could look at it that way, but you could also look at it like this: you're getting *more* from your government than other citizens." Housel swept his arm toward the window. "Three times more. You're getting food. You're getting housing. You're getting medical care. Uncle Sam is supplying other citizens with none of those things."

Something passed over Doi. His brow tightened and his chin jerked. "But they have their freedom, Mr. Housel. We have severe limitations."

Housel's voice rose. "Of course there are limitations. All kinds of limitations, imposed on all of us. Because of the war."

The men fell silent. Housel stewed in annoyance, as much at himself for letting the conversation go so far off the rails as at Doi for pushing it there. "So," he said after an uncomfortable moment. "Where were we?"

"The fence."

Right, the fence. "Look, I can assure you that if it was up to me the damn thing would not be going up."

"But it *is* up to you, Mr. Housel, isn't it? It certainly isn't up to any of us. We can draft petitions, write letters to the *Sentinel*, that sort of thing. Make noise. But you're the project attorney here. You've got clout. Isn't it your job to offer legal advice to the project director?"

"Well, that's *part* of my job, Mr. Doi." He knew he should stop there but couldn't resist a jab. "When I'm not busy helping members of your community with their problems, legal and otherwise." He paused. "Without charge."

Doi sat still, impassive.

"But this fence situation is out of my hands. It's out of the WRA's hands. This is not a WRA fence, Mr. Doi. It's an army fence. I've gone carefully through the regulations and the WRA's memoranda of understanding with the army—believe me, I've looked carefully—and I've found no prohibition of an army fence along this particular boundary."

"Have you found an *authorization* for an army fence along this particular boundary, Mr. Housel?"

Doi could also jab.

"I would not expect to see an authorization for such a thing in a memorandum of understanding. The army has general policing duties, so that permission would be assumed unless it were specifically negated."

Doi rose from his chair and took a step toward the door. "Mr. Housel, you may be right that this is an army fence and not a WRA fence. Perhaps that is visible from the outside. From inside, it looks the same either way. And the barbs are just as sharp."

Housel promised to look back through the regulations and agreements for a loophole in the morning. After Doi left, Housel spent a few moments looking out his window. Although it was only half past three, the early December shadows fell long across the snow. Details of the forest and snowfields on Heart Mountain were already hard to make out; soon the mountain would appear only in silhouette. Smoke curled from countless mess hall chimneys receding toward the horizon. The evening meal was not far off. Housel wondered what Mary Elaine had on for them for dinner at home.

Housel got to the office early the next morning and plunged back into the fence issue, scouring the regulations for language that might help. The situation was getting more serious. A handful of evacuees had signed up to build the fence, but the military policeman at the gate this morning told him they were now refusing to work, leaving the army stranded. Housel could see the suspicion in the MP's eyes and could only imagine that his superiors were more than just suspicious. These army guys could find treason in a bowl of rice.

He felt the evacuees deserved more freedom to move about the center, but it wasn't really up to him. It was up to Chris Rachford. He didn't want to keep spinning his wheels with the documents if the project director didn't want to fight the fence, so he closed the binder of regulations, returned it to its spot on the bookshelf between an IRS manual and the Wyoming criminal code, and walked across the hall to poke his head in Rachford's door.

"Do you have a minute, Chris? It's about this fence situation."

"Sure, come on in." Rachford gestured toward a chair. "Yeah, things are really heating up out there."

"Yeah, I figured our friends at the MP station wouldn't be pleased if the workers didn't show up to set the posts."

Rachford shook his head. "That's not what I'm talking about. I mean the sleds."

Housel cocked his head slightly, perplexed. "The sleds?"

"The sleds. Didn't you hear? Yesterday afternoon? Out on that hill the kids have been sledding on?"

An image of little figures on the snow out by guard tower 5 flashed across his mind: those kids he'd seen on his way back from lunch with Gop Goppert.

"Yeah, I saw some kids out there yesterday, Chris. Looked like they were having a grand old time. What happened?"

"They *were* having a grand old time, Jerry—until the MPs pulled up in trucks. Seems they told the kids they were out of bounds and lucky not to be getting shot at."

"No way," said Housel.

"Yes indeed. They put the kids in the trucks and drove them all the way around to the army station out by the front entrance. Must have put the fear of God into them. The parents were summoned and treated to a harangue about keeping their kids clear of where the fence is going in."

So that's what this was really about, Housel realized: Not the sleds. The fence.

"I guess they really mean business, Chris."

"So it would appear."

They sat in silence for a few moments. Housel thought about whether to press Rachford on the issue. He decided against it.

"If they want their fence, OK, let 'em have their fence," said Rachford. "But jeez, the bastards didn't even give the kids their sleds back."

CHAPTER THREE

FEBRUARY 1943

HEART MOUNTAIN, WYOMING

The finger whistle pierced Jerry Housel's swirling thoughts like a dart. In his rearview mirror, he glimpsed a military police officer at the gate, his looped thumb and finger still in his mouth. Housel pounded the brake and the car slid to a stop. *Did I drive through the gate?* he asked himself. He had no recollection of doing it. Yet here he was, outside the gate.

The soldier was now walking toward the car. Housel rolled down his window and frigid air blasted in. "Mr. Housel, you need to stop and show your ID," the young soldier said.

"Yes, yes, of course, I'm so sorry. I don't know how this happened."

"We know who you are, sir, but we still need you to come to a stop and show your identification, give us a chance to eyeball the car. Those are the rules."

Yes, the rules. The project attorney knew the rules; he had just been lost in thought.

"It's not you, sir; we know you're OK, but there's no telling whether one of the Japs might be hitching a ride with you in the back seat. Without your knowing it, under a blanket, or suchlike."

Housel checked the urge to roll his eyes. These army kids. It was always "the Japs" with them. He couldn't really blame them; this is what they heard from their commanders, and they had no basis to think differently. They spent all their time outside the fence, never chatting or working with the evacuees the way the WRA staff on the inside did. Still, the idea of an evacuee staging a great escape under a blanket in the project attorney's back seat was farfetched. "I think that's a pretty unlikely scenario, Private, but I take your point. Like I said, I'm very sorry. I know I'm supposed to stop. Guess I was off somewhere in my mind and just blew past you without realizing it."

The soldier's gloved hand came through the window, puzzling Housel until he realized it was for his ID card. The exercise seemed pointless, but maybe that was the point. Housel dug out his ID and passed it to the soldier, who made a show of scrutinizing it before handing it back. "Thank you, Mr. Housel. Have a nice evening."

Housel rolled his car out to the Powell Highway and turned northward toward Powell and home. It was just a little thing, but he felt stricken by blowing past the gate. Was this kind of thing happening more frequently? He supposed it was.

The first month of 1943 had not been easy for him. He'd always liked New Year's, the spirit of a fresh start, but this year had felt different, with a tense, jangly energy in the administration building. The Poston Relocation Center in Arizona had been paralyzed by a strike just before Thanksgiving, and Housel had read the internal reports about it with a sense of alarm. That one had ended quietly—nobody injured—but not two weeks later a full-blown riot crippled Manzanar. Housel's gut had gone sour reading the reports from his counterpart there. They'd had to call in the army. A couple of poor Nisei kids had been killed and some others wounded. Housel couldn't help wondering how he'd handle a situation at Heart Mountain if trouble broke out. Riot control had not been in the law school curriculum at the University of Wyoming.

Heart Mountain was tranquil by comparison to Poston and Manzanar, but Housel worried it was a false tranquility, like the calm surface of a Yellowstone geyser pool before an eruption. A week didn't go by without rumblings of a work stoppage in one department or another—the mess hall workers, the motor pool, the firefighters. The Issei were angry that WRA policy barred them from office in the center's government. Some were turning their anger on their own kids for daring to try to lead the community, calling the Nisei government the "baby council." Factions were tearing at each other over who should run the community enterprises—the stores, canteens, barbershops, shoe repair shops, and beauty salons. A lot of money was at stake; the enterprises had turned a profit of $50,000 in the latter half of 1942 alone. There was the Kagetsu faction and the Nakanishi faction and neither could stand to be in the same room with the other, let alone trust the other to manage the community's money.

The sign marking Ralston's little train depot slipped by and Housel realized he'd made it halfway to Powell without even noticing his surroundings. *Stay focused*, he thought. *The road's icy. Don't want to end up in a ditch.* But within moments, his mind was back on the center. These twelve- and fourteen-hour days were longer than any he'd put in back in Washington at the Federal Trade Commission. And he'd been single then; now he had Mary Elaine waiting for him at home—and waiting and waiting. He felt guilty walking in the door most nights, to say nothing of when he had to go to the office on weekends.

He saw a sign indicating two miles to Powell and groaned. He'd done it again—driven most of the way to Powell when they didn't live there anymore. They'd moved to Cody in mid-January. Housel was on automatic, driving his old commute. Third time in two weeks. With a sigh he pulled into a ranch access road over the rumble of the cattle grate to turn around south, past the center, to his new home in Cody.

"Home" was now a hotel, the Green Gables Inn, just a block or two past the Irma Hotel on Cody's main drag. Their stay in Powell had come to an abrupt end in mid-January when Mary Elaine's brother decided Billings wasn't for him and asked for his house back. They'd cast about for a rental home in Powell, found nothing, turned their sights to Cody, found nothing. A room at the Green Gables in Cody was their only option. The inn was nice enough, clean and neat, but their room was small, and the bathroom was down the hall. It was much less space than they'd had at the house in Powell, and a lot less private. Hardly the setup that a newlywed couple dreams about.

And then there was the fact of trying to live an ordinary life in a hotel set up as a John Ford Western. The menu in the Green Gables' little dining room left no doubt who it was for—the crowds from the coasts who kept the inn's "no vacancy" sign swinging in the breeze all summer. If ya had a hankerin' fer "range stew" with "trimmin's" and "fancy doin's" like "deep sop" or "fly catcher," why, pardner, the Green Gables was where ya should hitch up yer hoss! It was all very shoot-'em-up and Buffalo Bill, and Housel didn't doubt it tickled the city folk passing through to the geysers and the bison. But a couple of weeks into their residency at the Green Gables, he was starting to find it tedious. At the end of a tough day like today, the whole chuckwagon gimmick was just exactly the wrong thing for his mood. Like a sidewinder in yer hen skins after a long day of driving the dogies, one might say.

After his roundabout commute, Housel parked and rushed straight into the dining room. He found Mary Elaine alone at a table, reading a book. She looked up at him, pointed to her watch, and shook her head.

Housel wasn't one to gripe, but he unloaded a little on Phil Barber at the office the next day. Mary Elaine had been snippy with him as he left the inn that morning, and the road out of Cody was an icy mess, so when Barber asked how he was doing, the truth slipped out rather than the usual platitudes: He was tired of living out of suitcases. He was tired of being cooped up in one room and having to don a robe just to get a glass of water. He missed Mary Elaine's home cooking. He missed his privacy. And they couldn't stay at the Green Gables indefinitely, so they were going to have to go through the rigmarole of another move.

"There's another option, you know." The community services director poured himself some coffee and tipped an empty cup toward Housel, who declined. "You could live here on the project, like a lot of us do."

"Here, at the center? With Mary Elaine? In the staff apartments?" Housel flushed slightly.

"No, Jerry, in a guard tower." The New Yorker's quip reddened Housel's cheeks a bit more. "Yes, of course in the staff apartments! Where else? It's not the Ritz-Carlton, but it's surprisingly livable."

This would never work. The mayor's daughter? Living with the Japanese here on the project?

"Well, I can certainly see how it works well for you, being here by yourself and all . . ."

"I'm here as a bachelor but a lot of guys are here with their wives. Some even have kids, Jerry. They make it work."

"But those people aren't locals, Phil. We are. Isn't it better for me to be out in the community, keeping my ear to the ground? Hearing what the ladies tell Mary Elaine in the grocery aisles?"

Barber nodded.

"I'll think on it," he fibbed, as he stepped out of Barber's office and into his own.

A secretary had left a copy of the center's newspaper, the *Heart Mountain Sentinel*, on his desk. It was remarkably professional for a paper put out by evacuees—spiffy logo; columns as straight as schoolhouse rulers; big, well-composed photos with concise captions; careful typesetting. At a glance you might mistake it for any small-town newspaper. But it wasn't just the look that you noticed; it was the content. Each week the paper impressed Housel with its reliable reporting, careful editing, and mature editorial voice. Apparently, there was grousing from some evacuees that the paper was in the hands of "JACL types," who were supposedly too close to the administration and who pulled their punches. That's not how Housel saw the Japanese American Citizens League, though, and anyway, could anyone really expect the WRA to sponsor a forum for troublemakers?

Today's headline was huge: "Plans Mapped for Registration." The story deserved the big typeface. This registration program promised to be a big step forward for the WRA and the evacuees both. Back in February 1942, when the president signed the executive order that got this whole thing started, the army insisted that you couldn't tell a loyal Japanese from a disloyal one. The WRA had never bought into that theory, but the army was driving the policy at that point. Now, a year later, the army had come around to the WRA's way of thinking: you *could* tell a loyal from a disloyal Japanese. Housel had to chuckle at the army's about-face, but they had their reasons. They were setting up a Nisei combat unit to deploy in Europe, something the JACL had been pushing for. It struck Housel as a very good idea: What could prove the patriotism of these people better than military service? But the army couldn't just go handing a rifle to any Nisei who happened to volunteer. They needed a way to sift out the ones you couldn't trust. Hence, registration.

It wasn't often the WRA saw eye to eye with the army, but here it did. Back in Washington the decision had been made—well above Housel's head—to push for "all-out relocation" from the centers. The agency didn't want the evacuees getting comfortable in their barracks and settling in for the duration. It wanted them out of the centers, spread across the country from the Rockies to the East Coast and the Great Lakes to the Gulf of Mexico. But how could the WRA expect communities to welcome Japanese Americans if it couldn't guarantee that they were safe? Hence, registration.

Housel knew the WRA had another reason to make a show of weeding out the loyal from the disloyal. The agency was under public attack. The strike at Poston and the upheaval at Manzanar had made national headlines. You couldn't open a paper back in early December without seeing some flaming story about mayhem caused by mobs of "pro-Axis Japs." Some went so far as to label it a celebration of the anniversary of Pearl Harbor, which was ludicrous. Congress was riled up, and they blamed the WRA. Senators couldn't get to the floor fast enough to accuse the agency of coddling the evacuees with plush accommodations and gourmet meals. Some wanted to abolish the agency and turn the centers over to the army, and Housel knew as well as anyone that the army wouldn't support the evacuees with community governments, schools, and social services like the WRA did. The truth was stark: for its own survival, the agency needed to show it was sifting the good from the bad.

The *Sentinel* article said little about how this "registration" process was supposed to work, and Housel didn't know much more than was in the paper. All headquarters had told the project attorneys was that army teams would be spreading out with questionnaires for every evacuee over sixteen to fill out. It had the makings of a mess, and would be a lot for the community to absorb. Housel worried it might give the troublemakers a chance to gin everyone up, which would be a shame, because he could see that separating the sheep from the goats was in the community's best interests, whether they realized it or not.

Housel set down the newspaper to plunge into the stack of files on his desk. First up was a sticky situation with the construction of the center's high school. He'd negotiated a deal with a contractor for an hourly rate of $1.12½, but now the Labor Department was saying this kind of work deserved a buck twenty-five. Housel had to figure out who was on the hook for the extra twelve and a half cents. Then he turned to a question about whether the Community Services Division could sponsor Japanese language classes, which Phil Barber thought a fine idea but which made Housel nervous. By midmorning he was working his way through a bunch of files of evacuees who needed help applying for California unemployment insurance when someone rapped loudly on his office door.

"Come in!" he said cheerfully.

Phil Barber leaned in slightly, holding the doorframe. "Looks like we have a meeting."

Housel thought he'd cleared out the whole morning for desk work. "We do?"

"Yup."

"Is it about the Japanese language classes? Because I think I've got an answer for you on that."

"Nope. It's Mr. Doi."

The lawyer felt his shoulders tense. *Way to ruin a morning*, he thought. "Is it about the legal aid thing?" They were in the final stages of their plan to shut down Doi's legal work for evacuees, and Housel knew he wouldn't go down without a fight.

"It seems to be about furniture," Barber replied. "At least on the face of it."

"Furniture?" Housel looked up to the heavens.

"Easy, Jerry. I know Doi gets under your skin. Give him a chance."

"OK, Phil. Give me a minute to collect my thoughts. Your office?"

"No, the meeting room. It's not just Doi. He's brought the judicial commission with him."

He was really not going down without a fight. Housel sighed and nodded weakly. "OK, the meeting room. I'll be there in five."

Housel was two months into his plan to contain and neutralize Kiyoichi Doi—two months of moves and countermoves that would impress a chess grandmaster. At the outset Doi seemed as ubiquitous to Housel as horse pucky in a corral—head of the committee drafting the community's constitution, head of the judicial commission, head of the legal aid office that had been providing services to evacuees since they arrived in August. Under WRA rules, legal aid services were for the Project Attorney's Office, and they were to be provided gratis, not for the fees Doi was rumored to be charging on top of the WRA paycheck of nineteen dollars a month he collected for running Legal Aid. So Doi's Legal Aid Office would have to be shut down and its cases transferred to Housel's office.

Housel's next move was to rule that no evacuee could hold elective office while also working in a WRA administrative office. There was exactly one person holding both kinds of positions: Doi. Housel was giving him a choice: he could be a politician or a lawyer. Not both. He couldn't imagine Doi giving up his community leadership roles. Surely he'd give up Legal Aid so that he wouldn't lose those.

But Housel had underestimated him. Within days of the announcement, representatives of the residential block managers and the temporary community council—an Issei and a Nisei—dropped by the administration building. They'd heard that an evacuee couldn't hold elective office while also getting a WRA paycheck as an administrative employee, and they thought the rule unfortunate. Negotiations over the community constitution were in a delicate spot, they said, and it would be a terrible shame if a disruptive move by the administration blew up the process. It felt to Housel like a bit of a threat, but there was pressure from Washington to get these community constitutions ratified. So Housel backed down. Score one for Kiyoichi Doi.

Housel's next move was to transfer the staff of the Legal Aid Office to his own. Several stenographers, secretaries, and legal assistants were to leave the courthouse—Doi's domain—and migrate over to the administration building. He was careful to make a show of inviting Doi to join them—working beneath him, of course, which he knew Doi wouldn't do. Score one for Jerry Housel.

A few weeks later, Housel launched his final maneuver. He sent movers to the courthouse to pack up all the office equipment. Desks, chairs, typewriters—even the wall calendar came over to the administration building. Housel dropped by the Legal Aid office at the end of moving day to find a sad-looking room with only a few pencils and notepads strewn across dust-covered floorboards.

This was check, but Housel wanted check*mate*, so he wrote to headquarters for permission to shut down even pro bono work if he discovered Doi doing any. WRA regulations forbade "private enterprise" by evacuees, and Housel hoped Phil Glick in Washington would confirm that working for free would fit that description.

But now this sudden meeting suggested Doi wasn't quite ready to resign the match. Housel dawdled in his office for as long as he felt he could after Phil Barber left. Keeping people waiting was a good way to show who was in charge, and the longer he could postpone the inevitable, the better. Eventually he summoned his strength and strode down the hall to the meeting room. As he entered, several of the commissioners in Doi's entourage rose to half-standing, but Doi stayed square in his seat. Phil Barber gestured to an empty chair at his side for Housel.

After an awkward silence, Housel forced the corners of his mouth into what might pass for a smile and tossed out a comment about the cold weather. Doi gazed at Housel but said nothing. The room again fell silent.

Phil Barber stepped in to get the conversation going. "Jerry, the commissioners have some concerns about their office space in the courthouse."

Doi finally spoke. "How, sir, do you expect the judicial commission to deal with the important business of this center without chairs, desks, or typewriters?"

Seeking out the eyes of all the commissioners, and not just Doi's, Housel pointed out that the furniture in the courtroom itself remained untouched. "We have nothing but respect for the work of the judicial commission. You all know that furniture is in high demand. Our goal in redistributing some desks and chairs was not to undermine what you gentlemen do. Not at all. It was just to shift resources to where they're most needed. With Legal Aid closing, and its business moving over to my office, there simply was no reason to keep all of that furniture in the space that Legal Aid used to occupy. That's all there was to it."

"And where is the judicial commission supposed to do paperwork when we are not in session in the courtroom, Mr. Housel?" Doi kept his gaze fixed on the project attorney. "Am I to do my dictation on the witness stand?"

Barber cut in. "Now Mr. Doi, you know there's a small office space next to the courtroom with a desk. We're happy to keep a secretary on the WRA payroll there to support the work of the commission."

"A full-time secretary, Mr. Barber?"

Housel saw where this was going. Doi had been using the Legal Aid space to see his own paying clients and was looking for a way to keep his business going now that the space was bare. Housel had to admit, the man could negotiate.

"A *part-time* secretary, Mr. Doi," Barber replied. "For when the commission is hearing cases."

Housel jumped in. "You know as well as I do that much of the time the commission has no cases to hear. There's no point in paying a secretary who has no work to do, is there?"

"We beg to differ. Cases take time to prepare. Subpoenas for witnesses must be typed. Evidence must be cataloged. Transcripts must be proofread." Doi paused. "Perhaps if you had more trial experience, Mr. Housel, you might perceive the need more clearly."

Several of the commissioners shifted in their chairs.

Barber again stepped in to defuse the tension. "I imagine we could authorize a few additional hours per week, Mr. Doi, for those sorts of tasks. On an as-needed basis."

The Nisei lawyer stood and squared his shoulders. "Mr. Barber, Mr. Housel, my fellow commissioners and I are resigning, effective immediately. We will notify the community that the work of the judicial commission is suspended until new commissioners are selected."

Housel wondered if this was news to the commissioners, who glanced at one another but remained seated.

Doi looked to his left and his right at the commissioners. "Gentlemen?" As one, they rose to join their chairman.

This was a move Jerry Housel had not anticipated. The resignation of the entire judicial commission would be a huge setback for the community. It could even spark the kind of flame that had already scorched Poston and Manzanar. He glanced at Phil Barber, whose face showed the anxiety Housel felt.

Housel extended his palms to soothe the air in front of him. "Gentlemen, gentlemen, please. Take your seats. Let's keep talking. I'm sure we can work something out."

Doi eyed his colleagues, and after a beat they eased back into their chairs. They waited for Housel to make an offer.

Housel cleared his throat. "Perhaps we can make some upgrades to the courtroom, gentlemen—some curtains for the windows, maybe a stand for the stenographer." Looking directly at Doi, he added, "And a gavel for the chair."

Several of the commissioners eased back in the chairs and smiled. "That would be most welcome, Mr. Housel," said one. "A real improvement."

"And?" said Doi.

"And . . . and . . . and I'm sure we can find a way to get some secretarial support at the courthouse at least three days a week when the commission isn't in session."

Doi smiled and nodded. "Yes," he said. "Yes. I believe that would be most appropriate." He turned to his colleagues. "Do you agree that this shows a proper respect for the important work of the Heart Mountain Judicial Commission?" The men nodded in unison.

Housel waited for a thank-you, but it was not forthcoming. His stomach went acid. Had he just been played? Had he given up too much? But Phil Barber was smiling, and he took it as a signal that he'd done the right thing.

"Well," said Doi. "The weather has really been quite something, hasn't it? Mr. Housel, are the winters always like this?"

"This has been a pretty bad one so far, Mr. Doi."

The chitchat continued for a few minutes until Barber rose to usher the group out. When they were gone, he turned to Housel and thanked him for being flexible.

"I don't know, Phil. One man's 'flexible' is another man's 'weak.' I think we may come to regret this. We shall see." He clapped Barber lightly on the arm and stepped out into the hallway. For several long moments he brooded outside the door. The Legal Aid Office was gone, but Kiyoichi Doi was probably still in business.

When he returned to his desk, the mail was waiting for him. Among the letters was an envelope bearing the return address of WRA headquarters—a reply from Phil Glick to one of Housel's recent weekly updates. He opened it first.

WAR RELOCATION AUTHORITY

WASHINGTON

Office of the Solicitor

February 16, 1943

Dear Jerry:

This will reply to your report of February 4, 1943.

I continue to follow the Kiyoichi Doi story with interest. You inquired about whether pro bono services by an evacuee attorney would constitute an impermissible private enterprise.

Mr. Doi is not violating any WRA regulations if he is not charging any fees for the services he is offering. I don't think we should prohibit him from giving legal advice to residents of the Center so long as he is not charging fees.

However, we can do a number of things to discourage him. First, we can do everything we can to educate the evacuees to come to the Project Attorney's Office when they want legal advice rather than to Doi. Secondly, I don't see why we have to make facilities available to him. If no office space were available to him, he would have to conduct his practice from his living quarters, which would make it much more inconvenient for him. Also, we can refuse to assign a stenographer to him to handle his work. The girl working for him can be assigned to other work; and if she refuses to do other work, make it clear to her that she is not working for WRA so long as she is working for Doi and will receive no salary.

Of course, as I am sure you realize, it is desirable to handle this as tactfully as possible. The office space and the stenographer's assistance can be taken away from Doi with the explanation that this is being done not because we wish to inconvenience Doi but because it is against WRA policy to assign office space or give other assistance to professional people who do wish to conduct a practice on their own without charging fees, since to do so would

be to imply official sanction which WRA feels it should not give
in view of the fact that these people, in conducting their practice,
will not be responsible to WRA.

   I am sorry to hear that your living arrangements have been upset
just as you and Mary Elaine must have been getting nicely settled.
I hope you will not have too much trouble after your month or so at
the Green Gables Inn is up.

Sincerely,

Philip M. Glick

Solicitor

Housel rocked back in his chair, kicking his feet up onto his desk and locking his fingers behind his head. Maybe his campaign against Doi was not yet over. He pictured the Nisei lawyer trying to counsel his clients in the cramped space of his barrack apartment, with its makeshift closets and thin walls. A smile spread on Housel's face. Headquarters had his back. That might prove helpful.

That evening, Housel was spared having to grub up on the vittles at the Green Gables. Mary Elaine caught a ride up to the center from Cody with a couple of other WRA wives and joined her husband for a quick dinner in the staff mess hall. After dinner they jumped in their car to head up through Powell and over to Lovell in Big Horn County, a beet-growing town of 2,000. They were there for a basketball game.

This wasn't just any game; it was a charity match pitting the Heart Mountain All-Stars against the Lovell Westwood Indians, with proceeds going to the March of Dimes. It was hard to overstate what this little game meant, the first time a Heart Mountain sports team was heading out of camp to play a team "on the outside." Center officials had been trying to line up a match in a neighboring town for months but couldn't find an opponent. Finally, Lovell came through with an offer for this charity game.

Housel wasn't surprised Lovell had reached out the first friendly hand. The little Mormon town had opened itself up to the evacuees from early on, hiring scores of workers to bring in the beet crop back in the late summer and fall. Housel had helped negotiate some of those farm labor contracts and had watched it dawn on the people of Lovell that the evacuees were, for the most part, regular people, people like anyone else. He wished Cody and Powell would figure this out too.

The teams were on the hardwood in the Lovell High School gymnasium when Jerry and Mary Elaine Housel took their bleacher seats in the visitors' section. It had the makings of a lopsided game, with the Heart Mountain boys on the losing side. The Lovell community team was a regional power-house, two-time winner of the annual church tournament in Salt Lake City and nearly undefeated in the current season, its only loss a close game in the season opener against Billings. Lovell had every advantage over the hastily assembled Heart Mountain team: height, practice, and experience. Ham Hamasaki had done all he could with his handpicked crew, but they had never played as a team before and were coming into the game with just a week of practice on the dirt-and-ice court in block 7. During practices the coach had sent his boys inside every twenty minutes to avoid frostbite and numb fingers. But what they lacked in experience they made up for in enthusiasm. Housel saw a couple of players out there, Wally Funabiki and Babe Nomura, who looked like they could do some damage.

With a capacity crowd in the gym, the March of Dimes stood to do well on ticket sales. But the fan turnout was as lopsided as the likely final score. The home bleachers didn't have an empty seat, and lots of Lovell supporters spilled over into the visitors' section as well. The Heart Mountain group occupied just a couple of rows—a contingent of Caucasian schoolteachers and a handful of Housel's fellow administrators. They were doing their best to make noise for the camp squad. Phil Barber was attempting a call-and-response cheer, shouting "Heart!" and then cupping his ears to encourage a big "Mountain!" from the others. The group seemed to be getting the hang of it, and the boys out on the floor smiled and waved when they noticed it.

From the tip-off it was clear the Heart Mountain All-Stars' spirit would be no match for Lovell's smooth execution. The home team's fast-breaking offense seemed to put four points on the board for every two posted by Heart Mountain. Tasuka Yamada brought Housel to his feet with a couple of nice layups early in the game, but the Lovell squad answered both in duplicate. Late in the first half, Tosh Shiozaki stripped the ball from a Lovell player near midcourt and rifled a pass to Yamada, who faked a shot and then flipped it back to Wally Funabiki for a heroic swish from twenty feet out. Housel whooped so loudly that heads turned, and Mary Elaine shushed him in embarrassment. But he wasn't about to quiet down. How sweet it would be if their scrappy little band of evacuees pulled off an upset! What a shot in the arm it would give to the whole community back in the center.

At halftime, Housel went to get Cokes for himself and Mary Elaine. Near the refreshment stand he bumped into Frank Brown, Lovell's mayor. He thanked the mayor for inviting the Heart Mountain squad up to Lovell to play. "You probably don't even realize how important a signal this game is sending across Wyoming," he said, "or how grateful the evacuees are for the opportunity."

"Least I could do, Jerry," the mayor responded. "Your folks saved our hides last fall at harvest time. Most of our beet crop would've rotted away in the ground if hadn't been for Heart Mountain, what with so many workers off in the service. Good labor they are. Quick and careful. And not ones to gripe."

The men chatted about the highlights of the first half for a while. The mayor playfully offered the project attorney a bet on the outcome—something he winkingly said a good Mormon shouldn't do—but Housel didn't like his chances and didn't bite. Brown then turned the conversation in a more serious direction.

"I wanted to give you a heads-up about something coming your way, Jerry. I bumped into Oliver Steadman last week over in Powell." Steadman was the elected county attorney for Park County. "He's on the warpath about how much your camp is costing him."

"Yes, I know. He's requested a meeting with the governor about it, and I'm heading down to Cheyenne for it tomorrow."

"The way he sees it, nobody wanted the Japanese here in the first place. Nobody asked for this camp. You guys just came in and plopped it down. Literally doubled the population of the county overnight. And now your people are needing divorces and death certificates and marriage licenses, committing crimes, putting big demands on the court and the county jail, and it's all one big free ride. Steadman said he's not about to bankroll the federal government for their project—your project—and that if the WRA wants county services he's going to see to it that you pay for them."

"What a load of nonsense, Frank! Park County is making money hand over fist on the backs of the evacuees. I pulled together some calculations. Do you realize how much we're putting into the local economy every month? *Forty thousand dollars.* That's a conservative estimate. Sales tax, purchases from local businesses, license fees, you name it. Park County isn't suffering for having the center here. Not one bit."

"I know it, Jerry, believe me. Like I said, your people kept us afloat last fall at harvesttime. You don't need to convince me."

"I need to convince Steadman is what I need," Housel replied. An idea raised his eyebrows. "You know what would be helpful? If you said something to him—told him how you see things. How we're putting in way more than we're taking out. I haven't been able to make any headway with him. He says I spent too long in Washington, that I've lost my Wyoming common sense."

The Lovell mayor shook his head. "I'll be happy to put in a word, Jerry, but I don't think it'll do anything. Remember, when you came out here today you crossed the county line. Oliver Steadman has no more reason to listen to me than to Gary Cooper."

Housel gave a grim nod and looked at the floor.

"Now, you know who he might pay attention to?" A waggish grin lit Brown's face. "A mayor of a town in *Park* County. You wouldn't happen to know anyone like that, would you?" He scanned toward the bleachers where Mary Elaine was chatting with the women in front of her.

Housel knew Brown was only being playful, but the reference to his father-in-law stung a little. Managing family relations had proven to be one of the trickier aspects of being Heart Mountain's project attorney. There were certainly benefits to being Ora Bever's son-in-law; some people returned his calls a little quicker than they otherwise might. But the center was a delicate subject around the Sunday dinner table, one Housel preferred to avoid. He knew they didn't see eye-to-eye about it, but he was never sure how much of his father-in-law's bluster about "the Japs" to believe—how much was real, and how much he just brought home from the office with him.

"I believe I know someone who fits that general description, yes," Housel replied, giving Brown a mock punch in the arm. "I'll give that some thought." In truth he suspected he wouldn't.

The second half of the game played out like the first. The WRA contingent in the stands shouted their throats raw every time one of the Heart Mountain boys got a basket, but there just weren't enough to keep pace. The Lovell Westward Indians ended the game with forty-six points to the Heart Mountain All-Stars' twenty-two. But the score was secondary; what mattered was that the game had taken place at all. Both sides played clean and the final handshakes at center court were warm. On the spot, the mayor of the tiny neighboring hamlet of Byron issued an invitation to the All-Stars to play his town's Independents in another benefit game a few nights later, which Coach Hamasaki gratefully accepted.

A light snow was falling as Jerry and Mary Elaine Housel left Lovell High School for the drive back to the Green Gables. Housel would have to take it slowly. They talked about the spirit and skills of the Heart Mountain players and chuckled over Phil Barber's cheerleading efforts. As they passed through

Powell, Mary Elaine wondered aloud whether she could convince her father to invite the Heart Mountain team as Lovell and Byron had done.

"Really?" said Housel, shooting her a quick sideways glance. "Are you joking, or are you serious?"

"I'm being serious, Jerry." She sounded a bit insulted.

"These days he's sounding a pretty different tune, honey. You hear him just like I do. There's all this talk in town about keeping out the Japanese, barring them from shops. They want us to cut way back on the number of day passes we issue. Your father's not doing anything to tamp any of that down so far as I've heard."

Mary Elaine gazed out the passenger window at the snow sweeping by.

"In fact, honey, what I'm hearing is that he's actually stirring that talk *up*. That he's talking to the mayor of Cody about a joint resolution of the two towns calling on us to stop issuing passes altogether."

She turned to her husband. "You're not being fair. You know Daddy doesn't believe each and every word he says about the center, about the evacuees. You know he's smarter than that, and more worldly."

Now it was Housel's turn to watch the snow sweep by.

"It's his *job*, Jerry. He's the mayor. He can't go running around speaking his mind to every person he meets in line at the feed store. He's not free to just say what he thinks about every single thing that comes along."

They drove a ways in silence.

"If anyone should understand that it should be you."

The comment stung. "You're right, honey. I'm sorry." Housel reached across and patted her arm. "I do understand. Very well."

A man with a purpose and a bit of luck could do the drive from Cody to Cheyenne in a day, but Jerry Housel split it in two. Four hundred thirty miles on two-lane roads was a long way even under sunny summer skies, but every segment of the trip to the capital in the winter was a gamble. Sure, you could get a tire fixed in Greybull and gas in Thermopolis, and probably even a sandwich in Chugwater, but between those little dots on the map was nothing. A badly timed blizzard could do a man in and had been known to do so. Casper, with its 18,000 residents, was the metropolis at the midpoint, so that's where Housel spent the night.

The distance and the icy roads notwithstanding, Jerry Housel was glad to be getting away from the center for a few days. An army team had arrived at Heart Mountain to launch the registration program a couple of days before, and he could already tell things were not going quite as smoothly as the folks in Washington expected. Big groups of evacuees were gathering in mess halls. Petitions were said to be circulating. The project director had tried to short-circuit problems, issuing a statement that the registration was "not a matter to be decided by a majority rule in block meetings." Housel doubted it would have much impact. The other side of the state seemed like a good place to be for a while.

Housel headed straight to the capitol building upon arriving in Cheyenne, just in time for his early-afternoon meeting. Around the table in a richly paneled conference room were Governor Lester Hunt, just over a month in office after edging out the incumbent Nels Smith in the 1942 election; U.S. attorney Carl Sackett; state auditor Scotty Jack; and Park County attorney Oliver Steadman, who had requested the meeting. *Not a friendly crowd*, thought Housel as he took his seat.

Steadman spoke first, ticking off a list of services that the county and the state were providing to the evacuees at Heart Mountain—criminal courts, probate courts, jail cells, beds in the state's insane asylum—all, he argued, a terrible drain on the county and the state. If the federal government thought Park County was such a great spot for a relocation center, then it should have to foot the bill.

Housel stifled a grin. *Right into my trap!* With a flourish he reached into his briefcase and pulled out the tally he'd mentioned to Lovell's mayor at the basketball game. He had a copy for each man around the table. It showed that the center's community stores and services were sending around $1,100 in sales tax to the state treasury each month. The WRA was buying at least $10,000 in goods and services each month. The evacuees themselves were spending at least $1,000 per month in Park County shops and businesses. And this was all on top of the $2 million the army had pumped into the local economy when it built the center in the first place.

The governor put on his reading glasses. After a minute he looked up at Steadman. "These numbers put your concerns about jail cells and probating wills in a little bit of a different light now, don't they?"

Steadman looked flustered. He ran his index finger slowly over each line of the statement, mumbling that some of the estimates seemed high.

"Would you concede, Mr. Steadman, that you are focusing more on the money you see going out than on what's actually coming in?"

Well put, Mr. Governor, thought Housel, his grin now breaking through a little.

"Perhaps," grunted Steadman.

"I don't see a problem here, gentlemen, at least not one that needs solving right now. Mr. Steadman, why don't you keep a tally of what the county is spending over the next few months, and Mr. Housel, I'd appreciate your updating the numbers on this very helpful accounting as well. If you can't work things out by the end of the fiscal year I'll certainly be happy to get involved, but I hope that won't prove necessary." The governor rose, handing the accounting back to Housel. "Thank you for coming, gentlemen—and Mr. Housel, would you please stay a moment?"

After the others were gone, Hunt told the project attorney that he was still waiting for some information he'd requested from the WRA right after taking office. "Every time one of your Japs leaves that camp, my people need to know about it," he said. "I want to know who is leaving and where they're going, and if their destination is inside this state, I want an exact address."

"That could be tricky, Governor Hunt. We don't compile that information at Heart Mountain. WRA headquarters in Washington does that—not just for us but for all ten of our centers."

"Jerry, that's not my problem. That's your problem."

"Well, I will certainly make that request, but I can't promise you the data on a weekly basis. Even monthly might prove difficult."

"That won't do at all. I need to know the whereabouts of *every single one* of these people if they're not behind the fence at your camp up there." He poked Housel's lapel in rhythm with his words.

"May I ask your reason, sir? It might help me make a case to Washington."

"Certainly. The time is going to come—and soon—when I get wind of your Japs trying to buy land here in Wyoming. I need to know where they are so that I can let you people know and you can go out and grab them before a deal gets too far along."

The pleasure of Housel's little victory over Steadman ebbed. "Sir, if I may, there are two problems with what you're asking."

"I'm all ears."

"Well, first, sir, if the person is a U.S. citizen, he has the right to buy land here in the state, the same as anyone else."

"Don't we have a law against that?"

"No, sir, I don't believe that we do."

"Well, we should. I know other states do—the states out on the coast where these people all came from. They figured this out long ago. We're behind on this."

Housel weighed his words. "Respectfully, sir, those laws only prevent aliens from buying land, not U.S. citizens. I am quite sure it would be unconstitutional to keep a U.S. citizen from buying real estate."

The governor did not look interested. "You said you had two problems, Jerry?"

"Yes, sir. The other problem is about getting one of our evacuees back into the center after we've released him."

"And the problem is?"

"We can't do that. Once a resident has satisfied our leave regulations and been granted what we call 'indefinite leave'—basically a permanent pass—we don't have the authority to arrest him and bring him back."

Incredulity flared in the governor's eyes. "Then the FBI can do it."

"Not if he's committing no crime, sir. And even if he commits a crime while on leave, the FBI can't bring him back to the center. They can arrest him where they find him and keep him locked up there for a trial if he can't make bail. But they can't bring him back to Heart Mountain."

Hunt gave Housel a long look. "Lawyers!" he spat.

Housel smiled, thinking that the governor was teasing, but Hunt's gaze was flat.

"I'm going to keep asking for this information, Jerry. Tell your agency to expect it." Hunt extended his hand. "And tell them that we're going to introduce a bill in the legislature to keep your people from buying land. And from voting, too, for that matter. Let 'em vote in California or Tokyo or wherever they're from. And tell your people that those bills are going to pass, and that I'm going to sign them."

"Yes, Governor Hunt," said Housel, clasping his hand firmly to communicate a resolve he was struggling to muster. "Respectfully, I might suggest that you talk with your attorney general about those bills. Those laws would not be constitutional, at least for our U.S. citizens at the center. I'm confident your attorney general will confirm that."

"You obviously don't know the attorney general very well. I think he'll tell me no such thing. And to be honest, it makes no nevermind to me if he does." He released Housel's hand and then patted it. "Sometimes you lawyers take too narrow a view of things. Laws send messages, Jerry. You know that. It's the message that counts." The governor paused. "When was the last time you heard of a court declaring a *message* unconstitutional, counselor?"

Housel shrugged. Tough crowd down here in Cheyenne. Who was he to take them all on? The courts would work it all out in good time.

"Have a safe drive home," Hunt said as he turned to leave the conference room.

Housel followed Hunt through the door. The governor's secretary was waiting for him, arm extended. She held a note.

"Call your office, Mr. Housel. They're looking for you and they say it's urgent."

She allowed him to make the long-distance call to the project director from her desk. Housel didn't like what he heard: the registration process had bogged down, almost to a standstill. Evacuees were demanding information about the language of the questionnaires and about the consequences of their answers. Some of these were legal questions, the project director said, and nobody was sure how to answer them.

Housel went straight to his car. He'd have to do the drive back in one long leg, darkness and black ice be damned.

Eight perilous hours later he found himself across a desk from Ray McDaniels, the army lieutenant whose job it was to bring off the registration program at Heart Mountain. In the couple of days Housel had been gone, McDaniels had worked with Guy Robertson, the new project director who'd replaced Chris Rachford, to give registration a big kickoff. But they were immediately swamped by a torrent of questions flowing from anxious meetings in mess halls all over the center. People wanted to know why they were being made to fill out a document called an "application for leave clearance" even if they had no plans to leave. People wanted to know what uses the army and the WRA intended to make of their answers. People wanted to know what would happen if different members of a family answered questions differently. Young men wanted to know if this was a trick to get them into the army against their wishes. People just weren't coming in to register.

Housel's head was pounding and he felt dizzy. This was all new to him. The only thing he could think to do was to try to buy some time. "Lieutenant McDaniels, thank you for coming to me, but I think you should take big questions like these to Guy. This is project-director-level stuff, I'm afraid."

"Mr. Robertson told me to come to you."

Rats, thought Housel, and he made a show of looking through some papers to buy a little time.

Ah, he thought. *Headquarters. Send it upstairs.* "I'll do my best to get you answers as soon as possible. I'll get right on this. First thing in the morning I will write to the solicitor's office in Washington for clarification."

"You don't understand, Mr. Housel. There's no time for that. We're supposed to get this wrapped up within two weeks, and I doubt we have more than a few hundred of these people registered. I need to break this logjam. These people need to understand that this program isn't optional. These questionnaires aren't a customer satisfaction survey. These forms are *mandatory*." The soldier banged his fist on the desk with the last word.

"Of course." Housel nodded vigorously. But in truth, he was unsure: *Was* it mandatory for the evacuees to fill out these forms? On whose say-so? What if they refused? Housel realized that he had no idea.

The two men looked across the desk at each other. Housel played for time, getting up for a glass of water.

"So what can we tell them, Mr. Housel?"

"About what, Lieutenant?"

"About the consequences for urging people not to register! What can I say will happen to these busybodies who are telling people not to register?"

Everything in Housel's training was screaming at him to avoid a quick answer. It wasn't even clear to him that the soldier was his client; the army had its own lawyers. It wasn't clear to him that the evacuees had an obligation to fill out these questionnaires. And it wasn't clear to him that an evacuee would do anything illegal by discouraging others from complying.

There were just so many things he did not know.

He thought about the strike at Poston, the riots at Manzanar, the military police rolling in. His head throbbed as he searched for an answer.

"Well, uh, in principle at least, there's . . . there's the penal provisions of the Selective Service Act, Lieutenant McDaniels."

"Penal provisions?"

Housel explained that the draft laws didn't just require people to register; they also made it a crime to interfere with the process. It had actually been a while since he'd looked at the text of the law, but he knew that was the nub of it.

"And what's the penalty?"

"My recollection is that it's up to five years and a ten-thousand-dollar fine. I'd want to check to be sure."

"And we can tell them this? That anyone who interferes with registration or threatens anyone about it or spreads rumors about it can be charged?"

Housel paused.

"Well, in principle, uh, yes, Lieutenant. I believe you can. That would be one option."

McDaniels popped out of his chair and extended his hand. "Thank you, Mr. Housel. That's very helpful indeed."

Housel rose slowly, shook the soldier's hand, and eased back into his chair. He looked at the wall and then thought to add a word of caution. "I believe this puts you on safe ground, Lieutenant, but I do want to check with Washington to be sure."

But McDaniels was already out the door.

CHAPTER FOUR

MARCH 1943

HEART MOUNTAIN, WYOMING

Jerry Housel was feeling pretty brilliant for having ironed out the divorce lawyer situation with Gop Goppert over lunch at the Irma back in December, because by early March the marriage problems were coming at him fast. Barely a week went by that he didn't get word of a breakup in one block or another. These barracks were pressure cookers. A marriage already on the rocks before evacuation wasn't likely to thrive here. Occasionally a sympathetic ear over in Social Welfare was enough to bring a husband and wife back together. Often, though, camp threw too many obstacles in the marital path and divorce was the only solution.

Divorce in a relocation center was tough to manage. There was only so much distance the WRA could put between a husband and wife who were splitting up. Tougher still was when a married woman found a new "friend." It was a western cliché, Housel supposed, but this town truly wasn't big enough for the men on the corners of such a triangle. One of them simply had to be sent away.

Just recently they'd averted this kind of crisis with a couple named Tatsuno who lived in block 22. Mrs. Tatsuno had shifted her affections from her husband Seiichi to one Paul Yanari, a bachelor living in the next block over. They did a bad job of hiding it, and word got around that Seiichi Tatsuno his brother Kazuo weren't taking kindly to Yanari's romancing. Threats were flying. Housel had jumped in and put the Tatsunos in touch with Gop Goppert, who set to work getting them a speedy divorce. Any day now, the interloper Yanari was scheduled for transfer to the Topaz center in Utah, where he had relatives and, more important, where he'd be out of the reach of the Tatsuno brothers.

Housel was also pleased with himself for finally squeezing Kiyoichi Doi out of the legal aid business. It had taken quite some doing. He had plastered the *Heart Mountain Sentinel* with reminders that evacuees could bring their legal problems to the Project Attorney's Office. He'd hired a couple of men away from Doi's orbit and given them responsibilities for advising evacuees on tax and business matters. He'd trimmed down the schedule of the secretary ostensibly supporting the judicial commission but actually just doing

Doi's typing. Every now and then he dropped by the judicial commission building to make sure Doi wasn't seeing clients. As best Housel could tell, he had finally outmaneuvered the Nisei lawyer.

With Doi out of business, the couple now sitting in front of him had no choice but to come to the Project Attorney's Office, where they belonged. Shika Fujii, an Issei mother of four, sat with a man named Seiji Goto, whom she introduced as her "friend." He looked to be ten, maybe fifteen, years older than Housel. The notes in their file made clear the two were more than just friends. Goto had been spotted frequently at Mrs. Fujii's barrack while Mr. Fujii was away working in the fields in Montana. In theory he was there to do household chores and watch the Fujii children while she was out at adult education classes, but twice a cousin of hers stopped by to find Goto napping in his nightshirt. Social Welfare told Mrs. Fujii that the right thing to do, if the marriage couldn't be saved, was to divorce her husband and marry Goto. But Goto was balking at that plan. He seemed more interested in the role of paramour than stepfather.

After a few minutes of pleasantries, Housel dived into the matter at hand. There was only one person, he told Mrs. Fujii, who should be taking care of household chores and minding the children, and that was *Mr.* Fujii. If he couldn't perform these duties to her satisfaction, that was why the state had divorce laws, and she should avail herself of them.

He heard his voice quaver. Marital cases made Housel a little uneasy. He'd been married all of a year. Who was he to be dispensing advice?

"As for you, Mr. Goto," he said, doing his best to steady his voice, "until Mrs. Fujii obtains a divorce and you lawfully marry her, you should keep clear of her, keep clear of her children, and keep clear of her barrack."

Goto mumbled something about money and not having steady work. "I don't know about marriage, Mr. Housel. Kids are expensive."

"And so are lawsuits for the alienation of affections, Mr. Goto."

"For the . . . what?"

"What I mean is, Mr. Fujii could sue you in court, Mr. Goto. For interfering with his marriage. For quite a bit of money." He paused. "If I am understanding your current arrangement correctly, that is."

Fujii turned to her lover with a look that said, *See? I told you.* Goto looked away.

Housel decided to up the pressure. "The law will not allow you to enjoy the, uh, benefits of marriage, Mr. Goto, as it seems you have been doing," and here he glanced quickly to Mrs. Fujii, "without assuming its responsibilities."

He cleared his throat and theatrically gathered the papers in front of him. Goto now understood his choices and there was nothing more Housel could say here that Mrs. Fujii wouldn't say more effectively in private. "Let me know of your decision," he said, rising and gesturing toward the door. "Mrs. Fujii, should you choose divorce, I will promptly put you in touch with an experienced attorney in Cody."

Goto hung back as Mrs. Fujii passed out of Housel's office. He waited until her footsteps faded and then took a small, folded envelope out of his jacket pocket. "Thank you very much, Mr. Housel," he whispered, head bowed, as he extended the envelope across to the lawyer with both hands.

A five-dollar bill peeked out from the envelope's edge. Housel immediately handed it back.

"That is all I can afford," Goto said meekly, eyes toward the floor.

"I cannot accept it, Mr. Goto."

"Mr. Doi wanted twenty dollars," said Goto, still avoiding Housel's eyes, "but this is all I can manage."

"No, you don't understand. The WRA pays my salary. What we do here"—Housel swept his arm across his small office—"we don't charge for. My services are free to the community."

"Ah," Goto replied, eyebrows raised. He tucked the envelope back into his pocket, bowed quickly, and shot out the door.

So Doi's still out there, Housel thought. *Still hustling.* Housel had to hand it to the guy. He was nothing if not persistent.

Maybe Housel had jumped the gun in thinking he'd neutralized Doi. But he'd at least managed to channel most of the Nisei lawyer's energies into something useful—running the center's judicial commission.

The commission handled crimes—thefts, assaults, and the like. There was less of this sort of thing than Housel expected—a crime rate that would make any small town proud. This was something he wished the newspapers would cover, instead of the bogus stories they liked to run about how the WRA was coddling the evacuees. By and large the evacuees lived peaceful, law-abiding lives. The only persistent problem was gambling, unless you wanted to count the harmless Issei brewing sake on the sly.

But no barrel of apples is pure, and when crimes occurred, the center found itself in an odd spot. Heart Mountain was a federal enclave, but it was also within the boundaries of Wyoming. Every fistfight was potentially a double violation—of Wyoming law and of the center's own rules. WRA headquarters was clear that the serious cases had to go outside. The centers were not to be running murder trials. But the minor things—the petty offenses and misdemeanors—could stay inside the fence.

At a lot of the centers, criminal justice was meted out quickly—just a brief hearing by the project director. This was what the WRA's regulations seemed to call for. But that method struck Housel as a missed opportunity. One of the things the WRA was supposed to be doing was Americanizing the evacuees. How better to do this than by helping them run their own municipal court system? Sure, it was cumbersome, but it worked at Heart Mountain, and Housel was proud of it.

The process had several layers. First, police chief Rosie Matsui and his evacuee police force investigated and made an arrest. Then a joint evacuee-staff body, called the Preliminary Hearing Board, took a look at the evidence to make sure the case was worth bringing to trial. Next came a trial before the judicial commission. Finally, the case headed to the project director's desk with a recommendation. If he disagreed with a recommendation, he could go his own way. But he rarely did. He usually deferred to the judicial commission, which the commissioners—and, Housel believed, the center as a whole—noticed.

It had been an unusually busy couple of weeks for the commission. It had handled charges against two teenagers for pilfering wallets out of the latrines and against a sticky-fingered Nisei bachelor whose roommates kept waking up to find their belongings missing—combs, shaving kits, decks of cards, and the like. Then the commission had turned to a tough case that had the makings of a real blowup. Two hungry Los Angeles teenagers tried to score a second steak dinner by sneaking into a mess hall that wasn't their own. When an evacuee from Santa Clara wised up to them and blocked the door, the beef-addled boys knocked him around a little. It was a garden-variety assault, the kind of case that would have been quickly resolved were it not for the bad blood between the center's Los Angeles urbanites and the more rural crowd from Santa Clara. The groups weren't quite the Hatfields and McCoys, but there was tension that made the case a flash point. Housel worried the case might spark the kinds of protests that had convulsed other centers. But lo and behold, when the commission convicted the boys, the Los Angeles faction accepted the verdict. This was, to Housel, the genius of the judicial commission. It gave the evacuees a big enough say in their own affairs to keep the peace.

Housel made it a practice to drop in on the proceedings from time to time, and he had to admit that Kiyoichi Doi was doing an admirable job as chair. He kept the proceedings moving, but with a surprisingly light hand. He maintained an air of impartiality.

Today, though, was different. Housel had popped in on the trial of Toshiharu Tago and Kanda Oharu just to make sure that all was well, but within twenty minutes he could tell that something was amiss. The two Issei defendants, both mess hall workers pushing sixty, were charged with stealing sugar, raisins, and a pot to brew up some sort of Japanese moonshine. This wasn't the first such case, but whereas others had pled guilty, Tago and Oharu were insisting on a full-blown trial. That was why Housel heard Doi explaining the presumption of innocence as he entered the courtroom. Oddly, though, Doi was still at it ten minutes later, rhapsodizing about the ancient Anglo-American commitment to due process and the principle that freeing 100 guilty men was better than convicting a single innocent.

When Doi reached John Adams's defense of the Redcoats after the Boston Massacre, Housel leaned toward the man to his right, an older Nisei he often saw in the courtroom gallery. "How long has Commissioner Doi been at it?" Housel whispered.

"Do you mean his whole speech or just this stuff about innocence?"

"Just about the presumption of innocence."

The man shook his watch out from under his sleeve. "Hmmm. Maybe twenty minutes?"

Housel blinked. "No, really? Twenty minutes?"

The man nodded, an amused smile spreading across his face.

"What?" said Housel. "Why are you smiling?"

"Let's just say Commissioner Doi himself might not be a stranger to the brewer's craft."

"Ah."

"Or so it's said," the man quickly added.

Housel listened for a few more minutes, until Doi started in on the writings of Sir William Blackstone. He stood, gave his neighbor a friendly wink, and left.

Saturday night was date night for the Housels. Some young couples managed to get out for a meal or a movie on a weeknight, but how they managed it was beyond the Housels. Despite his best intentions Housel often found himself stuck in the Project Attorney's Office into the evening hours, and between church activities and checking in on her parents in Powell, Mary Elaine was rarely free herself. Saturday was their evening together.

This week it was dinner and a movie. *Once upon a Honeymoon* with Cary Grant and Ginger Rogers was playing at the Cody Theatre, and Mary Elaine let it be known that she wouldn't mind seeing it. From the title, Housel wasn't enthused—he imagined a frilly affair, long on newlywed hijinks and short on substance—but Mary Elaine reminded him that their own honeymoon wasn't so long ago, and Housel felt he'd be a cad to say no. Their best bet for dinner was the Mayflower Cafe, just a few doors down from the theater. It was convenient, and you could get a nice trout dinner without paying a fortune.

They settled into a booth near the jukebox on the back wall. Mary Elaine threw in a coin and punched in a few soothing tunes to help them settle in. Housel took his wife's hand over the gentle beat of "Moonlight Cocktail." They stayed with silly things to keep the mood light. They chuckled over the the high school marching band's smelly misfortune in being positioned behind rather than ahead of the horses in Buffalo Bill's Birthday Parade. Mary Elaine caught her husband up on some of the crazier citizen complaints her father had shared from the mayor's office mailbag. Housel regaled his wife with the story of a kerfuffle over the evacuee swing band, whose trumpet section, according to a stinging review in the *Sentinel*, always drowned out the singer. Letters to the editor flew back and forth until one writer compared the band unfavorably to the junior high school orchestra, and that's where the newspaper decided to let the matter rest.

Their conversation floated along on the strains of Glenn Miller. They laughed and bantered as young couples do, sharing town gossip and planning a trip into Yellowstone when the snow eventually cleared. When they rose to pay their bill and head to the theater, Housel felt lighter on his feet than he had in weeks. Out on the sidewalk they ran into friends from church, the Garveys, who were out to the movies, so they walked to the theater together.

"Is Bobbie overseas yet?" Susan asked Mary Elaine, touching her elbow in concern. Mary Elaine's younger brother Bobbie had enlisted in the Army Air Force just a few weeks earlier, and when the son of a local mayor enlists, it makes the papers.

Mary Elaine explained that Bobbie was still stateside for training, but it wouldn't be long before he'd be in the air over the Pacific.

"It's nice to see some men doing their duty," Arthur said, shooting a glance at Jerry Housel.

"Arthur!" blurted Susan, grabbing her husband's hand with a look that said *not now.* "Cold for March, don't you think?" she chirped a bit too brightly.

Mary Elaine jumped in to assist with the rescue, saying she'd heard the temperature would plummet back below zero within days. Housel dug his hands into the pockets of his coat and watched his feet cross the cracks in the sidewalk. This wasn't the first time someone had poked at him for not joining the service and he doubted it would be the last.

But Arthur was not finished. "Did you hear about Bill Brady? Missing in action in the Pacific."

Naturally they'd heard about Bill Brady. The young man was the nephew of Milward Simpson, the most prominent lawyer in town and a recent candidate for the U.S. Senate. Park County boys had gone missing before and the towns had mourned, but Bill Brady's profile was higher. For the war to touch such a prominent local family delivered a special kind of shock.

"Awful," Mary Elaine said.

"Just tragic," Housel added.

"And Earl Best's kid too," Arthur added. "Killed in action in North Africa."

They walked a few paces in silence.

"Earl Best is up there at the Jap camp with you, isn't he, Jerry?"

"Yes, Art, he's a steward in our food operations."

"Strange that a guy would want to help feed Jap POWs here while the Krauts are shooting at his son."

Housel grimaced. How many times had he had this conversation? Trying to explain that the evacuees weren't the enemy, weren't POWs, weren't even technically Japanese, at least the younger ones? He opened his mouth to reply but this time it was Mary Elaine grabbing her husband's hand to ease the conflict.

They bought tickets. "You two go on in," said Mary Elaine. "I need to freshen up and might need a moment."

"We can wait," Art Garvey offered, but the women exchanged a glance of understanding that it was better the couples sit apart, and Susan steered her husband toward the theater.

As the newsreels flickered on the screen a few minutes later, Housel heaved an audible sigh, and Mary Elaine reached for her husband's hand on the armrest. "Don't give what Arthur Garvey said another moment's thought," she said softly. "He's being ignorant. You're doing your part, right here at home."

"Not in the eyes of some people," he muttered.

"In the eyes of the people who matter, honey. In *my* eyes."

Music swelled in the darkened theater, a rich violin melody, and the opening credits began to roll.

"Let's just enjoy the movie," she whispered, leaning in close to his ear. "Remember. It's about a honeymoon." She squeezed his hand, pecked his cheek, and turned to the screen just as the opening credits ended.

A clock appeared, with a swastika revolving where the hands should be. The music turned ominous as a map of Austria filled the screen, soon replaced by Nazi banners fluttering on ornate Viennese buildings and German soldiers in crisp lines filing past saluting crowds.

Now it was Housel's turn to whisper in his wife's ear. "Some honeymoon."

"Oh, give it a chance, Jerry," she replied without taking her eyes from the screen.

It was indeed a honeymoon story, though a wild one. A gold-digging Ginger Rogers marries an Austrian baron, a closet Nazi. Their honeymoon takes them to Warsaw, where the baron sets to aiding the German invasion of Poland. Just when Ginger Rogers realizes the scale of her mistake, Cary Grant sweeps in to whisk her from the marriage on a wild escape across Europe, complete with false passports, leaps from ocean liners, and a brief stint in a concentration camp.

The audience seemed to enjoy the story, laughing at the antics and gasping at the twists and turns. But the Housels sat quiet. When the lights came up, they let the Garveys leave first; Mary Elaine gave them a little wave as they passed. During the walk back to the Green Gables they agreed that it wasn't much of a movie, what with its clichéd characters and farfetched plot twists. Some of the distance they covered in silence. Garvey's digs replayed in Housel's mind rather than scenes from the film.

Over breakfast before church the next morning, Housel noticed a little headline in the *Cody Enterprise*, tucked in the bottom corner of a page opposite the classifieds. "Navy Recruiters to Visit: College Men Sought." Gripping the paper with two hands to muffle the sound, he tore the little story from the paper and tucked it into his wallet.

Jerry Housel liked Rosie Matsui, the chief of police at Heart Mountain. Technically an Issei—he'd come to the United States as a kid back in the 1910s— he was young enough to be able to relate well to the Nisei and command the community's respect. Normally Housel looked forward to seeing him. But the look on the police chief's face when Housel arrived at the office on Monday morning signaled bad news.

"I'd say good morning, Rosie, but something tells me the morning hasn't treated you well."

"Not just the morning, Mr. Housel, the whole night. Big trouble with our triangle case."

Housel sighed. He thought he'd scared Seiji Goto straight—that he'd have the sense to stay away from Mrs. Fujii now that he saw what he was risking. "What did Goto do now?" he asked.

"Not that triangle, Mr. Housel. The other one. The Tatsunos."

Housel was confused. "I thought we solved that one. Didn't we? Weren't we sending Yanari far away from Mrs. Tatsuno? To Topaz?"

"Yes, but not fast enough. The Tatsuno brothers got to him first. Last night, at his barrack." Matsui slowly shook his head, as if to say that Housel might not want to know the details.

"How bad is it?"

"Bad. Yanari's in the hospital. Lost a lot of blood."

Housel dropped into his desk chair and gestured for Matsui to take a seat. "All right, Rosie, let's hear it."

The story was harrowing. Tatsuno and his brother had heard Yanari was about to leave for Topaz, and somehow they'd gotten it in their minds that Mrs. Tatsuno was going to try to grab their children and head off to Utah with him. The two men went to Yanari's barrack to make him sign a promise not to obstruct Tatsuno's relationship with his children. But Yanari just crumpled it and tossed it into the flames of his charcoal stove. Tatsuno grabbed Yanari and they tussled. Tatsuno's brother pulled them apart, but Tatsuno spotted a metal pipe hanging near the stove and brought it down hard on Yanari's skull.

"We've got Tatsuno in custody," the police chief said.

"And did you get a statement from Yanari?"

"The doctor wouldn't let us near him. Said it's a deep wound. They'd already given him twelve hundred cc's of blood—almost a third of a gallon."

That was a lot of blood. Housel rose and stepped behind Matsui to a table with a couple of small stacks of books—what passed for Heart Mountain's law library. He picked one out, sat back down, kicked his feet up onto his desk, and began leafing through the pages of the Wyoming Revised Statutes. In another room, two typewriters clacked away in ragged rhythms. "This is obviously assault and battery," he said under his breath, "but let me see what it takes for aggravated assault." He hummed tunelessly as he ran his finger across the index.

"Whatever it takes, Mr. Housel, we've got it here."

The lawyer looked up, eyebrows raised.

"Yanari's right arm is paralyzed. Doctor says he can't talk."

That must have been one hell of a metal pipe, Housel thought.

"Yanari might not make it, is what the doctor said." Matsui eyed the book in Housel's lap. "He might not survive."

Housel looked back down at the index, no longer humming, searching for second-degree murder and manslaughter rather than aggravated assault.

"If Yanari dies, this case will definitely have to go outside, Rosie, to Park County authorities. WRA regulations are crystal clear on that."

"Naturally, Mr. Housel."

The men sat in silence, each looking off into a different distance. Somewhere along the hallway a telephone rang unanswered.

"And if he survives?" the police chief asked quietly.

Housel closed the statute book and returned his feet to the floor, sitting up straighter in his chair. "If he survives, we should probably still send it outside."

Matsui cocked his head slightly, a signal Housel read as caution.

"Look, Rosie, at a minimum, if we keep it internal, Guy Robertson is going to have to handle it." Headquarters had made clear that whatever experimenting the centers wanted to use with procedures for minor cases, serious cases were for the project director and the project director alone to resolve.

Matsui cocked his head once again.

"What, Rosie? What are you trying to say?"

"The community's with Tatsuno, Mr. Housel."

Now it was Housel's turn to cock his head, but in confusion.

"Yanari and Mrs. Tatsuno have been pretty shameless about this thing for months now. Yanari had this coming to him. That's what I've been hearing— and not just from a few people but from most everyone. "

"Huh," Housel said, his index fingers and thumbs tapping a triangle on his lips. "Huh," he said again.

"No one's surprised Tatsuno roughed him up; they're surprised that it took this long."

"So, are you saying we should take this to the judicial commission, Rosie? Something this serious?"

The police chief nodded.

"And what if the commission gives Tatsuno a slap on the wrist or even acquits him? Are you saying the people will accept that? That we won't end up with a mob of protesters out in front of this building, like they've had at Manzanar and at Poston?"

"All I can say is Yanari had it coming to him, Mr. Housel. That's what I'm hearing."

Housel rose and extended his hand to Matsui as the police chief snapped up from his chair. "Thanks, Rosie. We'll see if Yanari pulls through, and I'll talk to Guy Robertson. We'll make our decision once we see which way this is heading."

Matsui donned his cap and left the office.

Housel took a deep breath and let it out slowly. He was proud of the judicial commission at Heart Mountain. It might not meet WRA specifications, but it worked. It got the evacuees involved in their own government, which was what WRA said it wanted. If Rosie Matsui was right about the community— and Housel would have to do some checking to be sure—then maybe this actually was a case for the commission to handle. Headquarters would squawk about it. But if he really believed in the commission—and he really did—then maybe this was worth the fight.

March 21, 1943

AIR MAIL
Mr. Philip M. Glick
Solicitor
War Relocation Authority
Barr Building
Washington, D.C.

Dear Philip:

1. On Monday the Preliminary Hearing Board voted to refer the
Tatsuno triangle assault case to the Judicial Commission for
trial. The victim, Yanari, is continuing to improve slowly and is
regaining use of his right arm and is also getting his speech back.
Rosie Matsui believes he may be able to appear at the hearing a
week from today, but if not he may ask for a continuance until such
time as Yanari can appear.

A good number of the residents know the background and history
of this entire case and they do not feel Tatsuno is seriously at
fault. A long petition signed by many residents familiar with the
case was presented to the Commission yesterday requesting leniency
for him. It is quite possible he will be acquitted on grounds of
sufficient provocation and self defense.

2. The debut of delightful spring weather here has come concur-
rently with the fruition of investigations and recommendations
by a committee of staff members on work hours and efficiency at
the project. If the weather holds as we believe it will the emphasis
from now on will be on agricultural work and related activities.
Effort is also being made to increase the general output in all
parts of the project and to get away as much as possible from the
indifferent and irresponsible attitude toward work that has
grown among large numbers of the residents. The warm stimulating
weather comes at a good time to implement the efforts of the
administration to make the entire project a hard working,
efficient organization.

Sincerely,
Jerry W. Housel
Project Attorney

WAR RELOCATION AUTHORITY

WASHINGTON

Office of the Solicitor

March 28, 1943

AIR MAIL
Jerry W. Housel
Project Attorney
Heart Mountain Relocation Center
Administration Building
Heart Mountain, Wyoming

Dear Jerry:

This will reply to your report dated March 21. I am sure that the advent of spring weather in Wyoming as in Washington makes for better working conditions and gives new inspiration for added effort. Your suggestion that the time of year makes it appropriate to urge that regular working hours be kept by all the employees is an interesting one and I hope it works out.

The continued story on the Tatsuno divorce case and its aftermath is a Sunday supplement thriller. It is, of course, extremely unfortunate that the parties could not have been separated in different centers before an attack occurred.

It seems that this case might well be one of the sort that ought to be referred to the outside authorities for prosecution. Certainly that is true if Yanari dies, and even if he does not die the fact remains that the case is an extremely serious one. Even though it is generally felt that Tatsuno was not basically at fault, it still might be undesirable to allow a case of this seriousness to be disposed of without regular judicial proceedings in a regular court.

Please keep us informed on developments in connection with this case.

Sincerely,
Philip M. Glick
Solicitor

April 9, 1943

AIR MAIL
Mr. Philip M. Glick
Solicitor
War Relocation Authority
Barr Building
Washington, D.C.

Dear Philip:

After a trial lasting four days, with a packed courtroom and
people hanging their heads in the windows to follow the proceedings, the Judicial Commission delivered its decision in the
Tatsuno case. They decided that the younger Tatsuno should be held
not guilty and that the elder Tatsuno (the husband who inflicted
the blow on Yanari) should be found guilty. There was considerable
question as to what sentence the elder Tatsuno should be given,
but it was unanimously decided that a sentence to confinement for
30 days with suspension of 15 days would be proper. The sentence,
though we might think it short for such a brutal attack, was well
received by the residents.

You may wonder why we handle our criminal cases here with the
Judicial Commission rather than in strict conformity with WRA
regulations. While it is difficult to get the residents to assume
primary responsibility for many phases of center administration,
our judicial system is one in which the residents themselves have
assumed primary responsibility for the trial and punishment of
offenses and it has functioned on the whole very well.

Now that they have assumed such responsibility, I trust you
will agree that taking it away from them would be ill-advised.

Sincerely,
Jerry W. Housel
Project Attorney

CHAPTER FIVE

MAY–JUNE 1943

HEART MOUNTAIN, WYOMING

Sunrise this time of year, late in the spring, was just before six. That's when light touched the tops of the mess hall chimneys and flared the white bellies of the swallows flitting among the barrack eaves. But the summit of Heart Mountain, a good couple thousand feet above the valley floor, caught the eastern rays much earlier. If you kept a patient eye you could capture the moment the uppermost rocks burst out of purple-gray silhouette into flaming peach, like the strike of a match. After a minute or two the whole mountaintop shone like a beacon above a valley floor still nestled in the last grays of night. But it would still be minutes until the full height of the guard towers glowed in the sunlight and the streetlamps above the peaks of the barracks clicked off for the day.

Jerry Housel took all of this in from behind the steering wheel of a 1940 Ford half-ton pickup idling near Heart Mountain's poultry pens. He'd been out driving since shortly after five, shuttling feed from storage near the depot over to where the animals were kept. Feed delivery didn't figure in his job description, and the project director had stressed that nobody was strictly required to pitch in on the farm while the evacuees were on strike. But Housel felt a sense of duty. If the office types all stuck by their desks during the crisis, didn't roll up their sleeves and get dirty, what kind of example would that set for the rest of the staff, let alone the evacuees?

Yes, this was a crisis—the biggest work stoppage since the center opened. First the evacuees in the motor pool had walked off the job, and then the farm-workers went out with them in sympathy, and now the center was in danger of imploding. With the motor pool boys out, nothing was getting delivered—no coal for the stoves, no food to the mess halls. That was why Housel was out in a truck—to stave off disaster while the strike was being settled.

Housel rolled down his window and hollered for someone to come over and hoist the sacks out of the truck. A kid from Powell approached, the son of friends of Housel's in-laws, just a couple of years out of high school. His day job was managing property in the Community Services Division—movie projectors, sports equipment, and the like.

"Not quite what you signed up for, eh, Mr. Housel?" the boy shouted as he stepped up onto the wheel well to jump into the truck bed.

"Nor you, Jimmy—nor you!" Housel responded out the window, and they shared a smile.

He turned back to the steering wheel and waited for the truck to be emptied. *How on earth did I get here?* he asked himself as he shifted the truck into idle. This question was cropping up in his head every day recently, most days more than just once or twice. Always without an answer.

The labor trouble had begun five days earlier, when Henry Kiyomura, foreman of the tractor drivers, walked over to the motor pool building to talk to the mechanics. Late spring was key planting time at this elevation in northwest Wyoming, and tractors were in serious demand. They were also in disrepair. The drivers jimmied under the hoods to try to keep the engines running, but their tinkering could only do so much. Sometimes the hand of a real mechanic was called for.

Everything that followed might have been avoided if Elbern Linderman hadn't been the man to field Kiyomura's request. The assistant chief of the motor pool in charge of vehicle repair, Linderman was not known for cordial dealings with the evacuees who worked under him. From what Housel had heard, Linderman turned down Kiyomura's request for a mechanic, but rather than just leaving it at no, he added some choice words. Kiyomura stormed away, hurling a few epithets of his own.

By the following day the tractor situation had grown more desperate. Not only were the broken ones still broken, but the working ones were running out of gas. Kiyomura desperately needed them serviced, so back to the motor pool he went. This time Linderman wasn't there. Kiyomura told a mechanic in the garage to let his boss know he was a nasty so-and-so—that's how it was related to Housel, "a nasty so-and-so." Housel was pretty sure he could fill in the blanks.

Unfortunately, the mechanic did just what Kiyomura asked him to do.

The next day, Kiyomura went to lodge a complaint with Linderman's boss, C. E. Richey. When he arrived, Linderman was already huddled with Richey and several other white men in the supervisor's small office. No sooner did the Nisei step into the office than Linderman asked if he meant what he'd said. Kiyomura said he did, and that was that. Linderman threw a roundhouse punch at Kiyomura as he took off his coat, and in an instant the men were at it on the floor. Richey and the others looked on as Linderman, who had at least ten pounds and three inches on the Nisei, started to get the better of things. The tumult brought some evacuees toward Richey's office, but the supervisor locked his door, so they watched helplessly as Linderman smacked Kiyomura's head on the concrete floor.

The fracas went on for ten minutes. The white men in the office looked on until fortunes reversed and Linderman's was the head hitting the floor, at which point they pounced on the pair and yanked them apart. Kiyomura was banished from the office into the angry crowd watching through the office windows.

Needless to say, no tractors were serviced that afternoon. Neither were any driven.

At an emergency staff meeting late in the day, project director Guy Robertson settled on the idea of summoning Kiyomura and Linderman to shake hands and apologize. Robertson said that ought to keep the situation from getting out of hand, but Housel thought he was fooling himself. Nerves at the center had grown taut. He saw evacuees moving around in tight groups, leaning closer into their conversations. In Housel's view, no handshake—even if it could be arranged—would defuse this crisis.

And he was right. The next morning not a single evacuee reported for work at the motor pool or the transportation division. People were furious over a beating under the nose of a WRA division chief who did nothing to stop it. Posses of young evacuees were rumored to be prowling the center for Caucasian workers to rough up. Trucks and cars and buses sat idle in parking lots and pastures and among the rows of young vegetables.

Housel had watched strikes and riots break out at other centers for months. The weekly reports of the project attorneys at those centers had been harrowing to read. Now his luck had run out: Heart Mountain looked to be barreling toward bloodshed. He wanted no part of it.

After another couple hours in the truck, Housel dropped it back at the motor pool and hustled to the gate to meet Meyer Rankin, a Cody lawyer who was handling a couple of the project's divorces. A skeleton of a man in his mid-forties, Rankin did nothing to hide his dislike of the Japanese at Heart Mountain; he was one of the center's most vocal local critics. But business was business, and these divorces helped pay the bills.

No sooner did Housel shake Rankin's hand than the Cody lawyer thrust a newspaper at him. "I take it you've seen this?" he asked.

Boy, had Jerry Housel seen it. It was a recent issue of the *Denver Post* folded to box off its headline: "Food Is Hoarded for Japs in U.S. While Americans in

Nippon Are Tortured. Openly Disloyal Japs Pampered." There had been talk of little else at Heart Mountain since the story ran, among administrators and evacuees alike.

"What in tarnation are you people doing here, Jerry?" Rankin demanded as they began walking toward Housel's office. "This is outrageous! People are furious."

"Come on, Meyer, please don't tell me you're falling for this nonsense," said Housel. "You should know better." The article was part of an exposé series by *Post* writer Jack Carberry, who claimed that Heart Mountain was stockpiling all manner of fancy foods for the evacuees, luxuries that ordinary ration-conscious Americans could only dream about. Papers all over the country had picked up the story, triggering an avalanche of criticism from outraged citizens and headline-hungry politicians.

"Carberry is a *sportswriter*, Meyer!" Housel did his best to steady his voice. "His beat is high school football! He doesn't know the first thing about this place. Never so much as stepped through the gate you just walked through. The closest he came to the center was a room at the Irma Hotel, where he banged out a bunch of nonsense and then hightailed it back to Denver."

They walked along the dirt road a few steps.

"I'm not sure I'd even trust that bastard to tell me the score of yesterday's White Sox game," Housel added.

"He's got a source, Jerry." Rankin stopped and ran his finger along the story, half mumbling the words as went, until he hit the spot he was looking for. "Right here," he said, tapping the page and holding it up for Housel to see. "Earl Best. Says here he's a steward in the dining unit. Are you telling me somebody in the food operations here isn't in a position to know that food is being hoarded?"

Housel pushed the paper back to Rankin. "Best *was* in the steward's shop— past tense. We fired him—incompetence and a bad attitude. Not to mention food seeming to disappear when he was alone on duty. Best went to the papers after we fired him, Meyer. He's the textbook disgruntled employee." He added another thought a bit more quietly. "Plus, his kid just was just killed in action in North Africa. The guy might not even be in his right mind."

"Are you telling me—lawyer to lawyer—that luxury foods are not getting stashed away here?"

"That's exactly what I'm telling you, Meyer."

They resumed walking. After a few moments, Rankin took another tack. "True or not, these stories have got you in some serious trouble around here. Cody is not happy with the way the WRA's managing the camp, granting the Japs passes to come into town. I'm told that they feel the same way up in

Powell." He cast a sidelong glance at Housel. "Though I suppose you don't need *me* to tell *you* how they're feeling up in Powell."

Housel winced at the reference to his father-in-law. He wasn't sure whether people were bringing up Mary Elaine's father to him more frequently or whether he was just growing more sensitive to it. Outside the center, in Powell and in Cody, townspeople seemed to think Housel was carrying their views to the WRA. Inside the center, his colleagues seemed to think he might be carrying the WRA's position to the mayor, though none of them came out and said it directly. He was a bridge. But there's only so much weight a bridge can bear.

"Anyhow," Rankin continued, "I expect people will have plenty to say about all this tonight at the special council meeting. Will I see you there?"

Housel sighed. The mayors of Powell and Cody were convening a joint session of both towns' councils to consider some sort of resolution about the center. He didn't know what the resolution would say about the evacuees, but he was pretty sure they weren't planning to hand the evacuees the keys to the cities. Guy Robertson hadn't asked him to attend but Housel assumed the project director would be pleased if he were there as the WRA's eyes and ears. As far as Housel was concerned, he would rather be anywhere else on the planet. Like on a ship in the Pacific, for example.

"Doubtful, Meyer," Housel replied. "I'm pretty sure Mary Elaine and I have a church meeting tonight." He flushed slightly, wondering if it was a special sin to fib about church.

"Well, I'm sure you'll hear about it one way or another."

A group of notebook-laden teenagers passed them by at a near run. "Must be late for school—the school complex is up that way," Housel said, pointing west, in the general direction of the mountain. But Rankin was no longer beside him. Housel turned around and saw that Rankin had stopped a few paces back.

"What the hell's that thing?" Rankin asked, gesturing toward a tall wooden structure in an open lot some thirty yards away.

Four posts, nearly as high and wide as telephone poles, marked the four corners of a square. Green army blankets were lashed tightly around the base of each pole. Split logs ran between the tops of the posts, forming the sides of the square. Longer diagonal poles crossed in the middle as an X-shaped roof.

"Looks like some weird kind of gallows, Jerry."

"That's the dohyō," said Housel.

Rankin stared blankly.

"The sumo ring."

Rankin shook his head slowly.

"The place where they do Japanese wrestling," Housel added in a tone he hoped wasn't patronizing.

"I know what sumo is, Jerry," said Rankin with annoyance, and he continued shaking his head.

It was now Housel's turn to stand uncomprehending. "What?" he asked with a shrug of the shoulders. "What's the problem?"

"You're letting them do this Japanese stuff in here?" Rankin spat. "Sumo wrestling? You've got to be kidding me!"

Housel looked away.

"What else do you let them do, train kamikaze pilots?"

This is probably not the best moment to mention the haiku poetry classes, Housel thought.

"If you think you've got troubles from these stories about hoarding food," said the Cody lawyer, shaking his newspaper at Housel, "you better hope the papers don't hear about you guys supporting all this stuff." Rankin kicked a rock in disgust. "Aren't you people always going on about how you're trying to Americanize them? And all the while you're letting them build Japanese wrestling rings and lord knows what else?"

"Look, first of all, Meyer, we are actively supporting all kinds of American things here—football, baseball, basketball, theater shows, English lessons, Boy Scouts and Girl Scouts, I could go on all day. But more to the point, the Japanese activities we allow help to keep the evacuees busy, and they keep the center quiet. And there's plenty we don't permit. The stuff we allow is harmless. None of it's got anything to do with the emperor or the war or anything of that kind."

Rankin stared at Housel for a long moment before speaking. "Tell me something, Jerry. Stop spouting the party line and tell me the truth. Do you really believe that?" He gestured toward the sumo ring. "That this is harmless?"

"I do, Meyer," said Housel. "I really do." He tried to look Rankin straight in the eye but couldn't. *The man might just have a point,* he thought.

Rankin's client was waiting for him in front of the administration building when they arrived. Housel showed them to an empty room where they could meet in private, got a cup of coffee, and went to his office to get started on the day's correspondence. He hadn't been seated for more than a few seconds when Guy Robertson poked his head in.

"Don't get too comfortable there, Jerry," said the project director. "I've got something for you."

"The motor pool boys?"

"The motor pool boys."

Housel knew there was no escaping that situation but had hoped he could squeeze in a few hours of work on other things before it caught up to him. No such luck. He gestured weakly for Robertson to take a seat and leaned back in his chair, hands behind his head.

"Well, don't look so enthusiastic, Jerry," Robertson said with a wink.

"How bad is it?"

"It's bad. The strike's just the motor pool boys and the farmworkers right now, but we're hearing it could spread today. Turn into a general strike."

This was just what Housel feared—another step along the path to violence.

Robertson explained that he'd written up a proposal to share with the motor pool boys to try to settle things, but when he showed it to the block managers, who were acting as go-betweens, they just shook their heads and refused to deliver it.

"So what's your next move?" Housel asked.

Robertson smiled. "You're my next move."

"Me?"

"You. But don't blame me. Blame the block managers. They said you have the best shot at solving this thing."

Housel knew he should feel flattered. He felt nauseous.

"Don't let it go to your head, though. It's not you; it's your diploma. The block managers think that whatever a lawyer tells the motor pool boys will sound more professional and more profound. That it'll carry more weight."

Housel could only blink.

"Obviously they haven't met many lawyers," Robertson chuckled, but Housel couldn't even produce a smile.

Robertson leaned forward, hands on knees. "Can I count on you here? Will you do it?"

Will I do it? Housel thought, turning his eyes to his office window and absently watching a magpie land on an electrical wire. His mind wandered to an ocean scene, gulls circling over the bow of a navy ship. The idea of such a meeting struck him the same way as tonight's joint council meeting—something he'd rather avoid. But how could he say no? This was his job.

"Sure, Guy. I'll do it. Of course."

Robertson leaned back again, relieved. "Thank you, Jerry. You're a real professional."

Housel shrugged and looked away. "So, what am I proposing to them?" he asked after a few moments.

"Let's think on that a little, Jerry," said the project director, rising from his seat and walking over to the window. "That's a tough one." He stood there in silence, hands in his pockets. Housel picked up a rubber band and began snapping it absent-mindedly against his thigh. Voices rose up in the hallway and then receded as people passed the office door.

"I think I've got something, Guy."

"Great. Shoot," said the project director.

"I hope you won't be insulted," said Housel. "It involves bypassing you, at least for the time being."

"If it works, I'm for it."

Housel reminded Robertson that three officials from Washington were due to arrive at Heart Mountain in a few days on other business—two WRA men and an army liaison officer. They would all be at the center for at least a week. "What if we ask them to serve as an investigating committee while they're here?" Housel suggested. "You know, talk to the men directly involved in the fistfight, talk to the motor pool boys, talk to the farm people, and then write up some recommendations to you?"

Robertson turned away from the window, crossed his arms, and tapped his chin in thought.

"This would give you some distance from the situation, signal to everyone that you want to get to the bottom of it, and give the motor pool boys a little time to cool off."

The project director continued tapping his chin.

"And in return for the independent investigation, the boys would agree to go back to work pending the outcome."

"It's clever, Jerry," said Robertson. "Do you think they'll respect what your little investigating team recommends?"

"Only one way to find out," Housel replied. "The evacuees don't need to know why these guys are coming. We could tell them we summoned them just for this."

Robertson straightened and nodded once, firmly. "Right. Let's try it. The worst that can happen is we buy some time."

Housel stood and the men shook hands. "Thanks, Jerry," said Robertson. "The motor pool boys have chosen some representatives to deal with us on this, a committee of ten. I'll have my secretary set up a meeting this afternoon." The project director walked to Housel's door. "Keep me posted," he said, and strode out.

Shortly after lunch, Housel's secretary knocked and told him the motor pool committee was ready for him in a room down the hall. Housel stood and took a deep breath, exhaling loudly. "Wish me luck," he said, picking up an accordion file from his desk and walking toward the door.

"Good luck, Mr. Housel!" said the secretary brightly.

The administration building had no conference room large enough to host eleven people around a single table, so Housel walked in on ten men arrayed awkwardly around three sides of a table designed for six. A single empty chair—obviously for the lawyer—sat empty on the fourth side. An evacuee's watercolor of Heart Mountain at dawn graced one wall; a forgotten calendar showing December 1942 hung from the back of the door. "Good afternoon, gentlemen," said Housel, scraping the empty chair back from the table.

Perhaps four of the ten Nisei returned the greeting; two haltingly stood. The others stayed slouched in their chairs, straight-faced. Housel suddenly realized he was used to evacuees rising when he entered a room. Not this group. This would be a different sort of meeting.

The motor pool workers introduced themselves. Housel jotted down their names on a legal pad—Kay Yoshinaga from Mountain View by way of block 24, Carl Shimizu from San Jose by way of block 27, Tom Mitsunaga from Cupertino and block 26—but they moved along too quickly, and Housel couldn't scribble fast enough. All Nisei, all looked to be in their twenties or early thirties.

"Enjoying your time off, boys?" Housel asked with a smile. An icebreaker, but the ice didn't crack.

Tom Mitsunaga, who looked to be the oldest of the group, cleared his throat. "Mr. Housel, thank you for taking time to meet with us today. We've got a serious situation on our hands here. I hope you understand that."

Housel said that he did.

"I hope you know things are moving toward a general strike pretty quick."

"Well," Housel said, gently raising a palm, "let's not get ahead of ourselves."

"And people are looking to us for a signal on what to do."

Housel's pulse quickened against his collar. These boys meant business. "I can understand why people are looking to you, Tom, and the rest of you boys. You're the ones with the biggest grievance. You're the ones whose buddy got roughed up."

Another of the Nisei, one whose name Housel hadn't caught, leaned forward. "We're the ones who are getting roughed up every day, Mr. Housel, by Linderman and his bosses. At least with words: 'you Japs' this and 'you Japs' that."

The others stirred and mumbled in agreement.

Housel nodded in understanding. "I'll be the first to admit it, boys: some of our people at this center are not especially—how shall I put it?—enlightened."

"You can say that again," said someone under his breath.

"But I'm going to ask you to hear me out for a few minutes here. I very much want to get to your concerns, but I would like you to hear me out on this general strike idea first." The lawyer paused to look again across the row of faces. "Will you grant me that courtesy?"

Tom Mitsunaga swiveled left and right in his seat to get a sense of his group. Housel followed Mitsunaga's gaze and saw several of the young men nodding, though almost imperceptibly. Mitsunaga turned back to Housel and offered a slight bow of the head. Housel could proceed.

Housel rose. "I understand your issues, boys. Really, I do. The insults, the pay problems, the disrespect—all of it. But I'm not sure you understand what's at stake, what would happen if we had a general strike here at Heart Mountain now and people on the outside heard about it. Which they would."

Pacing back and forth on his side of the table, the lawyer began to tick off the risks, tallying each on a finger. First, the WRA and the Japanese American Citizens League had persuaded the army to accept Nisei volunteers. How did the motor pool boys think army brass would react to news of another general strike at another center, after the turmoil at Poston, and at Manzanar, and at Tule Lake? Number two, there were hotheads in camp—people less responsible than the group around the table—who were looking for any excuse to get physical. How did they think the military police at the gate would react if violence erupted? Number three, regular folks in the Midwest were warming to the evacuees coming into their communities. So were some colleges and universities. What would news of a general strike at Heart Mountain do to their hospitality?

The motor pool committee followed Housel as he paced, their heads swiveling as if watching a slow-motion tennis match.

The lawyer continued what was turning into a lecture. Everyone hoped the military would someday lift the exclusion orders and let the evacuees go back to the West Coast. How did they think the racists and the fearmongers on the coast would react to news of a strike at Heart Mountain? The newspapers were full of bogus stories about how the WRA was pampering the evacuees, serving them pheasant under glass. How did they think readers would react to a strike for higher wages? Politicians were pushing to abolish the WRA and turn the centers over to the army. Was that what they wanted? Did they think their lives would be better under military control?

Housel hadn't planned a word of this. The thoughts were just pouring out of him, a litany of fears and worries that he recognized as his own even as he pinned them on the motor pool boys. But he could see they were landing heavily on his audience, each new concern pushing the men a bit deeper into their chairs.

"And one last thing," said the lawyer, coming to a stop behind his chair.

"Let's talk about our neighbors just to our north and south. Did you see the article in the *Sentinel* about the meeting that's taking place tonight? Where the mayors and the councilmen from Powell and Cody are getting together to talk about the center?"

A couple of the men nodded, but most shook their heads, eyes downcast.

"Well, they are. They're having a big meeting—both towns together, which as far as I know has never happened. Gentlemen, these food hoarding stories in the papers have got everyone spooked. I know the stories are nonsense, but people out there are believing them, and they don't like it. They're also not thrilled that we give you and your families day passes to go into town to shop, or to do anything else really, apart from maybe cleaning their houses and working in their fields. There's no telling what they'll do at that meeting tonight."

Housel pulled out his chair and took a seat.

"But whatever the councils have in mind right now," he concluded, "I can only imagine what they'd do if they heard you boys were ginning up a general strike." He looked from man to man, trying to gauge the impact of his words. Only Tom Mitsunaga met his gaze; the rest looked at their laps or fiddled with sleeves and shoes.

"Now, I've been going on for, let me see . . ." Housel trailed off, glancing at his watch. *Could that be right?* he thought. *Had he really been holding forth for nearly half an hour?* "Well, for quite some time. Let me hear your thoughts."

The young men traded glances in every direction, searching for one who might have something to say and the resolve to say it. Eventually the one who looked to be youngest piped up. "We know they can't stand us, Mr. Housel. We don't care what goes on out there. We care what's going on *in here*!" He looked around for encouragement, but only one other person muttered a word of agreement.

"Mits, that's enough now," interjected Tom Mitsunaga, raising his hand to silence the group. "This is a complicated situation. We have to care what goes on out there because it affects what goes on in here." He turned to face the project attorney. "What are you offering, Mr. Housel?"

The lawyer saw his opening and took it. "I've talked to the project director about this, Tom, and we feel there's a lot we don't know—not just about the fistfight but about your working conditions more generally. Or the farmworkers' conditions, or the truck drivers', for that matter. We know there are a lot of issues piling up, a lot of grievances. We don't want to do this as a one-off thing, to just put a little bandage on it. If we're going to solve this thing, we want to really solve it."

Mitsunaga nodded.

"So, here's what I'd like to propose to you gentlemen. As I said, I talked to Mr. Robertson about this and have his permission to offer it to you. A special investigating committee. Neutral, from the outside. To come in and look at everything—the whole situation. Nothing off-limits."

Mitsunaga nodded again. "And?"

"And after talking to everyone, make recommendations to Mr. Robertson about what happened, and why, and what changes to make to keep it from happening again."

"Including, um, personnel changes?" Mitsunaga asked.

Housel understood what he was asking: Could the investigators recommend that WRA personnel be fired? This was not something he'd discussed with the project director, but he could feel movement in the room. They were actually considering this proposal, taking it seriously. "I would suggest to Mr. Robertson that we place no constraints of any kind on what the investigating committee can recommend," he said, hoping to cinch the deal.

"And who would these investigators be?"

"We've recruited an excellent team, Tom, who say they're willing to come in if we ask them." Housel described the three men—the WRA's automotive maintenance supervisor from Washington headquarters and the field assistant director from the Denver office, along with an army lieutenant colonel responsible for liaison with the WRA on transportation issues. He expected the motor pool boys to squawk at the idea of an all-Caucasian committee, but they seemed to take it in stride.

"And finally, Mr. Housel, an obvious question: What do you want from us? If we agree to this investigating committee?"

"That you go back to work, Tom. And ask the drivers and the farmworkers to do the same."

This got a rise from the group. Housel was asking them to give up their leverage, and it rattled them. To recapture the momentum, he added, "At least while the investigators are here doing their work. Once they issue their recommendations, you'll obviously be in a position to reassess the situation."

The room filled with chatter as several of the young men began trying to address their group at once. Tom Mitsunaga raised his hands and shushed them loudly. "May we have a few minutes alone, Mr. Housel?" he asked, gesturing toward the door.

"Of course, Tom." The lawyer jumped out of his chair and scooted quickly to the door. "Take as much time as you like." He closed the door gently behind him.

Housel leaned against the opposite wall, arms crossed, and waited. Voices rose and fell over one another inside the meeting room. At one point the volume in the room spiked. A voice cut through—Housel thought it was the young kid's—saying something about "that bastard Linderman" and "out of a job." That was all he could make out before others shouted him down. When the din subsided, Housel heard the scrape of a chair on the floor. The door opened. Tom Mitsunaga stood in the doorway.

"We agree to your proposal, Mr. Housel. We'll see what this committee of yours has to say and then consider our options at that point."

"And head back to work in the meantime?" Housel asked.

"Yes, the boys will go back to work. For the time being."

Housel extended his hand. "Thank you, Tom, for being reasonable. We'll get to the bottom of this."

Mitsunaga gave Housel's hand a single short shake. "We shall see."

The lawyer stood at the door as the motor pool committee filed out, offering his hand to each as he passed. When they were gone, he stepped back into the room and dropped into his chair. A wave of relief washed over him—relief that disaster had been averted, at least for the moment, that trucks would soon be hauling food to the mess halls, and that his stint as an early-morning truck driver was at an end.

An afternoon staff meeting in Guy Robertson's office ran very late that day. The resolution of the strike was welcome news to everyone, but it knocked over its own row of dominoes: What would be the investigating committee's charge? When would their report be due? Where would they work while at the center? Whose secretary would assist them? Add to that the fact that the *Denver Post* had published another scandalous piece of Jack Carberry non-sense that morning, and there were more than enough issues to carry the meeting through the dinner hour. Housel felt spent and distracted. His mind wandered in and out of the conversation, slipping off to thoughts about joining the navy. But he didn't mind staying late. The longer he stayed, the better his explanation for missing the joint town council meeting.

A note awaited him on the coffee table when he got home: *Going to council meeting—home by 9:00 (???).* This was really the best of both worlds. He'd managed to avoid the scene completely, and he'd get a reliable rundown from Mary Elaine when she got home. He clicked on the radio for a bit of distraction, made himself a sandwich, cracked open a Dr Pepper, and absent-mindedly flipped through some materials he'd picked up about naval recruitment.

As the evening wore on, Housel grew agitated. By nine forty-five Mary Elaine was still out. Plainly the meeting was running long. As far as Housel was concerned, any town meeting about the center was too long by definition.

No good could come of this meeting, and the longer it ran, the more time there was for no good.

Shortly after ten, Mary Elaine walked through the door, dropped her handbag on the table, and gave her husband a peck on the cheek. But she avoided his querying eyes, which did nothing to ease his mind. She disappeared into the bedroom without saying a word. Housel heard the sound of water running and dresser drawers opening. After a few moments she emerged in nightgown and robe and slid into a chair across the table from him.

"Bad?"

"Bad."

They sat for a few moments without speaking.

"How bad?"

"Very bad."

"Tell me."

Mary Elaine sighed. "I won't even bore you with all the foolish things that got said, Jerry. You can imagine all of that yourself. But they passed a joint resolution, from both councils together, along with the mayor of Cody and Daddy, too." She looked away when she mentioned her father, and Housel reached out and touched her hand.

"What does the resolution say, honey?"

She rummaged in her handbag for a moment and pulled out a folded piece of paper. "I'm sure it'll be in the papers, but I tried to write it down because I knew you'd want to know . . . need to know. I think I got most of it." She unfolded the paper and read aloud. "After careful consideration of the problems arising by virtue of the Japanese visiting in the communities of Powell and Cody, and with the principal idea in mind of avoiding any trouble or difficulty in the future, it is unanimously agreed by all members of the town council in each of these communities that the visiting of the Japanese in the towns of Powell and Cody be held to an absolute minimum; that no visitor's passes be issued except when absolutely necessary and that they be accompanied by authorized escorts; that no permanent or so-called indefinite leaves be extended to the Japanese for visiting or working in the communities of Powell or Cody; and that this request in no way interfere with temporary leaves for Japanese who are engaged in gainful employment essential to the war effort and, particularly, necessary labor on ranches and farms."

Housel snorted. "So basically, they're telling us only to let the evacuees out to work for them."

"When you come right down to it, yes."

Housel tapped the tip of a spoon on the table. "You know we're going to have to respond in kind."

Mary Elaine cocked her head quizzically.

"I mean, if the towns are going to put the screws to us, we're going to have to put the screws back to them. Shut the evacuees down from doing anything at all out in the county. No farmwork, no housecleaning—nothing." Housel slammed the spoon down. "Make them feel the bite of it."

Mary Elaine sighed deeply.

"Bunch of half-wits," he muttered.

"Jerry!"

Housel looked up. Tears welled in Mary Elaine's eyes, and he realized his mistake. This wasn't just the councils; it was her father, too. "I'm sorry, Mary Elaine," he said, again reaching for her hand, "I didn't mean that. It's just . . ." Housel trailed off.

"I know, Jerry. I know." She took a tissue out of her handbag and dabbed at her eyes.

Housel slipped behind her, pulled her gently up to him, and wrapped her in a hug. They stood together, close, for quite a while. He thought about saying a few words about his day—the hours out on the truck, the aftermath of the fistfight, the threat of a general strike, the negotiations. But there was no need. He could sense that she was thinking what he was thinking.

"I think it's time, honey," he said softly.

She pulled back so that they were face to face and she could probe his eyes. She could see his decision in them. "Yes, Jerry." She pulled him close again. "I think it's time."

The next morning, he detoured to the Cody post office on his way to the center. After a brief pause—a moment to ask himself one last time if he was doing the right thing—he slipped his enlistment papers into the mail slot.

Suddenly time, which had been crawling, took flight. Housel's days became a blur of wrapping up things and readying others for his replacement, a law professor coming up from the University of Wyoming. Some of the projects Housel had worked hardest on remained unfinished. He'd never managed to persuade the evacuees to organize their stores as a nonprofit cooperative; they were limping along as a business trust instead, which made no tax sense and was taking a bite out of their profits. The community charter was still a work in progress even though most of the other centers had long since nailed theirs down. His successor would have to take these batons from his hand.

On the other hand, he'd put together a judicial process that really worked, a body that the evacuees felt they owned. He'd had to tussle with headquarters over it on one front and with Kiyoichi Doi on another but was glad he pulled it off. Managing Kiyoichi Doi out of his shadowy private practice and onto the judicial commission felt like an accomplishment in itself. And perhaps his biggest achievement had been the most recent: cooling down the motor pool boys, preventing a general strike. When the investigating committee came back with its recommendations after a couple weeks' work, Housel feared it wouldn't be enough. The motor pool wanted heads to roll; the committee suggested nothing more drastic than a few reassignments. But the boys accepted it. Housel still feared a blowup, still felt tension in the air. But if it happened, it would happen on someone else's watch.

Soon it was his last day in the office. There was little to do but say his goodbyes and put the finishing touches on his last weekly letter to the solicitor back in Washington. He had little to report; nothing important had happened during the week, and even if something had, there wasn't much he could do about it anymore. But Housel had a few valedictory thoughts he wanted to share. As he looked over the typed letter, he wondered whether he was speaking too forcefully. Nobody had asked him for his advice. Being a short-timer, though, had allowed him to see some things at Heart Mountain he hadn't seen, at least not clearly. Things that needed saying.

June 10, 1943

VIA AIR MAIL
Mr. Philip M. Glick
War Relocation Authority
Barr Building
Washington, D.C.

Dear Philip:
    This is my report for June 3 to 10, and since I am leaving today
it will be my last.
    1. My successor arrived Sunday and has been here with me all
week. He is acquainted with the local attorneys who have the
best libraries and has access to their books. He already is well
established here and I know he is going to do a good job.
    I am going to Billings tomorrow to see if an eye specialist
there can get my eyes up to 12-20 without glasses. A Naval Officer
Procurement Board which went through Cody last week encouraged
me to believe that the Navy might use me in their military government program if I can see well enough without my glasses to meet

the minimum standard. Hence I am going to concentrate on an eye strengthening and health building program for the next two or three weeks.

2. I believe WRA should recognize the scarcity of incentives to work in relocation centers and make a more positive effort to reinforce such incentives as may exist and supply new ones. WRA has been trying to encourage the evacuees to assume responsibility and initiative for getting tremendous jobs done. But what are the incentives for them to work? They have been uprooted from their homes in a hostile atmosphere, gathered together in relocation centers behind barbed wire fences far from their former homes, and right now they are every day having their property and life-time savings in the evacuated states taken away from them. It is understandable in these circumstances that the traditional appeals to patriotism that are effective among American people outside the centers should meet with less response among the evacuees.

The evacuees have nothing to look forward to or build towards in the centers. They did not want to come into them in the first place, and a good many of them want to get away as soon as possible. They cannot develop individual enterprises nor do much toward insuring their individual future security, however hard they work in the centers.

The low wages paid to the evacuees for working obviously provide little incentive.

3. If ordinary work incentives are largely lacking in relocation centers, work compulsions are non-existent. The Project Director cannot require any evacuee to work if he does not want to work. Food, shelter, and necessary clothing must be provided to all evacuees whether employed or not. Under these conditions what good does it do to say to a man who earns sixteen or nineteen dollars a month that you will fire him, when he knows that he will be fed and housed, and if necessary, clothed? How are you going to see to it that he works eight hours a day if he wants to work only six or four? How can you make him work diligently if he wants to play around or idle at his job?

4. The employment relationships between the WRA staff and the evacuees constitute one of the more important factors which have

developed into a difficult situation in this center. In the work
and hardship of the early days of the center, when upset evacuees
were readjusting to a new life and the administrative staff were
faced with great physical problems in providing basic needs, there
was a good deal of give-and-take among everyone. This cooperative
relationship between the staff and the evacuees prevailed until
the time of the registration questionnaires. The compulsory
registration and the manner in which it was initiated gave rise to
many doubts and fears on the part of the evacuees and a few of them
were able to stir up a large number, especially among the Nisei, to
resist registration.

When the registration program was finally pushed through, it
left considerable resentment among both the evacuees and the staff.
On the one hand the evacuees did not like being forced to answer
question no. 28 or to register at all; on the other hand, the staff
members responsible for registration were heckled, insulted, and
pushed around for the entire period by the evacuees agitating
against registration. The staff were, as a whole, disappointed in
the outcome of the registration, and unpleasantly surprised to
find so many disloyal individuals among the evacuee residents.

This in brief was the status of relationships between the WRA
staff and the evacuees at the time of the trouble in the motor pool
a few weeks ago. Press announcements and propaganda of the past few
weeks raised the tension considerably, especially among the staff.
The motor pool incident led to a further intensification of feeling
on both sides. A crisis which would undoubtedly have resulted
in calling the military police and probably bloodshed was very
narrowly averted.

5. I am convinced that the Heart Mountain Center is headed for
an incident of major proportions which naturally will have an
important and injurious effect on the entire program to relocate
evacuees out of the Center for jobs in the interior. I believe such
an incident may possibly be averted only under one of the following
circumstances:

a. Immediate announcement of a plan that would allow evacuees
deemed loyal by the War Department to return to the West Coast,
while continuing to exclude all others. Such a plan would offer new
hope both to the evacuees and the administrative staff. Evacuees

could look forward to much that they cannot see now. The staff could look for the day when the evacuee population in the center is either mostly good or mostly bad, and administrative procedures could be devised on a definite basis with that fact in mind.

(Of course, precisely because the intensity of feeling against Japanese people is now so great all across the nation, I suppose it is unlikely that a plan of this kind can be announced early enough to be of any help to us here.)

b. Revision of the policies on removing troublemakers from the centers, to make it easier for us to get rid of troublemakers on whom we are not able to obtain complete evidence by sending them to the WRA's holding facility at Moab in Utah. Right now the policy permits the removal only of an evacuee who is

> "in fact a responsible agent in fomenting disorder or threaten-
> ing the security of center residents, addicted to trouble-making,
> and beyond the capacity of regular processes within the reloca-
> tion center to keep under control."

The policy also requires a complete docket on each individual who is to be transferred to the isolation center, containing a summary of charges against him and the types of evidence available.

This policy seems to me almost to preclude transferring from the center those residents who really cause the most trouble. The evacuees who are at the bottom of our strikes and other problems are not the ones against whom charges are filed or against whom anyone will make statements or complaints. Usually they are the ones who sit back quietly without saying a word while their "front" men carry the ball for them.

If this policy is not changed, I am convinced that we will have trouble very soon as a result of the motor pool incident, and that we may have considerably more trouble later on. In my opinion the immediate need at this project is to establish in the minds of both the staff and the evacuees that the Project Director has sufficient power, authority, and means to take care of strikes and similar problems arising in the center which are agitated chiefly by evacuees who have declared their disloyalty to the United States.

6. I believe that it would be of considerable assistance to the project administration in the labor programs if we were to do away with practically all unemployment compensation. The abolition of unemployment benefits would add some stimulus to the desire to work and would help overcome some of the labor problems with which the project is faced.

7. We recently had an excellent Memorial Day program on the baseball grounds. The Boy Scouts and Bugle Corps, which is one of the best in the land, put on an exhibition and following that the Girl Scouts went through some of their marches. The girls were all dressed in white and carried yellow and purple pompoms. They looked very pretty out on the field. This was followed by the Campfire Girls, Girl Reserves, and Brownies marching. We were sorry the WRA camera men were not here to catch part of the program in the movie film they are making on relocation centers.

8. I have been thinking about the advisability of permitting in the center such out-and-out Japanese activities as Biwa, Goh, Kabuki Drama, Shinpa, Classic Dance, Odori (Dance), Operatic Singing (Kita), Japanese Penmanship, Poetic Chant, Shogi, Tanka, Sumo, and Judo. The WRA regulations indicate that these activities are permissible, and from what I have observed from them they are a potent influence for perpetuating Japanese influence and pro-Japanese sentiment among the evacuees in the center. Furthermore, the few people from the outside who attend these gatherings within the center are not at all favorably impressed and are not hesitant to let others outside know of their reaction. They have no way of knowing that a program at which Japanese only is spoken was not a rousing rally for Hirohito. The rather demonstrative and somewhat stern attitude which seems to be natural with the Japanese in their public speaking certainly accentuates this impression.

I believe we would be considerably better off in the long run if most of these traditional Japanese activities were strictly prohibited in the relocation centers.

9. Termination of my association in the legal fraternity of the excellent lawyers in the Solicitor's Office is not a pleasant prospect. I will miss the brilliant, conscientious reports of the other attorneys and the thorough, stimulating replies of the

Solicitor and his aides. I am not going to say goodbye. Rather I
look forward to the time when you visit Yellowstone Park and stop
in Cody to see me. Sooner or later everyone gets to Yellowstone.
So I will be looking for all of you, after the war if not sooner.

Sincerely,

Jerry W. Housel

Project Attorney

Housel read and reread his letter. In all his months of filing these reports he'd never written so bluntly. Diplomacy was an underappreciated aspect of being a lawyer, and he prided himself on his ability to be careful and measured. He hoped these final words wouldn't leave his colleagues with a bad impression. But these were things the men in Washington needed to hear. Housel was getting out before the blood spilled, but he had little doubt it would if things didn't change. He gave it one last scan for typos and then signed his name.

By the time Housel finished the letter the afternoon hour was late. His secretary had already said her goodbyes, so he left it on her desk for her to mail, paper-clipped to a little thank-you note. Briefcase in hand, he stepped out the office door for the last time, pulling it closed behind him. When he looked up, he saw Kiyoichi Doi approaching, right hand extended.

"Well, Mr. Housel, this is it, is it?" said the Nisei lawyer.

"This is it, Mr. Doi," said Housel, grasping Doi's hand. "I'm heading to Billings tomorrow. Then off to training in a few weeks."

"It has been a pleasure working with you," said Doi. "A real pleasure."

Housel realized in this moment that after wrangling Doi out of competition for clients with the Project Attorney's Office, he had warmed a bit to the Nisei. Doi had done a good job leading the judicial commission, his occasional verbosity notwithstanding. "You've got your leave clearance, haven't you, Mr. Doi? What are your plans? Do you think you'll go out soon?"

Doi shook his head. "No plans to leave anytime soon, Mr. Housel. Yes, I got my leave clearance, but I don't feel right going out just yet. There are some very important matters pending in the judicial commission, and some details in the community charter still need hashing out. I just don't feel it would be right for me to abandon the community when there's still so much to be done."

"Well, that's admirable. I wish you nothing but success, here in the center and when you eventually go out." He extended his hand for one more shake, and then turned for his final walk down the hallway.

Kiyoichi Doi watched as Housel made his way down the hallway, leaning into each doorway with a wave as he went. Soon Housel turned a corner and was gone.

Tomorrow morning Doi would come back to meet a new project attorney. He glanced at his watch and moved off briskly down the hallway, tracing Housel's footsteps. He had a paying client to meet back in his barrack apartment, an Issei who needed help with a lease agreement, and didn't want to be late.

BOOK TWO

TED HAAS AND THOMAS MASUDA AT POSTON IN ARIZONA

Novelists and poets, jurists and criminologists have frequently written of men convicted of crimes they did not commit. Many loyal Japanese-Americans must have experienced the poignant emotions of those convicted erroneously—at least at the beginning before the opportunity for relocation was offered.

—Ted Haas, "Impressions of Poston," June 10, 1943

CHAPTER SIX

LATE AUGUST 1942

POSTON, ARIZONA

Ted Haas became aware of the clattering of the easels in the back of the bus only when the smooth asphalt of the Colorado River Bridge silenced them. They were rickety contraptions, evacuee-made and probably no sturdier than the latrine buildings from which their stick legs and mismatched screws had been "borrowed." But they did their job, which was to keep the Poston Art Club's sketch pads up off the desert floor.

The sun was just starting to bleach out the stars in the eastern sky. It was very early on a Sunday, but even so Haas wished he were in the Project Attorney's Office. His boss from Washington, Phil Glick, was due to swing through Poston tomorrow for a quick visit, and the office was a shambles. Files and stacks of paper strewn everywhere. Haas flushed at the thought of Glick seeing the chaos—unless it would do some good for the WRA's solicitor to see the conditions in the cramped closet that passed for an office. Maybe Glick could accomplish what Haas hadn't, which was to convince the project director that he deserved space befitting the important work the office did.

But none of that mattered, because Haas wasn't at the office. He was on a bus with the members of the art club, chaperoning their sunrise trip across the river to the Whipple Mountains. Haas was always an easy touch when the evacuees needed a chaperone. It seemed crazy that an evacuee group couldn't leave the center on a little field trip without Caucasian supervision. These were adults. The only sabotage they could possibly pull off would involve watercolors and sketch pads. Their families, their friends—their whole lives, really—were back in the barracks at Poston. They weren't going anywhere. But the military police officers at the gates took the chaperone rule very seriously, so the art club wasn't going anywhere without one. The artists had promised him he'd be back at the center in time for lunch, so he'd booked them a bus and met them at five for the drive north to Parker and then across the river to the mountains fifteen miles west.

"California, here we come!" sang club president Franklyn Sugiyama with enthusiasm as the bus approached the bridge's midpoint, where Arizona ended and the Golden State began. "Right back where we started from!" came the response from a few tuneless voices. Most of the artists were dozing, and none seemed to share Sugiyama's cheer over entering California—or, more precisely, reentering it, since it was home for everyone on the bus except Haas. After a moment, the easels resumed their chatter on the dirt road at the bridge's western edge. Haas was again struck by how easy it had been to ignore something so obvious.

After twenty minutes the bus eased to a stop at the side of the road. Haas noticed blond rays already striking the jagged top of Savahia Peak. Sunrise was just minutes away. He stepped out to take in the Mojave Desert landscape around him as the evacuees extracted their easels and art materials from the bus and began setting up. Bats whizzed through a cool breeze. Two javelinas broke from a nearby thicket of prickly pear and agave and dashed off into the shadows.

Haas was a long way from home. The landscape he'd grown up in was urban: the Bronx through high school, and then upper Manhattan, where he'd attended City College alongside many other young Jews who had the talent for the Ivies but lacked the pedigree. After college he'd migrated twenty Manhattan blocks south to Columbia Law School, graduating in 1932 at the age of twenty-seven, and then 130 blocks farther to Vesey Street to open a practice in the shadow of city hall. Until age thirty-five, his idea of open space had been Sheep Meadow in Central Park.

But when he took a job as assistant chief of the Indian Law Survey in the federal Office of Indian Affairs in 1939, his vistas began to broaden. The job took him from reservation to reservation—from the Catawba in South Carolina to the Grand Ronde of Oregon—cataloging tribal laws and constitutions. Weeks with the Navajo and Jicarilla Apache had given him a deep appreciation for the arid beauty of this southwestern terrain.

And not just the terrain. At the Office of Indian Affairs, Haas had come to see beauty in the tribes themselves—the grace of their cultures and the tenacity of their institutions, even after centuries of persecution and broken promises. Haas had always thought he understood the plight of the minority in America—the Negro, the Jew, the Puerto Rican. His work at Indian Affairs taught him he didn't know the half of it.

As sunlight reached the ground beneath the art club and the late-August air began to warm, Haas wandered from easel to easel, stopping to appreciate the landscapes that were starting to take form. All of the artists gazed on the same scene—the ruddy volcanic thrust of Savahia Peak from the desert floor and the greener, lower undulations of the Whipples off toward the east. But what struck Haas was the difference in each artist's focus and perspective. Harry Yoshizumi's desert was a shock of crimson uplift with the desert floor just a hint of lightly brushed smudges of yellow sand and chartreuse scrub;

Tokotaru Tsuruoka captured the emptiness of the landscape with isolated saguaros receding toward a silhouette of low ridges. Firm lines and closely sketched details dominated Tom Tanaka's developing landscape—a hard realism where the others favored abstraction. After making the rounds, Haas stepped far back to bring all twelve easels into his line of view. From that vantage point it was a cubist vision—a landscape shattered into twelve vectors of melancholic beauty.

Haas looked at his watch. Already past eight. He returned to the bus to grab his briefcase. It was uncomfortably warm inside, far too warm for him to get any work done, and it would only get hotter as the sun climbed higher. He stepped back out, folded himself into the shade of the bus's big dog nose, and pulled out an incomplete draft of the articles of incorporation for Poston's barbershops and hair salons. He shouldn't have indulged himself with his little artistic tour. He had plenty of work to do, and this was the latest start he'd gotten on a workday in weeks.

Thomas Masuda did his best to brush the dirt and splintered twigs from his clothes as he stumbled out of the desert brush onto the road at the western edge of Poston I. He wished he had a pair of work gloves to protect his hands: the thorns of the catclaw acacias and cholla cactuses could tear your skin right open if you weren't careful. Maybe someone with years' experience plucking produce from fields had tough enough hands for all these desert daggers, but Masuda had the soft hands of a lawyer. He winced at every prick.

What he really wanted was a shower and a fresh set of clothes. At four in the afternoon, he could probably have a latrine showerhead all to himself, and that was tempting. On the other hand, Phil Glick was due in and probably wouldn't come through without sticking his nose into the Project Attorney's Office. Masuda was neat by nature but couldn't recall whether he'd tidied up his side of the desk he shared with Ted Haas when he left the office on Friday afternoon. And Ted's stuff always seemed to find a way of spilling over onto his side anyway. After a moment of indecision, he set off toward the office. He'd have to sneak in a quick shower before heading for dinner.

What an afternoon it had been. Word had spread through the mess hall at lunch that a young man had gone missing, a member of the truck driving crew, Mike Oita from Watsonville. Masuda didn't know him, but he recognized the name. Anyone who read the sports page of the *Poston Chronicle* knew it. Probably the best pitcher in any of Poston's three subcamps. If they ever pulled together a Nisei all-star team from all ten of the WRA centers, Mike Oita's wicked curveball would surely land him in the starting rotation.

But he'd wandered off from the Sunday morning Motor Division outing at the picnic grounds out toward the river west of Poston I, and when he wasn't back by noon, the alarm had been sounded. This was not a place you wanted to get lost on a summer day, what with the rattlers and scorpions underfoot. The *Chronicle* had just run an article warning about the Arizona brown spider and the black widow—two menaces Masuda had never had to contend with back home in Seattle.

And the heat. God, the heat. He'd be damned if it was a degree below the century mark today, and that was actually tame for the next-to-last day of August. Who knew how high the mercury would climb tomorrow? Today's searching had turned up nothing so far, and they had only a few more hours of daylight. Hopefully Oita wasn't too disoriented to find the river. Another full day in the sun without water could prove fatal even for a healthy young guy like Oita. *Head to the river, Mike, head to the river,* Masuda thought as he tramped toward the building hosting the temporary quarters of the project attorney.

In the office, Ted Haas was reading. He'd come straight over after getting back from the art club outing, eager to make the office presentable for Phil Glick's visit. But a recent issue of the *New Republic* had beckoned from atop one of the stacks on his side of the desk, and now, an hour later, he was still deep in the pages, the mess on his desk undisturbed. It was a late Sunday afternoon. If he couldn't sneak in a little pleasure reading now, when could he?

The scrape of a key in the lock startled him. Who would be trying to get into the Project Attorney's Office on a Sunday? Who even had a key?

"It's open," he shouted. "I'm here!"

The door swung open and Tom Masuda stepped in.

"Tom!" Haas recalled that he'd given Masuda a key even though he wasn't sure he was supposed to. "What on earth are you doing here on a Sunday?"

"I could easily ask you the same question," Masuda replied.

"I came in to clean up for Phil Glick's visit," Haas replied. Masuda eyed the magazine in Haas's hands and raised his eyebrows. "OK, I got distracted," Haas said with a guilty grin. "So sue me. Harold Laski has an interesting piece this week on Churchill and the uprising in India."

Masuda playfully raised his palms. "I'm not making any accusations, counselor," he said. "Keep reading if you like. I'm here for the same reason, to tidy up for Mr. Glick." The Nisei lawyer scanned the office. It looked like one of those comedies where a feuding husband and wife tape a line down the middle of a room. Haas's side of the desk was a mound of papers, WRA manuals, and accordion files. A chair against the wall behind Haas was the resting place for at least a half dozen back issues of the *New Republic* and the

Nation. Masuda's side of the desk wasn't spotless, but at least you could see the wood surface.

"Where in God's name have you been?" asked Haas, noticing the perspiration streaming down Masuda's round face, the smudges on his clothing, some sort of fuzzy little clump dangling from a temple of his eyeglasses.

Masuda looked down at his shirt and pants and realized he hadn't managed to brush off all the evidence of his hours searching the desert scrub. Haas hadn't heard about Mike Oita's disappearance, so Masuda told him the story.

"But it's hot as blazes out there," said Haas. "Why would he have wandered off alone?"

Masuda shrugged.

"Suicide?"

Masuda flinched. What an odd suggestion. That hadn't occurred to him. "Seems doubtful," he replied. "They say he was a good-natured fellow, athletic— he was scheduled to pitch for Watsonville when the season opens later this week. Doesn't seem like the type to end it that way."

"Well, I hope he turns up soon," said Haas. "I don't like anyone's chances in this terrain alone for too long." He turned his eyes back to the magazine but looked up again right away. "Do they need another set of eyes out there searching?"

Masuda smiled warmly. It was like Haas to think of helping out. More of the Caucasian staff should be this way. But Masuda shook his head. "No, Ted, I think they've got it covered. Anyway, we've got Phil Glick coming in tonight and tomorrow. You've got your hands plenty full with that."

Haas nodded and put down the magazine. He stood and surveyed his side of the desk. "Well, might as well plunge in," he said with a sigh.

"You do your side and I'll do mine," Masuda grinned.

"Don't gloat, counselor," said Haas. "A messy desk is a sign of a genius." The men chuckled and began sifting through papers.

"Knock, knock."

Masuda swung around from an open file cabinet in the corner. Haas swiveled sharply in his desk chair, scattering the files he'd had resting on his knees.

A short, slight man in coat and tie stood in the doorway.

"May I come in?"

"That depends on who you are," Haas said warily.

"Phil Glick, Ted." He stepped into the room and extended his hand. "I got here a little early. Checking out the center and I thought I'd stop by."

Haas jumped up and pumped his boss's hand. This wasn't how he'd planned their first meeting face-to-face. He cast a glance at Masuda, and then together the men's eyes swept the mounds of paper strewn across every surface. "Please, come in, come in. What a surprise—we weren't expecting you until this evening."

"I can come back if this is a bad time," said Glick, gesturing weakly toward a toppled set of files spread like dominoes on the floor.

Haas assured him that the moment was fine. "Have a seat, Phil," he said, gesturing vaguely toward a chair standing near Masuda that was covered with a jumble of office supplies—scissors, a tape dispenser, Haas's datebook. Masuda lunged to grab them so they wouldn't fall to the floor, dumping them in an open file drawer and slamming it shut.

"Phil, I'd like you to meet Tom Masuda. I've written you about him, do you remember? A most valued member of my staff here, a very capable attorney. From Seattle." Masuda shook Glick's hand. "Tom," Haas continued, "you probably have more experience in private practice than Phil and I combined, isn't that right?"

Masuda doubted it, but he smiled and shrugged. He glowed at being introduced to the solicitor of the WRA in such a flattering way.

The men exchanged pleasantries for a few minutes—about Glick's drive from Phoenix, about the heat, about the height of the dust devils in the fields along the road down from Parker. At a lull, Glick leaned in toward Haas and asked whether he had any business he wanted to discuss.

"Why, yes I do, Phil, thanks for asking."

Glick looked expectantly at Masuda and then the door. Masuda got the message and took a step toward the exit.

"Where are you going?" Haas asked. It irked him to see evacuees treating Caucasians as their superiors. "Please, stay! There's no reason for you to leave. Stay!"

Glick's eyebrows rose.

Masuda glanced at Haas and then at Glick and then back at Haas. Was Haas being serious? Maybe Glick wanted to share something that was only for Caucasian ears.

"Stay," Haas repeated. Masuda met Glick's eyes. Glick nodded, almost imperceptibly. Masuda leaned back against the filing cabinet.

"OK, Ted," said Glick. "I'm all ears. What's on your mind?"

"Look at this office," said Haas.

Glick looked around, then back at Haas.

"Do you think this is a fitting space for the office of this center's legal department?"

Masuda tensed again. Surely Ted was not going to squander time with the solicitor to complain about office space.

Glick looked around again. "Well, it's small, but it seems functional."

"Small?" said Haas. "Small? This is what you'd call *small*? Why, I've been in bigger phone booths."

Masuda laughed nervously, shooting a warning eye over Glick's shoulder that Haas did not see.

"Now, Ted," said Glick soothingly, "let's not get carried away. All of the project attorneys are having to make do with less-than-optimal quarters."

"Well, the others can fend for themselves," retorted Haas. "Our situation here is untenable." He ticked off the litany of responsibilities he and Masuda were shouldering.

At the tenth item on Haas's list Glick raised his hands from his lap to quiet him. "OK, OK. I get it. I will talk to Wade and see what I can do."

Haas nodded firmly. He had talked to Wade Head about this several times already, but the project director hadn't done a thing. Maybe a word from the solicitor would get Head's attention.

"So, Ted . . ." Glick stopped, as if to give the air a chance to dispel the talk of office space. "How are things otherwise? Do you have enough staff, enough support?"

"There doesn't seem to be room for anyone else, now does there?"

"Ted." Glick raised his hands in mock surrender. "I get it. I'm asking you now about your staff."

Haas opened his mouth to answer, but Masuda saw his chance to jump in and grabbed it. "I can tell you about that, Mr. Glick. We've got seven or eight attorneys among the residents here, spread over our three separate units. Only a few of them are affiliated with our office, though. Here in Unit 1 we've got Elmer Yamamoto, in addition to myself, of course, and there's a satellite office of a sort about five miles south of here in unit 2, with John Maeno and Kay Tamura. We don't have an official presence in unit 3, which is another five miles farther along, but one of us gets down there on a regular basis for office hours, to do legal aid work for the residents."

"And these are all licensed attorneys, Tom?"

"Yes, Mr. Glick, all licensed. And we have some people who were in the insurance business back home, and they're helping out with advice to the community. Some accountants too."

"These are all evacuees, Tom, aren't they? All Nisei?"

"Nisei and Issei both, sir."

"Just as it should be," interjected Haas, snatching back the reins of the conversation. "Phil, there are entirely too many Caucasians here. Too many. Every office of any significance here at Poston is run by a Caucasian, and even some of the less significant offices too. Completely unnecessary."

Masuda stiffened. *Should I be in on this?* he wondered. He sought Haas's eyes and asked, with a slight cock of the head toward the door, whether he should leave. Haas ignored the gesture.

"Have we learned nothing from our treatment of the Indian, Phil?"

Glick stared blankly back.

"Have we learned nothing from the reservation? For decades we put the white man in charge, cut down their tribal governments, forced them to go through an Indian agent for everything. And look where it got us—and got them."

"Well, that may be true for Indian policy, Ted, but . . ."

"It *is* true. This is what we're trying to undo in the Indian Service, Felix Cohen and I. We have a chance to do better with the Japanese. We can build this community up instead of making them depend on us!"

Glick tapped his index finger on his lip in thought. After a moment, he asked Haas what he would do differently.

"For starters, I would fire *me*, along with most of the rest of the Caucasian staff. And I would put the Nisei in charge, and the trustworthy Issei. We say our goal is to Americanize these people. How are they going to learn if we don't give them responsibility?"

Glick said nothing.

"Am I right, Tom?"

Masuda directed his gaze to the floor. He was not about to offer an opinion to the solicitor of the WRA on how many Caucasians at Poston were too many. And he was not about to tell Ted Haas that what people really wanted was not to run the camps but to leave them and go home.

"Well," said Glick with a sigh, "you know that's not in the cards. Sure, we don't want another Indian problem on our hands. But we're not going to prevent it by encouraging people to settle in and get comfortable. We're going to prevent it by getting people out of these centers as quickly as we're able. The loyal ones, at least. Prepare them for life on the outside and then relocate them eastward."

Haas turned away. "Whether they want that or not."

"It's all-out relocation, Ted. That's our objective now. Dillon has made up his mind."

Haas knew this was the WRA director's decision. He'd read the memoranda. But that didn't mean he had to like it.

He walked over to Masuda and put a hand on his shoulder, then turned back to Glick. "This attorney could do my job, Phil. Some of it he could do better. The legal aid work especially. Who do you think the average Issei would rather talk to about his financial problems, his marital problems? Me or Tom?"

The question answered itself, so Glick said nothing.

"Isn't that right, Tom?" Haas turned a warm smile to Masuda.

The Nisei lawyer blushed, focusing his eyes on an empty accordion file leaning against an adding machine. "Oh, I don't know about that," he said quietly.

And it wasn't just modesty. Masuda really didn't know whether he could do the project attorney's job—if they would let him anywhere near the job—if they knew about the legal problems he'd run into back in Seattle, right after Pearl Harbor. The FBI at his door, the accusations of working for Japan, the months in jail awaiting trial.

If Ted Haas and Phil Glick knew about all that, how would it not sap their confidence in him—as it had sapped his own?

CHAPTER SEVEN

NOVEMBER 1942

POSTON, ARIZONA

The Dow Hotel in Lone Pine amused Ted Haas from the moment he arrived on Wednesday, November 19, after a tedious day-and-a-half journey from Poston on a Trailways bus. With its two-story facade of faux-adobe plaster, its sloping, mission-style red-tiled roof, and its rocking-chair-studded arcade, the property looked comically out of place, someone's overeager attempt to convince you that you were someplace other than where you actually were, which was on a dusty street in a California mountain village that was one horse short of a one-horse town.

Today the hotel managed even more kitsch inside than out. In the lobby was a gaggle of Union army soldiers, petticoated damsels, and masked train robbers. Extras for a Republic Pictures film being shot in the nearby hills, Haas learned from the desk clerk. Spotting an Indian in the crowd, he approached and asked the man's tribe. "Italian," the man answered. "From East Harlem."

Hollywood, thought Haas, managing his overnight bag and briefcase through the front door. Would it really be so hard to cast actual Indians in these roles?

Haas took a seat under the arcade to await Bob Throckmorton, his counterpart at the Manzanar Relocation Center just up the road, who was coming to collect him for the long bus trip back to Poston. At Manzanar's gate, Haas was to meet back up with Mr. and Mrs. Tamura, the lovely and entirely harmless Issei couple he'd chaperoned to Manzanar two days earlier so that they could attend a family funeral. A few Manzanar evacuees transferring permanently to Poston might be along as well, or so Throckmorton had informed him. The group would pick up a southbound Trailways coach at Manzanar and settle in for the long, bumpy ride to Arizona.

Haas had spent most of the prior day comparing notes in Throckmorton's Manzanar office, savoring the chance to visit one of his fellow project attorneys in the flesh. Nobody at Poston—except, Haas supposed, Tom Masuda—really understood the challenges of the job. Those who could understand, the other WRA lawyers such as Throckmorton, were like monks in distant cloisters, connected only by the carbon copies of their letters to their common boss in Washington. Most of the men were little more than their signatures to Haas. Now at least he knew Throckmorton, and though they disagreed about several aspects of center administration during his brief visit, he felt a bit less alone.

Throckmorton picked Haas up in a WRA sedan and turned north toward the center, pointing out the new snow on Mount Whitney that was already dipping well below the tree line. But Haas, worried about missing the bus, had eyes only for his wristwatch. As Throckmorton turned the car west off Route 6, Haas spotted a small crowd and a large pile of luggage near Manzanar's front gate. He recognized Mr. and Mrs. Tamura right away. But who on earth were all the others? Haas counted eleven people besides the Tamuras and probably twice as many suitcases.

Throckmorton noticed Haas eyeing the crowd. "Oh, right, Ted," he quickly said, "about your trip back to Poston today. Do you remember yesterday, when I told you—"

"You said 'a few' evacuees might be coming along, Bob. This is what you call a few?"

In the middle of the group, a toddler on a young Nisei mother's swaying hip began to cry, while her two slightly older brothers tugged on opposite ends of a toy baseball bat.

Throckmorton shot Haas a guilty smile. "OK, Ted, it's more than a few. But we're in a pickle here. We need to reassign all of these people to Poston immediately."

One of the boys let go of his end of the bat, snapping it up into his chin. His brother tumbled backward onto his bottom. Both began to wail. Their mother rolled her eyes skyward.

"You know kids and buses," Throckmorton said too brightly. "I'm sure the motion will lull them right to sleep in no time."

Haas rolled his eyes but gave a weak thumbs-up. Sure, he would do it; why not? He had to return to Poston, and what difference did it make if two evacuees or twenty traveled with him? But once again he flashed with annoyance that the WRA demanded a set of Caucasian eyes—his or anyone else's—on these harmless people. Chaperoning duty was always such a waste of his time, and this time was no exception—a fool's errand to Manzanar that had him away from Poston at what felt like a delicate moment, when news of the brutal beating of an evacuee by unknown assailants had just broken.

Haas shook Throckmorton's hand warmly and then slipped out of the car to join the group of evacuees by the gate. The Tamuras greeted him with a smile, sharing a few words about the funeral they had attended. The lawyer then turned to introduce himself to the other travelers, making small talk about the challenges of getting any decent sleep on a night bus. The little boys hid from Haas behind their mother's knees, so he crouched and asked them about their baseball bat with exaggerated interest. Their young mother smiled with appreciation, grateful for the distraction.

Not long after, a southbound Trailways bus pulled up to collect them. Haas stowed his overnight bag and briefcase, keeping with him just his copy of *Escape from Freedom*, a new book by Erich Fromm he was investigating for an adult education series on totalitarianism he hoped to offer at Poston after New Year's. The bus swung south on Route 6, back toward Lone Pine. It would be a long, nearly straight shot down to Barstow, then an overnight run east on Route 66 across the Mojave Desert through Needles, and from there across the Colorado River into Arizona. Chatter erupted as the bus rolled past the Dow Hotel, the evacuees rising as one and pointing at a throng of Union army soldiers and cowboys milling around on the sidewalk. "It's truly the Wild West out here, ladies and gentlemen!" shouted Haas with a chuckle, and he told them of his Hollywood encounter in the hotel lobby earlier that morning. The passengers took their seats again, shifting and twisting to wring every drop of comfort from their firm backs and solid armrests. On the bench in the back the young mother read to her boys, quietly so as not to wake the toddler in her lap. Mrs. Tamura peeled an orange for her husband, who was already engrossed in a magazine. Haas gazed out the window, letting the bus shape and reshape his perspective on the snowfields and spires of the Sierras. After a few minutes, he opened his book and found his place.

But he could not concentrate on the page. His mind kept running back over the tensions that had been building at Poston and no doubt awaited him on his return. As early as October, rumors made their way to the Project Attorney's Office of evacuees threatening violence—and sometimes inflicting it—on others. The word on everyone's lips was "inu"—literally "dog," though "stool pigeon" was a better translation. Mostly the term was slung by Issei and Kibei at the more visible members of the Japanese American Citizens League. This made no sense to Haas; the JACL people were the ones he saw working hardest to make Poston a livable place. But in the eyes of the disaffected and the obstructionists, Haas supposed, things looked rather different.

Poston's trouble wasn't just in the beatings. Haas sensed it in the meetings of the Temporary Community Council, which were growing testier by the week. Tom Masuda insisted the problem was that the WRA wouldn't let the Issei stand for election to the council because they weren't citizens. Haas saw his point. You didn't need a PhD in anthropology to recognize that the

Japanese respected their elders. Haas had helped the Issei form their own group, the Issei Advisory Board, but it had no formal authority like the council did, so the two bodies were clashing more and more openly.

And then there was the boundary fence. One day in early November, piles of posts and bales of wire had materialized. People assumed it was to pen in the livestock the WRA had been promising since summer. Haas was irate to learn the materials were for fencing in the evacuees. He knew it would go over terribly with them, which it did. He circulated a petition against the fence among his neighbors in what he liked to call "Little Caucasia"—the staff residential area—harboring few illusions it would make a difference. And it didn't.

By dusk, Haas had managed to work his way through countless worries but only five pages. With a sigh, he closed the book on his lap. He would make time for Fromm's thoughts on totalitarianism some other day—if the situation he encountered back at Poston would allow it. He had his doubts.

After a long night of delayed connections and little sleep, Haas had trouble absorbing what lay before him as he rolled up to Poston in the morning. Army jeeps and weapons carriers stood in lines just outside the gate, their drivers milling around and sitting on hoods. A squad of military police officers stood in formation in front of the headquarters building while others ran to and fro, rifles in hand. Some distance away, groups of evacuees clustered around open bonfires. Strains of Japanese music wafted from record players. Here and there, banners resembling the Japanese flag fluttered from makeshift flagpoles.

Looks like a general strike, thought Haas.

He walked the evacuees in his care over to internal security to register their arrival, skirting the open field where several of the bonfires burned. Most of the people around the fires were older men. Haas heard little English being spoken. He exchanged a worried glance with the Tamuras, who had no more idea what had happened at Poston in their absence than he did. Mr. Tamura bowed toward a group by a fire, but they did not return his gesture.

Once the Tamuras and the Manzanar transferees were registered, Haas dashed across the street to his apartment in Little Caucasia to drop his travel bag in his barrack and then set out in search of Tom Masuda. He couldn't tell exactly what was going on, but it looked bad. He shuddered at the thought that his Nisei friend had had to handle the situation alone.

Haas eventually found Masuda in a mess hall, standing before a big and unruly crowd of evacuees seated on benches. He didn't dare enter, so he positioned himself outside under an open window, as close as he could get to the front of the hall where Masuda was speaking. Every so often Masuda paused for an interpreter to translate his words. Haas now saw that he meant it when he insisted that his Japanese was only mediocre.

"The FBI has made clear that they have no interest in prosecuting Uchida-san for the beating," Haas heard Masuda tell the crowd. "Now it's up to Arizona state authorities to figure out whether they want to pursue the case or not. That's what we're working on right now. And if the state doesn't pursue it, the project director still might decide to put him on trial here in camp."

A voice in English cut in. "They should just let him go! Nishimura-san got what he deserved!"

There was scattered applause after the Japanese translation and shouts of "Sono touri!" which Haas knew meant "That's right!"

Masuda said nothing as the crowd continued to talk among themselves.

"Why don't you tell us what *you* think, Masuda-san?"

The crowd murmured in agreement.

"What I think doesn't matter," Masuda said.

Grumbling. Another voice yelled something in Japanese. "You're a lawyer. We want to know what you think," Haas heard the interpreter say.

Again, the room grew quiet.

"I have no personal opinion to express," Masuda said quietly. "Uchida-san has told me that he wishes to face a trial so that he can clear his name. If that is what he wants, then I will try to help him have it."

A few moments later, the meeting broke up. Haas heard benches being dragged across the wooden floor and watched people trickle out the back. Haas kept his distance until he saw Tom Masuda leaving, alone. He whistled. Masuda looked up, smiled and gave a half wave, glanced around, and then walked briskly over to where Haas still stood under the mess hall window.

"Boy, am I glad to see you, Ted." The men shook hands. "How was Manzanar?"

"Forget Manzanar! What the hell is going on *here*? There's a crowd over by Administration, with bonfires. They've got phonographs playing marches, and I saw Japanese flags!"

"It's a long story," Masuda replied. "Let's head to the office and I'll try to fill you in."

Masuda explained that trouble had already been seriously afoot on Tuesday when Haas left for Manzanar. The beating he had heard about before leaving was more serious than anyone realized. The victim, a thirty-one-year-old Kibei named Kay Nishimura, was still in the hospital and the prognosis was uncertain. Eight hooded men had accosted Nishimura in his barrack with a metal pipe and then scattered. Suspicion immediately focused on George Fujii and Isamu Uchida, both Kibei, and Internal Security arrested them and put them in the center's makeshift jail.

"Wait," Haas interrupted, "*our* jail? Here at the project? They weren't taken to the county jail?" Haas asked.

"No, here at Poston. Uchida's still in there, in fact."

"And what happened at their probable cause hearing?" Haas wasn't sure whether federal or state procedures would apply to these arrests, but in both systems people had a right to a hearing within a day or two of arrest, to make sure there was enough evidence to hold them for a trial.

"There was no hearing, Ted. People were confused. Some thought the FBI was going to want to handle the case. Some in the center's administration thought the FBI would just turn the case over to state authorities. And some thought it should just be handled by our judicial commission here in Poston," Masuda explained.

Haas leapt out of his chair. "Are you kidding me?" He paced to the window and back, muttering to himself, and then made the round trip again, and then a third time. There had been inu beatings before, but they've never turned into a situation like this. "OK, Tom, keep going," Haas said, returning to his chair. "Tell me why things have spun so far out of control."

Masuda explained that the story was more complicated than usual. It was rumored that Nishimura wasn't just a JACL member but some sort of patriotic zealot, perhaps even an FBI informant.

"So people think he's a snitch," said Haas. "Is that enough to get someone brained with a length of pipe?"

"There's more. It goes back to California before the war. Nishimura was a rice dealer in the Imperial Valley. Unpopular, apparently. People say he didn't play fair with his customers, that he'd sometimes demand cash up front but then never deliver the rice." Masuda paused and lowered his voice, even though no one was around to overhear. "And it wasn't just his business. People say he ran around on his wife Fumi like Casanova and then forced a divorce on her and left her destitute."

"OK, so he's not a good guy," said Haas. "But where do Fujii and Uchida come in, and the metal pipe? Surely they can't just be customers who didn't get their rice?"

"You need one more piece, Ted. Fumi's brother is George Fujii. Nishimura and Fujii used to be brothers-in-law. There's a lot of bad blood there, Ted— a whole lot."

Now it was making some sense.

"As best I can tell," said Masuda, "nobody is particularly upset about what happened to Nishimura. Between the fraud and the philandering and the divorce and the rumors of collaboration with the WRA, people mostly think he got what he had coming to him. That's where the bonfires and the banners are coming from, Ted. People think we have no business detaining Uchida or Fujii. People think they're innocent."

"Do you think it's the pro-Axis gang, Tom, using this to make our lives difficult? Is that what's in back of this?" Haas always worried a little about a subset of the Issei and Kibei, men who had never developed much of an attachment to America and who seemed to want Japan to win the war. He knew there were evacuees who cheered when newsreels showed the bombing of Buckingham Palace, people who passed along every rumor of Japanese victories in battle. People who liked to make trouble for the WRA.

"It's a whole bunch of things, Ted," said Masuda. "They're definitely the loudest ones out there protesting. But there are also people at the bonfires because they genuinely think Nishimura's a bastard who got what he deserved." He paused, measuring his words. "And some folks are out there because they're just plain tired, Ted. Of everything."

Haas, who was up pacing the room, nodded eagerly. "Of course they're fed up." Suddenly he stopped. "And not just *they*, Tom. *You.* All of you are fed up."

Masuda flushed and fiddled with a button on his sleeve.

"If I were an evacuee, and if I were going through what you're all going through? I think I'd probably be out there with those people." He paused, squaring his shoulders. "Yes. I do. I'd probably be out there myself."

"Yes, Ted. I imagine you might." Masuda looked up from his sleeve and met Haas's impassioned gaze. "No, correction: I'm sure you would."

Haas nodded solemnly.

"Anyway," continued Masuda, "there was a call for a general strike, and it took root quickly. By the following day people all over camp were walking off their jobs. Only the mess hall staff kept working, and that was to keep the strikers fed. Then the Temporary Community Council got involved. They asked the Issei Advisory Board to meet with them, and pretty quickly both groups asked for the unconditional release of Fujii and Uchida."

"The Nisei group and the Issei group did that together?" Haas was impressed. Those two bodies didn't agree about much, and they never met together.

"Unanimously."

"And how did the project director respond?"

"Well, Wade Head was away on business—bad timing—so this all fell to John Evans as assistant project director, and he refused to release the men. So, the council and the board up and resigned on the spot."

"Oh no," said Haas, deflating. He had worked harder on Poston's internal government than just about any other task. It had become his passion project, a chance to continue the sort of work he'd been doing with Indians on their tribal councils. The sooner the Poston community felt fully responsible for their daily lives—and the more closely the Issei and Nisei could collaborate—the better. To lose the Temporary Community Council and the Issei Advisory Board in one blow felt like nothing short of a calamity.

"But another committee was formed to replace it," Masuda continued. "The Committee of 72, they're calling themselves, because that's how many delegates there are. Mostly Issei. Drawn from all the blocks in camp. That's who I was just speaking to back in the mess hall."

"And by what authority was this Committee of 72 convened?"

Masuda thought for a moment and shrugged. "By their own authority, I suppose. They designated an executive council of twelve to speak for them, to do the negotiating with the administration, all but one of them Issei."

"This is completely irregular," snapped Haas. "These are illegitimate bodies! They have no legal standing to do anything." He threw himself into his desk chair and propped up his forehead with thumb and forefinger. "And who in God's name is speaking for the Nisei?"

"That's a fair question, Ted. In the meantime, the army pulled up to the gates, itching to come in. I'm told they were really panicking, thinking they were about to be engulfed in a riot. But Mr. Evans didn't think it would help the situation to let the army in, so he said no, which means they've positioned themselves just outside the gate and around the boundaries, patrolling back and forth and making themselves look big and scary."

"Yes, I saw them on my way in this morning. Quite a sight." Haas began tapping his desk with a pencil, slowly at first, but with mounting fury.

Masuda pulled over a chair for himself, leaving Haas a moment to settle down. It was not until the point snapped and Haas tossed the pencil into the wastebasket that the Nisei lawyer resumed the story. On Thursday, he explained, John Evans released George Fujii on account of a lack of evidence. The FBI let it be known that they had no interest in prosecuting Uchida, but Evans thought the Yuma County attorney might want to take the case, so he held on to Uchida. "But today's Saturday and nobody from the county has come to pick him up," said Masuda, "so he is still just sitting in jail here."

"And I take it that releasing Fujii wasn't enough to settle things down?"

"Mr. Evans hoped it would be, but it didn't turn out that way. If anything, people just got more hard-boiled about the whole situation. They started building bonfires, one for each block. We started seeing makeshift flags with big red circles. Posters and signs with drawings of inu."

Haas lowered his forehead back into his hand.

"It's all or nothing for people right now. They want Uchida released, and if they get that, they say they'll call an end to the strike and tell people to go back to work. If they don't get that, they say they're staying put."

"Is that it?" Haas asked.

"Almost. There's one other thing." Masuda paused, shifted his weight, looked at the floor. "I'm representing Uchida."

Haas raised his eyebrows.

"Mr. Evans and some others pointed out that the man is going to need some advice and they asked me to do it, so I said yes."

"Do you think that's wise, Tom?" Haas knew Masuda had run into some sort of legal problem in Seattle before evacuation—some sort of charge stemming from some legal work he'd done for a Japanese client. In his file there was a mention of a trial and an acquittal, so Masuda was in the clear. But gossip lingers and these were suspicious times. Stepping into the public eye on behalf of a man charged with assaulting a leader of the Japanese American Citizens League was not without risk.

Masuda cocked his head. "Huh? Do I think it's wise?"

"I'm thinking of your case in Seattle, Tom."

Masuda blanched but recovered in an instant. "Oh, that?" he said with a flip of the wrist and a tight chuckle. "That was nothing. What do you know about it?"

"Not a lot. Just that you were charged for not registering as an agent of Japan before the war. And that you were acquitted."

The Nisei lawyer picked up a pencil and flipped it, baton-like. "Look, Ted, my office was in Seattle. I was on my own; the Caucasian firms weren't exactly clamoring to hire me after I got out of school." He caught Haas's gaze for a moment. "I'm sure you understand what I mean."

Haas did. He and many of his Jewish classmates at Columbia had faced a similar situation.

"And Caucasian clients weren't beating my door down either. Most of my work was in the Japanese community, for Japanese clients. That's it. That's the story. I suppose that after Pearl Harbor my work must have looked questionable all of a sudden, so they went after me, said I was an agent of Japan but hadn't registered as one like the law requires."

"Ah, I see."

"It was absurd," said Masuda with another forced chuckle. "And the jury saw through it. They acquitted me." He stopped flipping the pencil. "On all the charges."

Haas understood immediately what the Nisei lawyer was implying: it was hard to imagine a more complete exoneration than an acquittal by an all-Caucasian jury just a few months after Pearl Harbor.

"Look, Tom, you have nothing to explain to me. Or to justify. I trust you entirely. But I can't vouch for everyone around here. So be careful. You know how much you're needed here."

"I do," said Masuda, "and I appreciate it."

The men smiled warmly.

"Well!" Haas vaulted up from his chair and took a couple of steps toward the door. "I think I want to go see this strike for myself. See if I can figure out what it's really about. Come along with me, why don't you?"

Masuda crossed his arms and stayed seated. "Do you think that's wise, Ted?" he asked with a wink. "For me to wade out into the middle of the strike? In the company of our distinguished project attorney?"

Haas thought about it for a moment. Obviously it wasn't. "Touché," he said with a wink before flying out the door.

Rounding a corner in the corridor Haas saw John Evans, the assistant project director, stepping out of his office. Ordinarily cheerful and energetic, Evans looked pale and caved in on himself and lost in thought. Running things in Wade Head's absence was taking a toll. He brightened when he spotted Haas. "Look who's back from Manzanar! You're a sight for sore eyes, Ted! We could've used a lawyer here these last few days."

"Tom Masuda has been here the whole time, just down the hall."

Evans looked quizzically at Haas, as though he couldn't be sure if Haas was joking.

"I'm serious, John. Tom's an outstanding lawyer—brilliant, really. An important part of the success of my office. I'm not sure I know what I'd do without him."

"You do know about his charges, don't you? Spying for Japan?"

"I do, and they were not for spying but merely for failing to register as an agent of Japan. And more to the point, he was acquitted of those charges by a jury."

"Still sounds fishy to me," Evans said with a shrug.

The men walked slowly along the corridor in silence. After a moment, Evans asked Haas where he was going, and Haas explained that he hadn't yet had a chance to take in the scene near the jail and police station, where the protesters were camped out.

"I was headed that way myself," said Evans, "to put in an appearance. Strut our stuff a little, you know? Show them that that we still run this place and aren't backing down. Would you like to head over together?"

Haas nodded eagerly. "I've been stuck in buses most of the last few days, so I could really use the walk. You can catch me up on the way over."

"Negative on the walk, Ted. I'm going to drive. I think that would be wiser."

"Come on, man! It's only a few minutes on foot!"

"Yes, but if we need to, uh, extricate ourselves, we'll be glad to have the car," said Evans.

That's really strutting your stuff, Haas thought but did not say.

From the administration building the protests appeared only as ribbons of smoke rising over barrack roofs in the gray late-afternoon sky. But as Evans turned the car onto the rutted dirt of Sixth Street and headed west, Haas saw hundreds of people out past the midway near the intersection with G Street. At first, they looked like one great mass, but as the car got closer they resolved into distinct circles around many bonfires. In another circumstance Haas might have thought the fires were for warmth, because it was a cold day and evening was approaching, but a pole jutted upward from each of the groups with what looked to be a Japanese flag bearing a number corresponding to a residential block.

Haas was trying to count the numbers on the banners in ascending order when the car stopped short. "Bastards!" shouted Evans, and Haas looked ahead to see two burning logs blocking their path. In an instant Evans was out the driver's door, hurling words at the backs of several teenagers racing toward the crowds into which they clearly planned to disappear. The assistant project director gave chase for a moment but saw it was hopeless. He returned to the logs, knocking them into a ditch beside the road with the heel of his cowboy boot. "Little bastards," he grumbled again as he dumped himself back into the driver's seat and threw the car into gear. Giving the crowd wide berth, he pulled up beside the police station.

The two men climbed out of the car and scanned the assemblage. Haas's eyes quickly fixed on a makeshift stage at the far edge of the crowd. A performance of some sort looked to be taking place. The most direct path to the stage snaked through several of the block bonfires. Haas set off, waving away Evans's warning that he'd be safer skirting the periphery. "I'll meet you back at the car in fifteen minutes," he called over his shoulder.

Behind Evans, something caught Haas's eye. A cardboard sign hung on the exterior wall of the police station. Painted in black, the sign showed a dog eating what looked to be dollar bills. Beneath the dog was the legend "No Dogs

Allowed, Except on Chain." *Not terribly subtle*, Haas thought. The community word about the inu was that they were all on the take, reaping hidden cash for the information they slipped to the FBI and the WRA. He turned back to make his way toward the stage and began to notice sketches and caricatures of dogs throughout the crowd. Here was a huge cardboard cutout of a dog dressed in government-issued clothing. There was a poster of a dog being beaten and next to it a banner emblazoned with the image of a dog in a noose. Block 22 displayed a poster of a sad-looking man with a dog's face. Suspended from the block 19 pole was a cartoon of a dog with a frankfurter being dangled just out of reach in front of him. A drawing of a Japanese boy chasing a dog graced the flagpole of block 35.

As Haas approached the numbered banners, subtle features emerged. From a distance they appeared to show the bold red circle of the rising sun, a forbidden display of Japanese nationalism, but Haas now could see that in fact they didn't—not quite. Some of the circles were crisscrossed by faint black lines; others had delicate fringe patterns around their edges; still others embedded the bright circles within very faint squares and triangles. The banners were *almost* the Japanese flag—simulacra designed to edge as close as possible to the forbidden line without crossing it.

After a few minutes he emerged into the clearing where the little rostrum stood. A young woman at center stage was singing a traditional-sounding Japanese melody. An Issei man of perhaps fifty plucked at a square-bodied, long-necked shamisen. A small crowd sat in small groups in front of the stage taking in the performance. At the side of the stage an easel presented what looked to be a schedule of the day's entertainment. Haas couldn't make out any of it except the entry for seven thirty in the evening: a showing of the movie *How Green Was My Valley*. That was the only item in English.

Out of the corner of his eye, Haas caught a blur of movement. He turned to see two young men stalking toward him. "This is not a place for you!" blurted the taller of the two as they got close. "You should not be here! You should go!"

Kibei, thought Haas, noting the young man's accent. He identified himself and explained he'd come to understand the protesters' concerns. But his words seemed to bounce off the young men, who kept gesturing back toward the administrative area.

Just then, a small gray-haired Issei woman inserted herself into their group. Haas recognized her as Mrs. Shibutani, a woman who'd twice come to the Project Attorney's Office for help with a life insurance policy her late husband had left her. Mrs. Shibutani was animated, barking Japanese words at the young men and gesticulating with both hands. Immediately the two Kibei fell silent, the fight drained out of them.

The shorter of the Kibei turned back to him and muttered, "She says you are OK. She says you helped her with a money problem. Says you are a good hakujin."

A good Caucasian. This pleased Ted Haas very much. "Arigato, Mrs. Shibutani," he said, bowing awkwardly. The young men slunk away. Mrs. Shibutani stayed for a moment, bowed deeply to the lawyer, and then turned and walked back to where she had been sitting with what looked to be a group of Issei women friends. Haas listened for another moment or two but realized that the wiser course was for him to withdraw.

As he approached the police station, he noticed Evans crouching by the rear of the car. "I'm back, John!" he shouted, making himself heard over the din of a military march coming from a nearby loudspeaker.

Evans wheeled around. "The . . . little . . . bastards!" he shouted, like last time, but louder.

"What is it now?"

"They let the air out of my tires!"

Evans's body blocked the rear tire, so Haas looked at the front. Sure enough, the tire was nearly flat. He walked around to the other side of the car. Both tires flat.

Evans cursed under his breath and shouted into the open door of the police station for help.

Haas saw movement over at the edge of the laundry building in block 28, some twenty yards away. Several young faces peeked out from around the corner, alight with laughter. Haas looked at Evans crouched beside the car, then back at the youngsters, then back at Evans. These must be the culprits. He put his hands on his hips and squinted at them sternly. This only made them laugh harder. Haas had a tough time stifling a laugh himself.

He told Evans he'd be fine heading back to the administration building on foot and walked off, saying nothing about the kids.

Haas slept better than usual that night, though that wasn't saying too much. Every now and then the exhaustion caught up with him and he managed to string together six good hours. Weary from his grueling round trip to Manzanar and the chaos at Poston, he turned off his desk lamp around one thirty and didn't open his eyes until the obscenely late hour of seven thirty the next morning. Thoughts of the papers and files left unfinished on his desk across the room came surging up as sleep receded, so he got out of bed and sat down at his typewriter. Coffee was riling up his stomach these days, so he stuck with water to accompany the dinner rolls he'd swiped from the staff mess the night before.

The little Corona made quite a racket when Haas really got going, so at first he didn't hear the knock on his door about an hour later. Only when the knock turned to pounding did it jerk Haas out of his papers. At the door was a Nisei teenager he didn't recognize. "Mr. Head would like to see you right away," the messenger said. "In his office." Haas grabbed his coat—late November mornings could be downright cold in the desert—and dashed off to the administration building to see the project director.

"You're back!" Haas said cheerfully as he walked into Head's office.

"Of course I'm back, Ted. Nothing could keep me away from Roastin' Toastin' Poston!"

Haas smiled at the sobriquet the evacuees had given the center in the worst of the summer heat. He'd wondered whether the nickname would stick as temperatures dropped in autumn, but the nickname was still going strong in late November, so it was probably here to stay.

"Yes, roastin' and toastin', but the sun's not the only source of heat right about now," Haas said.

"You mean the bonfires."

"I mean the *anger*, Wade."

Head's smile faded. "You do have a way with words, Ted."

"Tools of the trade," the lawyer quipped.

Head summarized the situation for Haas as he understood it: Fujii released, Uchida still in custody, FBI uninterested, Yuma County doing nothing, general strike, Committee of 72, and a cross between a protest and a carnival outside the police station. Haas confirmed Head's account and said that the first order of business had to be the status of the prisoner Uchida.

"Uchida? Really? We've got a strike and Japanese music blaring near the police station and the MPs at the gate with their fingers trembling on their triggers, and you think the prisoner's the priority?"

"Wade, you do realize he was arrested six days ago?"

Head nodded.

"Without charges?"

Head nodded again.

Haas waited for the problem to dawn on the project director, but seconds of silence told him that particular sun wouldn't be rising anytime soon, so he continued. "We have no authority to continue to hold Uchida, Wade. A man suspected of crime has a right to be charged with an offense. Here in Arizona, that's supposed to happen within twenty-four hours."

"And?"

"Twenty-four hours ended five days ago!"

"And?" Head repeated, wondering with upturned palms and a shrug of the shoulders what the big deal was.

"Do you not see the civil liberties problem here, Wade? Do you want the ACLU breathing down our necks? Because they will be on top of us if they get wind of this; mark my words," Haas said, jabbing the desktop with his index finger in rhythm with each of the last syllables.

The project director rocked back in his chair, threw his hands behind his head, and looked off through his office window for a few moments. Haas untensed a bit, relieved that he'd made the point clearly.

"So what's your advice, counselor? That I just spring Uchida, like the Committee of 72 is demanding?"

"No."

The project director cocked his head and furrowed his brow. "I thought that was what you wanted, Ted. Twenty-four hours, civil liberties, and all that."

"I believe it would be a terrible mistake to release Uchida unconditionally right now."

"Well, you've lost me once again, Ted. Is this what they teach you in law school? How to make any simple point complicated?"

Haas ignored the dig. "The fact that this illegitimate Committee of 72 is the one making the demand is precisely why you shouldn't give in to it, Wade."

Head narrowed his eyes. "Oh, is that what this is about? Your obsession—uhh, passion—for democratic principles?"

"It's OK, Wade. You can say it. I plead guilty to obsession. If we are not modeling democracy for these people, then I don't know what we're even doing here." He stood tall out of his chair, tightening the usual slouch out of his shoulders. "I mean, I don't know what *I'm* doing here."

This was not the first time Haas had hinted he might quit, but the threat retained its potency. Head apologized and invited the lawyer to sit back down. Haas turned away toward the door, took a step, stopped, sighed, and returned to his chair.

"Go on, Ted. I'm listening."

In a cascade of words, Haas laid out his vision. To begin with, he argued, John Evans had made a terrible mistake in turning down the joint request from the Temporary Community Council and the Issei Advisory Board to release Uchida and Fujii the prior Thursday, while Haas was at Manzanar. It wasn't just that they had a legal right not to be held without charges. It was that the request came from a democratically elected Nisei council and a fairly chosen Issei advisory board—*working together*. "John had a chance to bring Poston together, and he blew it," Haas explained. "It was a perfect teaching moment. He could've sent a signal to the evacuees that the WRA will respect their preferences if they express them in an American way." Haas stood again and paced the room. "But what did he do instead? He turned them down flat!

And what happened then? They quit. Both of them—the council and the advisory board! Months of effort at laying the groundwork for democracy here, and just like that, *poof!* It's gone."

Head swiveled in his chair to follow Haas as he trekked around the office.

"And you know what, Wade?" Haas stopped in his tracks and turned to face the project director. "I don't fault them for quitting. We left them no choice! What else could they do? I'm sure I would have quit too if I had been in their shoes."

This was a provocation, and Haas knew it. He expected Head to push back, and the project director did take a quick breath as if to respond, but he paused and sat back, as though he'd decided just to let the train pass rather than step in front of it.

Haas rolled on. "Anyone could have predicted what has ended up happening here. Anyone who reads a little history. It's how revolution works: when the moderates falter, the radicals pounce. Now we have a self-crowned group of kings claiming to speak for the residents, and they've got Japanese music blaring and posters of dogs and rising suns!"

Head nodded.

"This faction obviously doesn't represent the heart of the community. It's just a slice of the Issei, with some of their Kibei minions along for the ride. The last thing we want to do is empower their rogue group by handing over the prize that we withheld from the legitimate one."

Head kept his silence, letting Haas pace around the office until he finally came back to his chair and plopped down.

"So what do you suggest, Ted?"

"I'm inclined to favor an idea that Tom Masuda came up with," Haas replied.

"Masuda? Really?" Head raised his eyebrows.

"Yes, Wade, Tom Masuda. A very smart lawyer."

"And that business back in Seattle? He may be very smart, but I think we need to be careful there."

"He was acquitted, Wade."

"Yes, I know that."

The room fell silent. After a long moment, Haas pressed forward with Masuda's suggestion: that the administration offer to release Uchida, but with conditions. Uchida would submit himself to a trial by the evacuee-led judicial commission for the assault on Kay Nishimura, and the Committee of 72 would commit to restoring a democratic form of government and a spirit of cooperation.

"Is Uchida on board with this?" Head asked.

"Tom has stepped in to represent Uchida in all of this, Wade. He tells me that Uchida would welcome a trial in camp so that he can clear his name."

Head settled into thought, tapping a pencil on his desk. Haas scrutinized his face for clues of a reaction but found none. The project director took a sharp breath, stood up, and stepped around his desk to walk Haas to the door, putting his arm around Haas's shoulders as they walked. "Thank you, Ted. You make a good case, as always. I'm to meet with representatives of the Committee of 72 later today. I'll let you know what happens."

"They want you, Ted."

The project director stood impatiently at the open door of Haas's barrack room. It was late afternoon, but the streetlights were already on, and the wind had stopped blowing sand against the windows.

"Say what, Wade?"

"They want you. They won't talk to me. They said they'll talk to you. And you can act as a go-between."

Haas didn't like hearing about the impasse but couldn't help warming with pleasure. He knew from years of experience that members of minority groups could quickly discern a Caucasian who respected them. Haas glowed with the knowledge that he was that man.

For the next two days, the lawyer was in constant motion, shuttling back and forth between the representatives of the Committee of 72 and the project director. Once they set to talking, Tom Masuda's idea quickly took root; both sides were looking for a way to step back from the conflict and calm the MPs who continued to stalk the perimeter. The project director agreed to release Uchida to face a Poston trial in exchange for a commitment by the Committee of 72 to bring the strike to an end.

By Thursday, two days after the agreement was announced and the protesters rolled up their banners, quiet returned to Poston.

It came just in time for Thanksgiving dinner. Each in their separate spaces, evacuees and staff sat down to a holiday meal. But Haas had trouble enjoying it, and not just because of his sensitive stomach. The buffet laid out for the staff was the finest meal he'd seen at Poston, beautiful roast turkeys amid fixings and trimmings. No way could the evacuees possibly be getting a spread like this, and they would get wind of the difference. It was a petty indignity. But sometimes it's the small things that do big damage.

He slipped out early with an apple pie for Tom Masuda.

CHAPTER EIGHT

FEBRUARY 1943

POSTON, ARIZONA

T om Masuda clicked off the desk lamp in the Project Attorney's Office, stood, and bent to touch his toes. He felt a spasm and groaned as he straightened, throwing his hands to his lower back. How many consecutive hours had he been in that chair today? It was nearly five thirty and he'd started the day at eight. Nine and a half hours. A secretary had brought him a plate from a nearby mess hall at lunchtime so that he could work straight through. A couple of trips to the latrine had been his only breaks all day. He bent for his toes again and flexed a few times until his muscles loosened enough to bring them within reach.

The loyalty questionnaires had the office buried in work, a line of anxious evacuees stretching down the hallway all day, clutching their forms and waiting for the chance to sit down with a lawyer for help. Masuda's day would have been easier if Ted Haas hadn't gone home sick at lunchtime. Haas had been feeling poorly in recent days—weeks, actually, once Masuda thought about it—and looked like hell in the office this morning, pale, with eyes etched in darkness. His usual flood of words had ebbed to a trickle since sometime after New Year's. Haas insisted he felt fine, said he'd never missed a day of work in his life, but Masuda threatened to close up shop unless Haas went home to rest, so he grudgingly complied. Masuda was glad his boss was taking a break, even though it left him alone in the office to deal with the masses.

Some of their questions had easy answers. Yes, a certificate of deposit was an "account" that had to be reported on the form if it was in a foreign bank. No, a ticket for running a red light was not a reportable "conviction of a criminal offense by a court." No, a trip to Hawaii was not "foreign travel" so it didn't need to be mentioned. In all likelihood, yes, membership in the Young Buddhist Association was an affiliation with a "religious group" that had to be listed even if the association's activities were mostly social.

Some of the questions were much harder. Could a person say he was willing to serve in the army if he simultaneously refused to say he was willing to "swear unqualified allegiance to the United States"? What would the impact be if members of the same family gave different answers to that question about allegiance? Were people stuck with the phrasing of the questions on the form, or could they jot qualifications or quibbles in the margins?

The day had been a long exercise in deep breathing. Some of the evacuees were coming to him with the most outlandish interpretations of the questions imaginable. He understood that the community had little reason to trust this process. And he knew people who were doing their best to stir everyone up, fanning the flames of anxiety, pitching nefarious interpretations of every word on the form. But there was a line between caution and paranoia, and lots of otherwise sensible people were crossing it. This was where Masuda could rely on his years of experience calming clients with levelheaded reason. He knew that registration was bogging down at other centers, with mass refusals and rumblings of strikes. Nobody wanted those things at Poston. What was needed was reassurance. He thought back to the maxim he learned in law school, that "possession is nine-tenths of the law." Often, he found, reassurance was nine-tenths of being a lawyer. That's what Masuda spent the day offering.

It was dusk as Masuda left the administration building for his walk home to block 31. The air was fresh and pleasant, but once the sun set it would get cold fast. You tell people you're living in the desert and they think of blazing sun, rattlers, and tall, gangly cactuses. Nobody thinks of the cold of a winter night-time. He paused for a few moments to take in the cooing of some mourning doves and the raisin-colored silhouette of Riverside Mountain, a few miles to the west, on the California side of the Colorado River.

The lawyer stopped at the mess hall near his barrack for a quick dinner. Ordinarily he'd meet up there with Kay but she had an evening Student Relocation Council meeting and had eaten early. The group was doing important work placing Nisei students into colleges across the country. He was proud of her for taking on a big role as secretary. It meant they occasionally missed a meal together, like tonight, but he didn't mind at all.

Dinner sat in rows of prefilled plates in the cafeteria-style serving area. On the menu tonight was some sort of pork roll wallowing in a puddle of gravy alongside a block of tofu, a couple of chunky slices of cucumber, and rice. Masuda eyed the plates and grabbed the one with the smallest serving of pork and the biggest block of tofu. Normally he would look for a friend or neighbor to sit with if he wasn't dining with Kay, but tonight he was exhausted and knew that if he sat down among a lot of people, they'd end up peppering him with questions about registration, the kind he'd been fielding all day. He took a seat alone at the far end of the hall where only a few older Issei bachelors and a couple of animated groups of teenagers dotted the tables.

Masuda was only a few bites into his meal when one of the old men leaned in to ask whether he had to fill out a loyalty questionnaire if he was submitting a petition to be repatriated to Japan. The man said he'd had enough of this country; things hadn't worked out the way he expected, and Japan was probably going to win the war. The lawyer explained that he did indeed have to turn in a questionnaire; repatriation was a separate process with its own forms to fill out. The old man turned back to his plate sourly, mumbling something Masuda could not catch. Soon Masuda noticed a couple of the other nearby men eyeing him. He was tired of talking about registration—just plain tired of talking, really—so he inhaled the rest of his meal and slipped out.

The dark single window in their barrack room told Masuda that Kay was still out. He stepped inside and flipped on the single light bulb dangling from the ceiling. Something small and gray scurried into a gap in the floorboards a few feet away, near his night table. Masuda sighed. He and Kay swept their 320 square feet of floor twice a day and wet-mopped at least weekly, but the critters still seemed to find their space enticing. He had no idea what they were after. It was the same gritty sand inside as out.

He set himself down gently in their wooden desk chair. Like much of the furniture in camp, it was a homemade contraption fashioned from wood left behind by the construction crews. Many apartments proudly featured works of high inspiration and craftsmanship, with smart, curving lines and lacquered surfaces. This chair did not fit that description. Masuda was a lawyer, not a woodworker. It had four legs, and a flat surface to sit on, and a back affixed at an angle approximating ninety degrees, give or take five or ten. It complained when you sat on it, but it held you up.

In the cream light of a desk lamp lay Masuda's own registration form. He'd been so busy advising clients about their questionnaires that he hadn't had a moment to fill in his own. He picked up a pencil, sharpened it, and got started, working straight through without stopping so that he'd finish before Kay got home.

STATEMENT OF UNITED STATES CITIZEN OF JAPANESE ANCESTRY

1. _Masuda_ _Thomas_ _Shinao_
   (Surname)   (English given name)   (Japanese given name)
   (a) Alias _none_

2. Local selective service board _Field Arty., Armory,_
   (Number)
   Seattle _King_ _Washington_
   (City)   (County)   (State)

3. Date of birth _July 15/1905_ Place of birth _Seattle - Wash._

4. Present address _31-5-B_ _Poston_ _Arizona_
   (Street)   (City)   (State)

5. Last two addresses at which you lived 3 months or more (exclude residence at relocation center and at assembly center):
   1272-E 69th St. Seattle Wash. From _1931_ To _evacuation_
   805-Marion St " " From _1930_ To _1931_

6. Sex _Male_ Height _66"_ Weight _195#_

7. Are you a registered voter? _Yes_ Year first registered _abt 1926_
   Where? _Seattle_ Party _non-partisan_

8. Marital status _married_ Citizenship of wife _American_ Race of wife _Japanese_

9. _Osamu Masuda - Hiroshima Japan - restaurateur_
   (Father's Name)   (Town or Ken)   (State or Country)   (Occupation)
   (Birthplace)

10. _Chise (Komatsu) Masuda - Japan - housewife_
    (Mother's Name)   (Town or Ken)   (State or Country)   (Occupation)
    (Birthplace)

In items 11 and 12, you need not list relatives other than your parents, your children, your brothers and sisters.
For each person give name; relationship to you (such as father); citizenship; complete address; occupation.

11. Relatives in the United States (if in military service, indicate whether a selectee or volunteer):
    (a) _Wm. Y. Masuda - brother - American_
    (Name)   (Relationship to you)   (Citizenship)
    Montana _laborer_
    (Complete address)   (Occupation)   (Volunteer or selectee)
    (b) _Merry Nimbu - sister - American_
    (Name)   (Relationship to you)   (Citizenship)
    Rohwer, Arkansas - housewife -
    (Complete address)   (Occupation)   (Volunteer or selectee)
    (c) _Mae Natori - sister_ _American_
    (Name)   (Relationship to you)   (Citizenship)
    Helena, Montana - housewife
    (Complete address)   (Occupation)   (Volunteer or selectee)

DSS Form 304A
(1-23-43)   (If additional space is necessary, attach sheets)   16—32565-1

12. Relatives in Japan (see instruction above item 11):

Osamu Masuda - Father - Japanese
(Name)   (Relationship to you)   (Citizenship)
Japan -   retired restaurateur
(Complete address)   (Occupation)
Chise Masuda - Mother - Japanese
(Name)   (Relationship to you)   (Citizenship)
Japan -   housewife
(Complete address)   (Occupation)

13. Education:

Name	Place	Years of attendance
(Kindergarten)		From ___ to ___
Wash. Grammar Sch.	Ellensburg, Wash	From abt 1915 to 1918
(Grade school)		
none -		From ___ to ___
(Japanese language school)		
Ellensburg Hi.,	Ellensburg, Wash	From 1918 to 1921
(High school)		
Univ. of Washington -	Seattle, Wash	From 1921 to 1929
(Junior college, college, or university)		

R.O.T.C. in Univ. of Washington - 1921-1923. Cpl. rating
(Type of military training, such as R.O.T.C. or Gunji Kyoren)   (Where and when)
attended one summer at Ft. Lewis - R.O.T.C.
(Years of attendance)
Summer School at Ellensburg - Normal School - 1 summer
(Other schooling)

14. Foreign travel (give dates, where, how, for whom, with whom, and reasons therefor):

15. Employment (give employers' names and kind of business, addresses, and dates from 1935 to date):

16. Religion Methodist   Membership in religious groups Epworth League,
Wesley Club, Y.M.C.A.

17. Membership in organizations (clubs, societies, associations, etc.) Give name, kind of organization, and dates of membership.

Seattle Bar Ass'n. 1929 to present date
Washington Bar Ass'n - 1929 to date
American Bar " - abt 1937 to date
Japanese Chamber of Commerce - abt 1933-1941
Japan - Society (Business) - abt '33-'41
    (Club)
Boy Scouts of America - abt 1917 or 1918 - for a yr.
Cosmopolitan Club (social club in Univ. of Wash.) 1921-29

Tillicums (men's social club in Univ. of Wash.) '23-'29
Japanese Student Club - Univ. of Wash. pres. + ex-pres. '21-29
Univ. of Wash. Alumni Assoc. president 1929 to date
(See. supplement)

18. Knowledge of foreign languages (put check mark (✓) in proper squares):

		Good	Fair	Poor			Good	Fair	Poor
(a) Japanese		☐	☐	☐	(b) Other _none_ (Specify)				
Reading		☐	☐	☐ none	Reading	☐	☐	☐
Writing		☐	☐	☐ none	Writing	☐	☐	☐
Speaking		☐	☑	☐	Speaking	☐	☐	☐

19. Sports and hobbies golf, fishing, hunting, foot Ball, tennis, skating, reading, card playing,

20. List five references, other than relatives or former employers, giving address, occupation, and number of years known:

Judge Wm Long - County - City Bldg. Seattle Wash - Judge of Superior Crt - 10 yrs
Judge John 9Kater - " " " " " - Judge of Superior Crt - 10 yrs
Ralph Horr - Smith Tower, Seattle Wash - former Congressman - 10 yrs
Adam Beeler - Lowman Bldg. Wash - former Supreme Crt judge 10 yrs
Robert Thurston - Liberty Bldg., Yakima, Wash. - attorney - & 28 yrs

21. Have you ever been convicted by a court of a criminal offense (other than a minor traffic violation)? No

Offense	When	What court	Sentence

22. Give details on any foreign investments.

(a) Accounts in foreign banks. Amount, $ none

Bank none   Date account opened

(b) Investments in foreign companies. Amount, $ none

Company none   Date acquired

(c) Do you have a safe-deposit box in a foreign country?

What country? none Date acquired

Contents   none

16—32565-1

23. List contributions you have m... y society, organization, or club:

Organization	Place	Amount	Date
Red Cross	Seattle Wash.		1933 – 1943
Comm. Chest	"	"	1933 – 1943
Salvation Army	"	"	1933 – "
Methodist Church	"	"	1933 "

Have contributed to numerous charitable + civic
organizations in Seattle, Wash –

24. List magazines and newspapers to which you have subscribed or have customarily read:

Seattle P. I.   Colliers
Seattle Times   Legal journals
Sat Eve Post   and decisions
Life
Reader's Digest
Read most of the popular magazines

25. To the best of your knowledge, was your birth ever registered with any Japanese governmental agency for the purpose of establishing a claim to Japanese citizenship? _____ No _____

    (a) If so registered, have you applied for cancelation of such registration? _____ (Yes or no)

    When? _____ Where? _____

26. Have you ever applied for repatriation to Japan? _____ No _____

27. Are you willing to serve in the armed forces of the United States on combat duty, wherever ordered? _____ YES

28. Will you swear unqualified allegiance to the United States of America and faithfully defend the United States from any or all attack by foreign or domestic forces, and forswear any form of allegiance or obedience to the Japanese emperor, or any other foreign government, power, or organization? _____ YES

2/19/43
(Date)

Thomas Shozo Masuda
(Signature)

NOTE.—Any person who knowingly and wilfully falsifies or conceals a material fact or makes a false or fraudulent statement or representation in any matter within the jurisdiction of any department or agency of the United States is liable to a fine of not more than $10,000 or 10 years' imprisonment, or both.

U. S. GOVERNMENT PRINTING OFFICE   16—32565-1

On a separate little sheet of paper, Masuda added several organizations to his answer to question 17 that he hadn't been able to squeeze onto the questionnaire itself—that he'd been on the Mayor's Fair Rent Committee in Seattle in 1941, that he'd chaired the Sea Scout Committee in 1940 and 1941, and that he'd been a member of the JACL since all the way back in 1926. He stapled the addendum to the top of the second page and then turned back to the first page to review all his answers.

On the whole he was pleased with them. He assumed ROTC at the University of Washington would look good to whoever was reviewing his answers. Surely his long list of clubs and organizations would make him look like an industrious, public-minded citizen. Being a JACL member would probably help at least a little. He'd been reasonably generous to charities. Lots of American hobbies like football and tennis and fishing. Surely there weren't many Japanese Americans who could give a list of references made up entirely of judges, lawyers, and former congressmen. And most important of all, he'd said yes to questions 27 and 28, the ones about military service and allegiance to the United States.

But the longer he scanned the questionnaire, the more his eyes returned to the couple of items that troubled him. His Issei parents lived in Japan. Could that work against him? Some of his clubs and organizations were in Seattle's Japanese community. They were totally innocuous organizations. The Chamber of Commerce and the Japan Society were basically business clubs, places to find clients for his law practice. But was that how the reviewer would see them?

And then there was question 21, asking whether he'd ever been convicted of a crime other than a traffic violation. He'd written no, and that was accurate. Something about it left him uneasy, though. He thought back to May, to that Seattle courtroom where he'd gone on trial. Little had he suspected back in the late 1930s that the services he rendered the Japanese consulate from time to time would land him in such trouble. Japan wasn't an enemy at that time, and the work was innocuous—reporting on public meetings and tracking bills affecting aliens in the Washington legislature. It took on a suspicious cast only when the war came. Would it be smarter for him to attach a sheet explaining that he'd been indicted for failing to register as a Japanese agent? That he'd spent months in jail awaiting his trial? And most important, that he'd been acquitted? Would volunteering that information make him look like he had nothing to hide? Or should he answer the question exactly as they'd worded it, about "convictions"?

He stood and paced around his small room. Better to be safe than sorry—

but which route was the safe one? If he mentioned the charges, would they focus on his innocence? Or would they zero in on the work he'd done for the Japanese consul that had gotten him charged in the first place? Which would matter more—that he'd been charged or exonerated?

These questions spun in his head as he circled his room until it dawned on him that he was behaving just like the anxious evacuees he'd spent the day advising. Fear was gaining the upper hand over reason. What would he counsel a client who came to him with this question? That's how he had to look at it. He would tell a client that he should just answer the question they were asking. That it wasn't his job to speculate about what they meant to ask.

No, Masuda resolved, he had not been convicted of a crime other than a traffic violation. That was his answer, that was what he'd written, and he would stick with it.

"Mr. Haas!"

Someone was rapping on Ted Haas's apartment door. "Mr. Haas! I have a message for you!"

Haas sat bolt upright in bed in the dark, heart thumping. He grabbed his alarm clock. Ten after four in the morning. He made his way to the door by the jerking beam of a flashlight through his window.

A messenger apologized for waking him and told him that a beating had just occurred in a barrack. Someone important. Hospitalized. Haas was needed at the police station. Now.

Haas closed the door and stumbled back to his bed. He wasn't sure he had the energy for this, whatever it was. Throughout January his health had slipped, and now in February he feared a crisis. There was blood in his stool, and he'd been vomiting. Without warning a sharp pain would sometimes tear through his lower abdomen, leaving him breathless. He'd told no one about any of this and had tried to keep up his work schedule, but people were starting to notice.

And it wasn't just physical. A familiar dull sadness was pressing in on him, bleaching the color from larger and larger swaths of his experience. Where he used to breeze without a thought from entry to entry in his datebook, he had recently begun noticing each of the tasks filling his day, registering their weight. Shadows of earlier struggles swept through his mind unbidden— panicked walks along Manhattan streets, the ceiling of his sealed and darkened room in the weeks after the bar exam—but he tried to push them away. Sometimes he'd managed to distract himself through these dips by throwing himself even more intently into his work. That was proving harder this time. Whatever was going on in his bowels kept putting him back in bed where there was nothing to do but think.

Haas threw on the shirt and pants he'd draped over his desk chair just a few hours earlier and grabbed a flashlight for the walk to the police station. The center was quiet. Barrack windows were dark and the morning shift in the mess halls hadn't yet arrived to stoke the fires and warm the grills. Only the yips and yaps of a coyote family and the pulsing double call of a killdeer broke the silence of the Poston desert night. But there was no mistaking the police station, even from a distance: light beamed out of every window and figures cast shadows as they brushed past one another on the front steps.

Haas walked down the main hallway past closed doors to Ernie Miller's office. Miller, WRA's director of internal security at the center, was an imposing figure. Easily six feet tall and muscular, he'd come to the job at Poston from years as a beat cop on the streets of San Francisco. From the start Haas had pegged him as one of the less enlightened members of the staff, which was to say, one of those most gripped by racial prejudice. Miller seemed open to trusting the Nisei but was wary of many Issei and had no time at all for the Kibei. He gestured for Haas to take a seat.

"Thanks for coming over. Sorry to have to roust you out of bed. We've got a situation here."

"Another beating?"

"Yes, another beating, Ted, but a big one this time. Multiple perpetrators."

"Where are they?"

"They're here. Three of them. We've got them in separate rooms. Haven't started questioning them yet. Wanted to bring you on board before we got started."

Haas wasn't sure whether to believe that they'd done no interrogating. From time to time he heard rumors of rough handling by Poston's Nisei police squad. He had tried to encourage better behavior by offering evening seminars on proper police procedure, but the cops answered to Miller, not Haas. At least Miller had decided to involve him tonight, so he decided to take Miller at his word rather than press for details about what might have gone on between the arrests and the station.

"Who's the victim?"

"That's why called you in, Ted. This wasn't an everyday dustup. It's Saburo Kido."

Whoa, thought Haas. Saburo Kido was the president of the JACL. This had the makings of trouble.

"Your messenger said he's in the hospital?"

"Unconscious."

It had just been a matter of time. If anyone walked around the center with a target on his back, it was Kido. He was a little guy, dapper, around forty years old. A lawyer, though he wasn't doing anything with the Project Attorney's Office. He probably had no time; as president of the national JACL he surely had plenty keeping him busy. It also kept him unpopular. In the wake of Pearl Harbor, he was one of several JACL leaders who urged the community to comply with evacuation and, rumor had it, fed the FBI names of "suspicious" Issei and Kibei.

This wasn't the first time Kido was coming in for a bruising. Back in mid-September, a gang swarmed him as he walked home from a social visit. They dragged him to the ground, stuffed his mouth with a gag, and kicked him in the head. Then, in November, Kido had loudly called on the government to draft Nisei evacuees out of the camps and into the armed forces. After that, threats became a regular occurrence, so frequent by January that the police began stationing a squad car near his apartment every night.

Tonight, Miller explained, the squad car hadn't shown up. Kido's enemies saw an opportunity and grabbed it. "When our men got to Kido's barrack at around two, they found him on the floor, unconscious, bleeding from wounds to his head and shoulder. A two-foot-long ironwood club was on the floor next to him—bloody, so we're pretty sure that's the weapon they used."

"Why do you say 'they'? Only takes one person to swing a stick."

"This was definitely a group effort, Ted. The neighbors' doors were all jammed with wooden pegs so they couldn't open. The light bulbs were out in the nearby latrines. They even took the mess hall gong down from its mooring and dumped it on the floor so no one could raise an alarm. This was carefully planned."

"Indeed," said Haas.

"Some of Kido's neighbors nabbed one kid right away, a Miyoshi Matsuda, twenty-one years old, cowering in a barrack nearby. Said he'd acted alone at first but then lost his nerve and gave up two others, kids named Tanaka and Inokuchi. We arrested them and brought them here."

Miller looked at Haas with an expectant smile. Haas sensed that he wanted praise, but this was just routine police work. He stayed silent.

"We had them together out in the main office," Miller continued, "but they were whispering to each other in Japanese, so we put them in separate rooms. We're sure there were others involved, but these three aren't talking, and none of Kido's neighbors got a good look in the dark." He pointed to some papers on his desk. "This is what we've got on Matsuda, Tanaka, and Inokuchi. All of them Kibei, just like you'd expect. Tanaka's twenty-three; Inokuchi's just nineteen."

Haas stood up to take a look at the files, but a wave of nausea dropped him back into his chair.

"You OK, Ted?"

"I'm fine," Hass lied. "I was in a pretty deep sleep when they came for me. Guess I'm still waking up."

Miller pushed the papers in front of Haas—registration questionnaires, payroll records, a couple of reports from Social Welfare. The lawyer saw nothing remarkable. They were all rural kids from the Los Angeles area. Not much education. They'd been doing farm labor since they'd been at Poston.

"So what's next, Ernie?"

"Well, we need to round up the other perpetrators quickly, before they can gin up alibis. We've got to get these kids to give up some names."

"And how do you propose to do that?"

The internal security man looked flatly at Haas, his mouth a stern line across his face.

Haas returned the gaze, waiting.

"Shouldn't be too hard," Miller said, nesting his clenched right fist in the palm of his left hand. "They're plenty comfortable right now. Make 'em a little less comfortable and we'll get the names right quick, I think."

Haas shot up out of his chair. The nausea washed over him again, but he choked it back. "Is anything of that sort going on in this building right now?"

Miller smiled. "Simmer down, counselor."

Haas leaned forward, his fingers in little tripods on the desk. "I need to know if anything like that is happening to these boys this instant."

Miller leaned in toward the lawyer. "This isn't one of your night school classes, Ted. We've got to put an end to these beatings. These Kibei gangs are starting to act like they run the place. And they're picking on the folks you like working with, the pro-administration types. I'm surprised you can't see that."

"I can see that perfectly well."

"Can you? Really? How long do you think it'll be before they go after your lawyer friend, what's his name? Tom Masuda?"

Haas stiffened. "You have information about threats against Tom Masuda?" His voice rose in indignation. "Against a staff member of a WRA office? And you didn't see fit to say anything to me?"

"No, nothing specific. I'm just saying—if we don't put a stop to these troublemakers, it's only a matter of time."

"I would like to speak to the prisoners individually." Haas swept to the door, then turned back to Miller. "And with an interpreter," he added, remembering that they were Kibei.

"All right, all right," Miller said, but he stayed in his seat and gathered up the files.

"Now. This instant."

"All *right*, all *right*," he repeated, pushing back his chair.

"I will have more names for you promptly," said Haas over his shoulder as he walked out of the office.

"We'll just see about that, won't we?" Miller replied to Haas's receding back.

By 7:00 A.M., as the early February sky began to brighten, Haas had extracted five more names from Tanaka and Inokuchi. An hour later, four of them were in custody. Miller called Haas back to his office, greeting him at the door with an extended right hand.

"I've got to hand it to you, Ted. You get them to talk, although how I'm not sure. We usually find these Kibei to be pretty hard-boiled."

"Basic interrogation techniques. I got nothing from Inokuchi so I told Tanaka that Inokuchi had fingered him. Tanaka caved right away and gave me two more names—George Inouye and Tadao Hasegawa."

"Sneaky," Miller said with more than a hint of admiration.

"Then I went back to Inokuchi and told him Tanaka had ratted him out as the boss. He then gave up Mits Kuromito, Kataru Urabe, and James Toya. Almost without missing a beat."

Miller bowed slightly, looping his right hand forward from his forehead in an exaggerated gesture of respect.

"Oldest technique in the book, Ernie. Maybe you should enroll in my night school classes."

Miller allowed a smile.

Just then loud footsteps and voices rattled Miller's closed office door. The two men rose and walked out into the main office area. Two Nisei police officers sandwiched a young Japanese American man, each holding an elbow. His teeth were chattering and his eyes were fixed to the floor. "This is James Toya," one of the officers said. "We found him in his apartment, shaking like a leaf."

"Bring him over here," Haas said, pointing to a chair beside a desk.

They sat him down and positioned themselves at his sides. He continued to tremble visibly.

"Thank you, officers. You can step away now."

The men sought their boss's eye, unsure whether to follow the lawyer's orders. Miller nodded slightly and the men reluctantly moved off to the other side of the room. Haas pulled up a chair in front of Toya.

"James, I'm Ted Haas. I'm the project attorney here."

Toya continued to stare at the floorboards.

"I'd like to ask you a few questions."

Toya did not look up.

"Are you hungry? Thirsty? Would you like some water?"

This got Toya's attention. He looked up at the lawyer and nodded almost imperceptibly.

"Officers, would one of you please get James here a glass of water?"

After glancing at Miller for permission, one of the men went into a side room and came out with a glass of water. He handed it to Toya, who guzzled it in a couple of gulps.

"Another?" Haas asked.

Toya nodded.

They repeated the pattern twice more. Each time the trembling suspect downed the water immediately. Each time his trembling eased a bit more. After the third glass, Toya looked up fully and met Haas's eyes.

"Tell us what happened, James."

The story came flooding out, detailed and vivid—how the men had gathered around midnight and set off for Kido's apartment around two o'clock in two groups, with some killing the lights and removing the mess hall bell and others pegging the neighbors' doors shut. How they'd set themselves up as lookouts, and how Matsuda and Tanaka had been the ones to burst in on Kido and thrash him. How a woman had screamed, and they'd all scattered in different directions.

"I can sketch it for you," Toya offered. Haas handed him a sheet of paper and a pencil. Toya sketched the configuration of Kido's whole block, showing the barracks, mess hall, and latrines, the direction from which they'd approached, the doors they'd pegged shut, the positions they'd taken up as lookouts. He handed the drawing to Haas, who passed it to Miller.

"Thank you, James," said Haas, bowing slightly. "Would you be willing to sign a statement?"

"Sure, Mr. Haas."

The lawyer rose and shook Toya's hand. He then turned to Miller. "If you'll allow me to speak to the others again, Ernie, I'm sure I can get statements from them as well."

Within two hours, the police had signed confessions in hand from six of the seven assailants. Only one, Kataru Urabe, the oldest at age thirty-seven, refused to make a statement. He insisted he'd just had the bad luck of being in the vicinity of the attack at the wrong time. Haas stayed at the police station long enough to hear Miller phone the Yuma County attorney with word that they had seven men who needed transporting to the county jail on assault charges. At that point, the adrenaline that had fueled the project attorney through the night and morning's events ebbed away. Overcome by nausea and exhaustion, he stumbled back to his barrack to collapse.

But the day was not over. A couple of hours later, a knock again jolted Ted Haas out of bed. This time it was Ernie Miller, with the news that the county attorney had arrived to take custody of Saburo Kido's assailants.

"So?" Haas blurted, half-awake and squinting in the midafternoon sun. "For this you needed to wake me?"

"I'm sorry, Ted; I didn't want to bother you. But they want you."

"Who wants me?"

"The suspects. The guys you questioned this morning."

Haas tried to get his foggy head to make sense of what the internal security chief was telling him. He had taken their confessions. Why would they want him? "Are they unhappy with the statements, Ernie? Do they want to retract them?"

"No, Ted. They want you to go down to Yuma with them."

Haas opened his mouth but what he was hearing made so little sense to him that he didn't know what to say.

"They want you to represent them. In court."

Haas cocked his head. "Come again?"

"They're saying they want you to be their lawyer."

"You know I can't do that. WRA regulations. Project attorneys aren't allowed to represent evacuees in court."

"I tried telling them, Ted, but they won't have it. 'We want Haas-sensei; we want Haas-sensei' is all they'll say."

"Even after I took their confessions?"

"Go figure," Miller shrugged.

"OK, Ernie, I'll be along in a few minutes. Maybe I can at least explain to them how the system works. But do me one favor while I'm getting myself together, would you? Go grab Tom Masuda. Most of these kids don't speak much English. Tom's Japanese isn't perfect, but mine is nonexistent."

Miller thanked Haas and sped off toward Masuda's block.

Tom Masuda was pulling weeds from the rows of green onions and daikon radishes in his barrack garden when he heard the crunch of approaching boots. He looked up to see Ernie Miller striding toward him, and his pulse quickened. What could the chief of internal security want with him?

"Pack an overnight bag, Tom—you're going to Yuma!"

"I'm going to Yuma?"

"You're going to Yuma. With Mr. Haas. To court, so you'll need to look presentable."

To court? thought Masuda, slapping dirt out of the knees of his dungarees.

Miller quickly explained: Saburo Kido beaten and unconscious, eight Kibei arrested, Yuma County sheriff on his way up to collect them on charges of assault with a deadly weapon.

"But I can't represent them, Chief. It's against the rules, and anyway, I'm not admitted to practice law in Arizona courts."

"You can speak Japanese, can't you?"

Masuda nodded.

"That's why Mr. Haas needs you. Now grab what you need and let's get a move on."

Masuda threw a few items in an overnight bag, left a note for Kay, and dashed to the administration building, where a small WRA bus and a Yuma County police sedan idled. Ted Haas half leaned, half sat on the trunk of the car, with an arm across his chest, his head bowed, and a hand across his forehead massaging the temples. Masuda approached quietly, seeing that Haas's eyes were closed.

"Ted?"

"Ah, Tom, you're here!" Haas snapped upright. "Glad you could make the trip. We should be underway shortly." He gestured toward the building. "The sheriff's in Administration, finishing up some paperwork on the transfer."

"Are you all right, Ted? You're looking . . . pale." In truth, Haas looked worse than pale; he looked depleted. Sickly.

"Oh, I'm fine. Up half the night working on this case, this assault. I suppose I'm a little run down from that. That's all."

"And how's Saburo Kido doing? Do you know?"

"Still in the hospital. Looks like he'll be there a while. Seems he lost quite a bit of blood. But he's regained consciousness, so that's a plus. Too soon to question him, though."

"Where are the suspects?"

Haas turned his eyes to the bus. "In there. Not putting up any sort of fuss. It should be a pretty simple case once we're down in Yuma. I got confessions from all of them except one, Urabe. Insists he wasn't involved. I'm not sure what to believe. The others all seem pretty proud of themselves, though. And Urabe's a good bit older. So maybe he really wasn't in on it."

"And how's their English, Ted? All Kibei?"

"All Kibei. A couple of them do OK in English; the rest really struggle."

"I don't know, Ted; my Japanese is going to get a real workout. I hope I'm up to the task."

"Oh, come on, Tom," said Haas, clapping Masuda on the shoulder. "You'll do fine. Probably the finest Japanese language interpreter the Yuma superior court has ever had!"

"You mean the *only* one they've ever had."

"I prefer 'finest,'" grinned Haas. "Anyhow, if you think I want you along just to translate, think again."

Masuda squinted. "But we're not allowed to represent evacuees, Ted. You know that."

"We can't represent them, but that doesn't mean we can't advise them—about the criminal law, about procedures, about jail time." Haas raised his eyebrows. "Don't you agree?"

It sounded a lot like representing to Masuda, but these guys were in more trouble than they knew and needed all the help they could get. Anyway, who was he to argue?

In Yuma, Tom Masuda accompanied the suspects to the county jail to help with their intake. After all were settled in their cells, he walked to the county attorney's office to meet up with Ted Haas, who'd split off to learn what he could about the following day's court proceedings. Then it was time to find a place to sleep—and urgently, because Haas looked to Masuda as though he might just keel over on the sidewalk.

The San Carlos Hotel at the corner of First and Main was a modern structure, and enormous, easily the tallest in town. *If it had one room, it had a hundred*, thought Masuda as they stepped into the lobby. Behind the desk a man sorted mail into rows of numbered slots. Masuda was experienced enough to hang back and let Haas do the talking, but it did not go well. The clerk, arms crossed, kept shooting glances at Masuda over Haas's shoulder, while Haas's voice grew louder.

After several minutes, Haas wheeled and stalked toward the front door. "Grab your bag, Tom. Let's get out of here."

On the sidewalk, he explained what Masuda already surmised, which was that the San Carlos did not accommodate people who looked like him. "He said your safest bet was Brown's Hotel, just over there." Haas pointed across

Main toward the river, to a single-story building with peeling paint and a striped awning. They watched a Negro man and woman alight from a car and disappear into the hotel through a screen door.

"Thanks, Ted. Looks fine. I'll head over there. I'll come back here in the morning, let's say around eight, and we can find a place to grab breakfast, if you're feeling up to eating."

Haas picked up his bags and stepped off the curb toward Brown's. "Let's go."

Masuda stayed put, gesturing weakly back toward the San Carlos.

Haas stopped after a few paces and looked back at Masuda. "Come on. A bed's a bed."

Masuda couldn't help but flash back to Seattle as he entered the courtroom the following afternoon. This was his first moment back in a courtroom since his trial and acquittal—unless he counted the makeshift community courtroom at Poston—and the tension that had imprinted in him surged up even though it was Saburo Kido's assailants and not him on trial. But there was little time for the memories to steep, because the judge quickly called the cases of the eight Kibei from Poston.

The judge asked him about his Japanese language abilities and then swore him in as the official interpreter. One after the other the Kibei defendants rose to be arraigned on charges of assault with a deadly weapon. Masuda could not help but notice that what was left of their bravado had evaporated in the stale night air of the county jail. One by one across the afternoon, they entered pleas of guilty and, through Masuda, spoke with quiet remorse about their attack on Kido. Only in the case of Kataru Urabe did the pattern break, with the judge dismissing the charge for lack of evidence.

By late afternoon, the judge had worked his way through all of the cases. The only remaining step was to impose sentence on the seven who pled guilty. Masuda felt better than he had in months—invigorated, alive, expert, useful. He and Ted Haas huddled with the defendants, explaining the range of prison terms they might expect, when the judge broke in.

"Counselor?"

Ted Haas stood bolt upright. "Your Honor?"

"No, not you. Mr. Masuda."

The Nisei lawyer popped up beside Haas.

"Thank you for your services today. This would have been quite a challenge without you."

"It has been an honor, Your, uh, Honor." Masuda winced at his awkward phrasing.

"The court will be happy to pay you twenty-five dollars for your services today."

Masuda flushed with surprise and pleasure.

"But you're not finished."

"Your Honor?"

"The court has one more service to ask of you. I do not feel ready to impose sentence on these defendants today. I would like to develop a better understanding of the events and of the personal backgrounds of each of these young men. May I ask you to prepare brief reports on each of them and file them with the court two weeks from today?"

"Most certainly, Your Honor."

"Thank you, counsel." The judge tapped his gavel. "We stand adjourned."

Masuda bowed slightly as the judge left the bench. Eyes wide behind his round glasses, he turned to a beaming Ted Haas.

"A good day's work, Tom. We were lucky to have you here, all of us."

"Thanks, Ted. And thanks for the opportunity. It felt good to be back in a courtroom. Although I've been worried that I'm doing too much."

Haas stopped gathering his papers. "Too much? How do you mean?"

"The WRA rule against representing evacuees in court."

"The only thing I saw you representing today was justice. If it's against the WRA's rules to seek justice, Tom, the problem is the rules."

The praise filled Masuda with warmth in the moment. But on the long drive back to Poston, the cold truth about the rules took its place.

CHAPTER NINE

JUNE 1943

POSTON AND LOS ANGELES

WAR DEPARTMENT
MILITARY INTELLIGENCE SERVICE
Washington

June 9, 1943

Mr. Thomas Shinao Masuda
Colorado River Relocation Center
Poston, Arizona

Dear Sir:

You have been found qualified to attend the next course to be given at the Military Intelligence Service (MIS) Language School.

As soon as you have been inducted and assigned an Army serial number, it is requested that you present this letter to your Commanding Officer and that you notify this office, by wire, of your station and Army serial number.

Provided you are qualified for full military service, orders will be requested immediately assigning you to the Military Intelligence Service Language School.

Sincerely yours,
ROBERT S. TRAVIS
2nd Lt., AUS
Assistant Personnel Officer, MIS

Thomas Masuda had been waiting for this news for months, ever since the MIS put out its call for volunteers with skills in Japanese. Nobody knew the details of what the outfit was doing in the war effort—it was an intelligence unit, after all—but everyone assumed it was something sensitive and important.

Maybe they were interrogating Japanese POWs, or translating documents, or helping break Japanese codes, or even infiltrating Japanese army or naval units as spies. The specifics didn't matter to Masuda; it was an opportunity to serve, to use his language skills to help win the war. His spoken Japanese was far from perfect, and his reading was nearly a lost cause. That's what the language school at Camp Savage was for—to take Nisei soldiers with decent language skills and turn them into experts. Masuda couldn't wait.

As he read and reread the short text, his mind churned with conflicting thoughts. Seen one way, the moment was perfect for getting out of Poston. The Arizona summer was upon them, with temperatures climbing to triple digits almost every day since the last week of May. More and more buildings at camp were getting chillers, but they were no match for the blaze of the midday desert sun. Camp Savage was just south of the Twin Cities in Minnesota— *Minnesota!* Masuda pictured cool lakes bordered by lush forests, cotton-ball clouds puffing across crystal blue skies. Was it really like that? Who knew? But was it better than the flattening heat of Roastin' Toastin' Poston? It had to be.

Odd as it seemed to say, a military life also seemed simpler, less layered. You had one mission and you were to go after it single-mindedly. What a welcome change from camp, where it seemed Masuda was expected to be all things to all people. Working in the Project Attorney's Office was complicated enough, what with someone from Internal Security dropping by one minute and an irate evacuee the next. But now the chair of the community council had appointed him Poston's "city attorney." What that entailed Masuda did not know—probably nobody knew. But it was another hat to try to balance atop an already tottering stack. The chance to doff them all in favor of one sleek army cap was enticing.

And yet the timing was also terrible. These days Masuda didn't just work *in* the Project Attorney's Office. He *was* the project attorney, or the acting project attorney anyway. Ted Haas had left the center on medical leave in mid-February and was still gone several months later. There was a reason Haas had been doing so poorly back in the late winter: an anal fistula, with all the blood and pain and exhaustion that went with it. Haas had gone to Los Angeles for surgery, saying he'd be back within weeks, but weeks stretched to months without much explanation. There were rumors of a second fistula and a second surgery, but it seemed an awfully long convalescence. Even now, in early June, Masuda had no idea when his boss would be back.

Therein lay the problem: If Masuda were to leave for Camp Savage, who would mind the shop at Poston? For several months, Masuda had been the top lawyer at this, the largest of the WRA centers, shouldering all of the position's duties and enjoying all of its privileges. Well, all of its privileges except the financial ones. Masuda's salary stayed at nineteen dollars per month, the most an evacuee could earn, rather than the nearly $300 per month paid to Ted. But money wasn't the point; responsibility was. Masuda had been the one in the meetings with the project director and other key officials. He had been the one dealing with local and state officials. He had been the one writing the weekly reports to WRA solicitor Phil Glick in Washington. The center was depending on him. If he left, the WRA would find some stopgap—a lawyer on loan from the home office or another of the centers—but that person would step in without understanding Poston and its history, without appreciating the evacuees and the challenges they faced.

Masuda had to give Ted Haas some credit on this score. For a Caucasian, Haas tried to see things how the evacuees saw them. That time the head of Community Welfare had stormed into the office, outraged about unmarried couples living together, Haas had really stood up to her. She wanted legal action, but Haas told her to forget it. The community had no big problem with common-law marriages, and Haas had been astute enough to see it, and that was that. Haas did that kind of thing often. In fact, it was Haas who'd lobbied to give Masuda the project attorney's job while he was hospitalized. Haas believed deeply that the evacuees could be trusted to run the center, just as he believed Indians could run their reservations.

It wasn't that Haas always got things right. He had too soft a spot for the WRA's hokum about needing to "Americanize" people who were already Americans. He often seemed to fool himself into thinking that the beauty the evacuees put on the outsides of their barracks—the carved nameplates and the rock gardens—signaled contentment within. But at least he made a genuine effort to see camp through Japanese American eyes, which was more than you could say for much of the rest of the staff.

Masuda couldn't help but look through Japanese American eyes, and this helped him finesse tricky situations that even the most well-meaning Caucasian would miss. A recent burglary case, for example. A woman filed a complaint against a man for stealing a mirror from her apartment. The case was careening toward a trial by the project director until Masuda figured out what was really going on. The burglary wasn't the real story; a breakup was. The two were married, but not to each other. Their affair had been so flagrant that their block forced the man to move to a different part of the center. The woman now wanted to break things off, so the man picked her lock to retrieve what he claimed was his, including the mirror in question. Masuda persuaded the couple that a criminal case would cost more in shame than the price of a mirror. What they really needed was a way to break up without losing the little bit of face they had left. He got everyone to agree to a quick, quiet order from the judicial commission that they keep apart, and that was that. All it took was a little kenmei—a little good sense—to work it through.

This was what worried him about joining the service. Ted Haas was a good lawyer, and he tried to understand the evacuees, but kenmei would always elude him. In any event, he was in the hospital, and no one knew when he'd be back. Who could fill Masuda's shoes if he left for Camp Savage?

The Nisei lawyer looked again at the letter from Lieutenant Travis. "Provided you are qualified for full military service, orders will be requested immediately assigning you to the Military Intelligence Service Language School." He allowed himself a smile. A tingle of pride ran down his spine. The MIS.

Poston would have to figure out how to get by without him.

IMPRESSIONS OF POSTON
Theodore H. Haas
June 10, 1943—Los Angeles, California

A hospital bed offers the patient new perspectives. Amidst the quiet and leisure of convalescence, he seeks escape from present woes by reminiscing. His body tired and wracked with pain, he often becomes more introspective as he appraises and reappraises his deeds revived by reverie. As the present fades, the past is recreated in vivid colors and sharp angular forms.

This spring while recovering from my operation, my mind recalled innumerable memories of my work during the preceding nine months as attorney of the largest Japanese American relocation center, at Poston, Arizona, which is operated by the Indian Service under policies formulated by the War Relocation Authority, a war agency, established by the President. I jotted down a few of the thoughts which galloped feverishly through my brain.

The first months were replete with drama. The lights go out while an evacuee surgeon is performing an appendectomy. Undaunted, he successfully completes the operation by candlelight. Just as the first Community Council is sworn in by the Project Director in an open air evening ceremony, a terrific sandstorm, followed by a torrential rain, scatters the gathering. Many of the councilmen take refuge in the nearby fire house and watch roofs ripped off and power and communications disrupted.

The vast majority arrived at the projects stoically determined to make the best of things. Amidst physical discomforts including confinement, overcrowding, dust and heat, their plight preyed upon their minds. A community mess hall for each block, inhabited usually by about 275 persons with several families living together in one room, prevented normal family life.

Most, in my opinion, were loyal to the United States. The loyal were exposed to the taunts of the comparatively few who were disloyal. A few lost their faith in America because of their experience. Let us analyze some of the predominant emotions of many.

Humiliation. Imagine how it feels to be suddenly uprooted from home, school and business and brought to a camp, enclosed by a wire fence and guarded by soldiers; to believe that in the minds of many—maybe most of your fellow Americans—you cannot be trusted during a national crisis; to be unable to demonstrate your loyalty to your country by enlisting in the armed forces; to be classified by the Selective Service as "IV-C" (the category for aliens); to be identified in the minds of many of one's countrymen with the Japanese enemies and to be regarded by the unthinking and ignorant as "prisoners of war."

Novelists and poets, jurists and criminologists have frequently written of men convicted of crimes they did not commit. Many loyal Japanese-Americans must have experienced the poignant emotions of those convicted erroneously—at least at the beginning before the opportunity for relocation was offered.

Bitterness. They pined for the fields of California and the broad expanse of the Pacific or beautiful Los Angeles. They contrasted their barren surroundings with the beauties of their native states. They were angered by the false stories believed by many on the outside that they were being pampered and living in luxury, not even subject to rationing. Many had suffered heavy property losses because of hurried or forced sales of property or businesses. A few were tricked into disposing of personal property at a low price. In some instances supposed "friends" misused property entrusted to them while some of the property stored in churches or vacant stores was injured, destroyed or stolen within a year. Furniture and machinery, which escaped floods, fire, vandalism

and thievery, were sometimes "borrowed" and used without permission. In some places community sentiment and the police con-
doned this conduct. Their income in the center was insufficient to
give them and their children a modicum of comfort.

What had they done to deserve this? Why were they herded into
camps and Germans and Italians left untouched? In their despair,
some thought of the discrimination against them during the peace.
They felt bitter toward many Caucasians, false friends who turned
against them in their hour of need.

Gratitude. They were grateful for the liberal friends and
religious groups who remained faithful to them and tried to
alleviate their sufferings. Many were appreciative for the
untiring work of certain government officials. How glad they were
to see Caucasian friends who visited them! How overjoyed to learn
that amidst the war hysteria, some trusted them!

Fear. They experienced hundreds of fears, fears about the
present and the future—some real, some groundless, many based on
false rumors which were rife. Many of their fears related to the
immediate situation. Stoves did not come until the temperature had
reached a low depth. They feared the effect of the wintry blasts on
the health of the children.

They felt very insecure. The future looked black for them and
their children. The prospect of spending several years in the
relocation centers was disheartening. Yet the papers they read,
mainly the Los Angeles and Phoenix papers, and radio programs
they heard, reeked with the strong feeling against them on the
coast and in the far west. They were told that one of the reasons for
evacuation was the fear of violence against them. Would not this
hostility increase as the war casualty lists increased? Would not
the hymn of hate against them become louder and more intolerant?

Would they be able to return to California before the end of
the war? Or even after peace came? Would they be deported to
Japan? Would they lose their citizenship? Were they men without
a country—distrusted alike by the land of their birth and the
country of their parents? Were they children of a lost generation—
without hope, to be hated, feared and scorned by their fellow
Americans?

Lethargy and Loss of Ambition. Some of the older people had through industry and ability built up prosperous farms and businesses. Now they felt that nothing further remained for them. They became accustomed to the camps and were satisfied under the circumstances to stay there, where they were at least assured of safety, food, shelter, and medical care.

The hopelessness of the future also dampened the ambition of many of the young and middle aged. All the young men at a symposium maintained that it was unwise to get married at Poston because of the insecurity of the future. Discouragement caused them to assume an apparent indifference. They became dissatisfied with themselves and their life, but did not know how to remedy their condition. It was difficult for many who were formerly interested in improving their mind to read or study. The shock of their adversity stultified them; paternalism reduced their initiative. A few saw no life but going to Japan and they dreamed of their new life in the Orient.

The young women on the other hand were more cheerful. In many cases they had opportunities in their work more satisfying than housework. The improved status of women in the United States appealed to them. When the relocation program gathered momentum, many young women felt unhappy because their parents forbade them to leave, because of a fear that they might get into trouble without parental guidance and because Japanese tradition of parental duty required the daughter to remain with her family until marriage.

Confusion. The conflicts in culture between the younger and older people, characteristic of immigrant groups, were accentuated, and added to the confusion of youth. The few who were disloyal argued, "We're all Japanese. They distrust all of us. All right, let's be Japanese then. Let's not cooperate. They'll send us back to Japan after the war anyway. Let's improve our knowledge of the Japanese language and culture. Let's teach it to our children and friends." The clash between Nisei, Kibei, and Issei ideologies and culture—the Japanese and American way of life—became acute at times. American plays and movies versus Japanese drama and Shibai. Baseball, judo, golf, boxing and sumo competed. There was a diffusion of cultures. Many country girls learned how to jitterbug. Many youths improved their Japanese.

Renewed Hope. The War Relocation Authority announced in the fall of 1942 a program of releasing on indefinite leave residents of the centers who secured positions in communities where local sentiment was found to be receptive to their coming. Special emphasis was placed on relocation in the Midwest. Private industry and agriculture are increasingly employing evacuees. Although most of the early requests were for domestic or farm labor, gradually there was an increased demand for workers in trades and offices and professional workers, and a variety of other occupations, including chick sexers and nursery assistants. Several religious groups have aided in this work.

The War Relocation Authority investigated all applicants for indefinite leave before their release. Their names are checked against the FBI's records and when necessary by the Army and Navy Intelligence Services. The adventurous residents who applied at the outset and left their friends and families with premonition wrote back favorable accounts of their new freedom and their treatment the same as other human beings. This has greatly improved morale in the centers and added impetus to the leave program.

Maybe there was still hope for the future. It seems strange that we must count as an achievement during a war, caused in part by the Nazis' false doctrine of racial superiority, that a few thousand Japanese-Americans are relocated comfortably amidst a minimum of discrimination.

The world is shrinking by the growing speed and ease of communications and transportation. All nations and races are becoming neighbors. If we cannot live amicably with 120,000 Japanese scattered throughout our land, it presages ill for our ability to live peacefully in a world of several hundred million Mongolians. If we perfect our democracy by ending racial and religious discrimination, it will serve as an example for the people of the world to imitate. Our hypocrisy relating to minorities must end.

Some of my memories are so very sad! Have sickness and pain affected my emotional stability so markedly? To check my feelings, I review historical parallels thus:

"Don't lose your balance. Compulsory migrations of religious,

national, and racial minorities have been frequent in peace and
war—for example, Huguenots, Armenians, Jews, Arcadians, Mormons,
Catholics, and the American Indians.

"The last four years of European history are blackened by
heartless deportations by the Nazis of masses of people, young
and old, rich and poor, men, women and children. During the past
six years, millions of Chinese have migrated westward after the
ruthless destruction of their homes."

I understand these tragedies more fully because I saw some of the
hardships of an evacuation executed with humanity and kindness.

To Tom Masuda's eye, downtown Phoenix was an eyesore, totally lacking in
Seattle's charm. The only saving grace was the pretty palm trees; apart from
those, there was not much to look at. The art deco Luhrs Tower at First and
Jefferson was the one modest exception. It had none of the elegance of the
Olympic Hotel in downtown Seattle, of course, but its columns, crests, and
arched entry gave it a touch of class that the surrounding low, boxy structures
lacked.

Unfortunately, the rear of Luhrs Tower had none of its facade's sophisti-
cation, and that's where Masuda was standing in line, waiting to enter the
armed forces recruiting station when its doors opened at eight thirty. His
military adventure was about to get underway, and he was having a hard time
containing his nerves. As the only Nisei in line—and probably in the entire
complex—Masuda knew better than to try to strike up a conversation with
those around him. He'd spent enough time in Phoenix on Poston business to
keep his head down and look away as quizzical eyes tried to discern whether
his was a Chinese or a Japanese face. One of the MPs at the door was already
casting glances his way. So Masuda contented himself with bouncing gently
from foot to foot and humming a Bing Crosby tune. Every few minutes he
patted his pocket to make sure that the letter from Lieutenant Travis hadn't
gone missing since the last time he patted his pocket.

Once inside, Masuda moved through the steps to induction quickly. The
letter welcoming him into the Military Intelligence Service jumped him to
the head of the line for his physical examinations. He'd heard stories of Nisei
volunteers running afoul of the height and weight requirements—in the sense
of being too short or too thin—but at five foot six he was half a foot above the

minimum, and at nearly 200 pounds, well, an upper limit was more of his concern. But the exams went off without incident, and a smiling handshake from the physician chairing the medical examination board let him know he'd made the grade. The doctor looked at Masuda's letter welcoming him into the MIS training program and directed him to a waiting area for army induction processing. Soft music was playing, free Cokes were on offer, and Masuda had his choice from an array of lounge chairs and divans. He chuckled at the amenities as he settled in to complete a stack of paperwork. This was surely the pinnacle of army comfort; it would all be downhill from here.

"Mr. Thomas Masuda?" A uniformed man at the opening of a cubicle caught the lawyer's eye and waved him forward with a clipboard. Masuda leapt up and walked briskly into the cubicle, noticing sergeant's stripes on the soldier's shoulder as he passed. "Have a seat," said the sergeant. Army posters covered the low walls; American flags stood in the corner and, in miniature, on the sergeant's desk. A single manila folder sat between the men on the desk. Masuda offered his filled-out forms across the desk, but the sergeant simply jerked his head to indicate where Masuda should set them down. He tried to present the sergeant with his letter of welcome to the MIS, but the soldier gestured that off as well. Masuda watched as the sergeant picked up the manila folder, studied whatever was in it—Masuda couldn't see—and then placed it back on the desk.

"Mr. Masuda, the army would like to thank you very much for coming in today. I'm sorry to let you know that we will not be seeking your induction at this time."

It took a long moment for these words to assemble themselves as a meaningful sentence in Masuda's ears. He cocked his head slightly but kept his smile locked. "I'm sorry?"

The sergeant repeated himself word for word.

"But there must be a mistake somewhere, sir," said Masuda, picking up the letter from Lieutenant Travis and again offering it across the desk. "I've been invited to the training program of the Military Intelligence Service up at Camp Savage in Minnesota. I'm due there in just a few days."

The soldier did not take the letter from Masuda's outstretched hand. It hung there uncomfortably.

"Again, Mr. Masuda, the army will not be seeking your induction at this time. You are free to return to the relocation center."

"Would you do me the courtesy of examining this letter, sir? The language is quite clear."

The sergeant took the letter and examined it. "Uh-*huh*," he said after a moment, tapping the paper with his index finger.

"What?"

"It says here, 'Provided you are qualified for full military service, orders will be requested immediately assigning you to the Military Intelligence Service Language School.'" He tapped the paper again. *"Provided you are qualified for full military service."*

Masuda stared ahead in bewilderment.

"You are not qualified for full military service at this time, Mr. Masuda." He passed the letter back. "That is what I am trying to tell you."

The lawyer slumped. "May I ask the basis of the disqualification, sir? I passed my physical with flying colors."

The soldier shook his head. He held up the manila folder, gave it a meaningful glance, and then met Masuda's eyes across the desk. "I am not at liberty to say, Mr. Masuda."

Masuda looked down at the letter now lying in his lap. A clock on the desk ticked several seconds away, and then Masuda brightened. "The MIS training program begins in just a few days. Wouldn't it be smarter for me to head up to Minnesota and wait there? In case this proves to be an error? I am prepared to pay my own way."

The sergeant opened his manila folder once again and glanced down at its contents. "I believe that would be quite pointless, Mr. Masuda." He stood and offered a hand, gesturing toward the door of the cubicle with the other.

The next thing the Nisei lawyer knew, he was on a bus heading west back toward Poston. How he'd stumbled his way from the Luhrs Tower to the bus station he could not recall. What could possibly have gone wrong? He had a letter of admission to the training program. He had passed his physical.

A thought flickered through his mind and singed his gut. The loyalty questionnaire. He hadn't mentioned his trial back in Seattle. Could that be it? Just failing to mention a charge of which he was innocent? For which he'd been exonerated by a jury of Caucasians?

Could that be the problem?

If that's it, he thought ruefully, *I'll never forgive myself.*

CHAPTER TEN

JULY 1943

POSTON, ARIZONA

Is *circle dancing universal?* Ted Haas turned this question over in his mind as his eye followed a curving line of Nisei girls on a surprisingly pleasant mid-August evening at Poston.

He'd grown up watching plenty of horas, circles of Jews in locked arms kicking and pivoting their way around crowded dance floors. The stylized promenade taking place in the field before him traced a wider arc than those. What the scene brought to mind more vividly were the Indian ghost dances he'd witnessed when he was out on the road with Felix Cohen working on tribal constitutions for the Office of Indian Affairs. Those often started with the dancers treading a wide, slow radius around drummers at the center. That's what these Japanese were doing, more or less. Upward of 100 women and girls were revolving in a circle half the length of a football field around a central platform with an amplified record player. *Humans have so much in common,* Haas thought. Pretty much anywhere you looked on earth, you'd find dancers in a ring around someone striking or plucking or blowing something.

He was trying his best to "take it easy"—doctor's orders back in late June when they finally released him from the hospital and let him return to Poston. No more nineteen-hour days, no more seven-day workweeks, no more middle-of-the-night memoranda. "Taking it easy" didn't come naturally; he wasn't one to while away an afternoon with the funny pages. Hiking was more to his liking, but out here the searing summer heat placed that out of the question. So he took in the center's musical and cultural activities whenever he could. These got him out, occupied him, and kept him in circulation with the evacuees.

And he learned things. This was the seventh lunar month under the Japanese calendar, the season of Obon, which Tom Masuda explained to him as a time when Buddhists honor their ancestors. The dance unfolding before him was bon odori, the traditional dance of Obon. Earlier in the day he'd attended a beautiful, solemn service before an altar, with incense, offerings, and chanted prayer. Tonight's event was more lighthearted. The field next to block 28 was festooned with pennants as colorful as the vivid kimonos of the dancers. The space glowed under spotlights that seemed to grow more brilliant as the sky slipped from dusk into night. Cheerful Japanese melodies lilted from the yagura, the wooden platform at the center of the circle. Children ran to and fro with hot dogs and shaved ice from the canteen.

It bothered Haas that so few WRA staff members had come out for the event. Staff turnout at baseball games and concerts was dependably good, which made the thinness of the crowd this evening that much more noticeable. Naturally, project director Wade Head was there, along with his top deputy. But apart from them, it looked to Haas as though the only staff to show up was a handful of schoolteachers. What a lousy message to send the evacuees.

As the evening grew late, Haas bumped into some friends of Tom Masuda's in the crowd and fell into conversation. The lawyer inquired about some finer points of the bon odori choreography and described a Northern Paiute ghost dance he'd once witnessed on a reservation in western Nevada. After a while, the talk turned to a topic that was on nearly everyone's minds: segregation. Those who had answered no to the loyalty questions back in the spring, or who had asked for expatriation to Japan, were to be segregated to the Tule Lake center in California. The loyal folks at Tule Lake, in turn, would be shifted to one of the other nine WRA centers, including maybe Poston. People knew the process was scheduled for the fall of 1943, but that was about the extent of it. Nobody knew the details.

In truth, Haas didn't know the details either—WRA headquarters either hadn't yet worked them out or hadn't announced them—but he was doing his best to reassure Masuda's friends when he heard laughter over his shoulder and felt a sharp tug at his elbow. A Nisei girl who looked to be maybe thirteen years old was pulling on his arm, shouting an invitation to join the dance, while several kimono-clad friends of hers convulsed in laughter a few feet away. "Come on! We'll teach you! Come dance with us!" they shouted, drawing the attention of other dancers, who stopped to join the chant. Haas felt a rush of delight at the invitation but was nothing but a spasm of jerking arms and legs as a dancer and had no desire to make a fool of himself. He also had his still-healing incisions to think about. The scene become a hilarious tug-of-war, with his elbow as the fulcrum, until big drops of rain began plopping into the dirt around them. In seconds the pace picked up, sending everyone scattering, Haas's young wooer included. A rare late-evening cloudburst: *Deus ex machina*, thought the lawyer as he trotted toward the police station nearby for shelter.

Haas collided with a dripping Wade Head inside the door. The project director threw his arms around Haas's waist to stabilize him. "Easy there, counselor, we don't want to have to send you back to the hospital!" he said with a smile.

Haas thanked Head for the helping hand and began pointlessly brushing off his drenched shirt. As more soggy souls threw themselves through the door, the project director grabbed Haas by the arm and pulled him back into a corner. "Listen, Ted," he murmured, leaning into Haas's ear, "I need to tell you something—something about Tom Masuda."

Haas didn't like that Head was whispering.

"You know that while you were laid up in Los Angeles, Tom got turned down by the army, right? Big mystery—he was accepted at the Military Intelligence School at Camp Savage, but they wouldn't induct him, and they wouldn't tell him why."

"Yes," said Haas, "of course I know. Tom was terribly disappointed. He wants so badly to serve."

"Well, mystery solved," whispered Head. "Just got the note today. There's intelligence info on him, Ted, and it doesn't look good. Something about working for Japanese interests in Seattle, back before the war."

"Wha-what?" Haas stammered. "Intelligence info on *Tom*?"

"Yes, on Tom."

"This isn't about that trial, is it? In Seattle, before evacuation? The one where he was *acquitted*?" Haas emphasized the last word to make sure Head recalled that key detail.

"Unclear, Ted. But Washington has revoked his leave clearance, so he's not leaving the center until we hold a hearing and get to the bottom of it."

"There simply has to be a mistake, Wade. I would trust that man with my life. Hell, he even ran the Project Attorney's Office for months while I was sick!"

"That's what the hearing's for, Ted. He'll have the chance to clear it all up, whatever it is. Clear his name."

Haas shook his head in disgust. "Doesn't seem right."

"No, it doesn't. But I have confidence in you, Ted. If anyone here can give him a fair shake, it's you."

"*I* will give him a fair shake? What do you mean, *I* will?"

"Look, this is obviously sensitive. I need you to do this. It's above anyone else's pay grade."

"But Tom's a friend, Wade. How am I supposed to interrogate a friend?"

"I have confidence in you." Head clapped him on his wet shoulders and gave him an affirming nod.

When Haas arrived at the office the next day, a single yellow envelope sat on his desk. Sealed with both staples and tape, it bore the word CONFIDENTIAL in red across both front and back. He closed his door, sat down at the desk, and sliced the envelope open with a letter opener.

FEDERAL BUREAU OF INVESTIGATION
Washington, D.C.

July 7, 1943

THOMAS SHINAO MASUDA

Reference is made to the request for a name check on Thomas Shinao Masuda. Masuda is a Japanese-American citizen who practiced law in Seattle, Washington. In 1941 he was the vice president of the North American Japanese Association and the Japanese Chamber of Commerce. This organization was dominated by first generation Japanese and was engaged in activities indicating sympathies of the Japanese government. It sponsored Japanese language schools and Japanese fencing clubs, which exercised a retarding effect on the Americanization of the second generation Japanese. It had also collected contributions for the Japanese war chest, and the officers were almost invariably pro-Japanese. Masuda was legal representative for the Japanese Consul, for numerous business concerns, and for Japanese clubs and associations. A number of his clients were suspected of being engaged in espionage activities, and he himself was reported to be very pro-Japanese and quite close to the Japanese consul.

Additional information regarding Masuda was received to the effect that he was visited quite frequently by an individual who was a known espionage agent, and it was also reported that he participated in the distribution of pro-Japanese propaganda which was sponsored by the Japanese Chamber of Commerce in 1937. In a signed statement Masuda admitted that he was not registered with the State Department as an Agent of a Foreign Principal, and that he had acted as an Attorney for the Japanese Consulate for four years, and in addition that he was the Attorney for the Japanese Association of Seattle, which organization distributed pro-Japanese propaganda. He further acknowledged that he

reported audience reaction to anti-Japanese propaganda, and that
such information was furnished by him to the Japanese Consul
in Seattle. Masuda also admitted that he had contributed $25
to the Japanese War Chest in 1939. Masuda was allegedly engaged
as a lobbyist for the Japanese Consul at the 1941 session of the
Washington State Legislature, and had also acted as a lobbyist
for the Consulate in 1937.

Haas looked out his office window, taking a deep breath and exhaling
slowly through puffed cheeks. Masuda had mentioned none of these details
to him in all the months they'd worked together. He'd mentioned his trial,
of course. Haas remembered it vividly because of the acquittal: What chance
had any Japanese American stood in court in the spring of 1942? The acquittal
was a stunning rebuke of the prosecutor's case; no doubt about that. But these
specifics, they were . . . concerning.

Haas looked back at the document. Two short paragraphs remained.

On January 28, 1942, he was indicted by a Federal Grand Jury,
Seattle, Washington, and charged with violation of the Registration Act, Section 233 of Title 22 and Section 98 of Title 18, United
States Code. Section 233 of Title 22 prohibits a person, not being
a diplomatic officer, not being a Consul officer, and not being
an Attaché, to act as an agent or representative of a foreign
government without prior notification to the Secretary of State
of the United States of America. Title 18, Section 98, prohibits a
person from having possession of or having control of property and
papers designed and intended for the use of a foreign government
or in aid of a foreign government.

Masuda was tried at Seattle, Washington, on these charges.
However, he was acquitted by a Federal jury.

He placed the report on his desk and pinched the bridge of his nose. A
burning twitch in his neck foretold a headache. This was a more complicated
situation than the acquittal had led him to believe. Sure, the verdict was
miraculous. But all it meant from a legal standpoint was that a prosecutor
hadn't managed to prove guilt beyond a reasonable doubt, the standard for
convicting someone of a crime in a criminal court. But these WRA hearings
weren't criminal trials. They were for figuring out whether a person was safe

to release. Nobody in the WRA seemed sure how much evidence was needed to deny leave clearance, but it surely was less than the amount needed to send someone to a penitentiary. So the acquittal, remarkable as it was for its time and place, wouldn't really carry much weight here at Poston.

The WRA had public relations to think about too. One mistake—one evacuee committing a crime while out on leave—and the newspapers would be on the agency like a swarm of wasps. The politicians would follow. It would be a disaster, particularly if the crime had even a hint of subversion or sabotage to it. That would be the end of the leave policy entirely; the gates of the centers would swing shut for everyone and stay shut.

Haas also had a personal reason to tread carefully. Reading the intelligence report gave him the distinct sensation of egg on his face. He had trusted Masuda and advocated for him with the rest of the staff. Had he known the details in this report he might have been a bit more circumspect. He might have taken Masuda aside and talked things over—assured himself that these were all just innocuous matters the lawyer had undertaken well before Japan became an enemy of the United States. Haas had no doubt he would have reached that conclusion if they'd had the conversation. But they hadn't. So it wasn't just Masuda's reputation on the line now. In a way, it was also his own.

Thoroughness was in order. He was sure Masuda would understand.

The next day, Tom Masuda stopped to pick up his mail on his way home from the office. He had just two items—the latest Montgomery Ward catalog and what looked to be a piece of government mail. The return address on the envelope said . . . the administration building right here at Poston? How odd. Probably a notice about pay schedules or some such.

Once home, he realized the mess hall wouldn't be serving dinner much longer, so he dropped the catalog on a chair and dashed off with Kay to grab dinner. Only when they returned did he think to open the letter. It was from Wade Head, the project director, and it wasn't just a form letter about pay schedules. The letter told him that he'd been denied leave clearance due to "certain information in the hands of the WRA" and that a leave clearance hearing had been scheduled in a few days' time. Dinner turned to lead in his stomach. What could this possibly be about? First the army rejection, and now this? His mind could fly back only to the Seattle courtroom where he'd been tried and acquitted. *Acquitted!* He wanted to shout the word so loud that everyone could hear it—even Dillon Myer in his office at WRA headquarters in Washington. Would they ever let him step out of the shadow of those accusations—the ones he'd beaten?

The letter offered one more piece of information about the hearing: Ted Haas would be chairing it. Now this was just downright bizarre. He'd crossed paths with Ted at least a dozen times today in the office. They'd been in two meetings together. But Ted hadn't breathed a word about it.

Why?

"Are you ready for me?" Tom Masuda poked his head through the conference room doorway.

Ted Haas wheeled and smiled a bit too broadly. "Tom! Come in, come in. Yes, we're all set." He extended his hand and Masuda grasped it.

Why are we shaking hands? thought Masuda.

This feels awkward, said Haas to himself. *We never shake hands.*

In an instant they unclasped, and Haas swept his arm toward the other men in the room. "Tom, you know these good gentlemen, don't you? Ralph, Ernie, Giles, Len?"

A five-member hearing committee? Masuda thought. They were normally three. *Something's not right here*, he said to himself as he briefly acknowledged each of the men.

Haas saw the worry in Masuda's eyes. "Quite a group of heavy hitters, eh, Tom?" These were some of Poston's top administrators—assistant directors, heads of divisions. "This was the hottest ticket in town! I guess you're just a popular man!" Haas always spoke quickly, but these words buzzed out of his mouth like bees from a hive.

For a moment the men stood in place, each looking at the other and none knowing what to do next. "Well, gentlemen, shall we sit down and get started?" asked Haas, gesturing toward the table.

The men played a game of musical chairs, even though there were enough seats for all. At first, they arrayed themselves around the table in a way that left Haas and Masuda on the same side, which was not going to work if Haas was to take the lead on questioning. The group stood awkwardly for a moment until Masuda grabbed the back of his chair, at which point Haas gestured to Ralph Gelvin across the table and the two men changed places. "This ought to work," said Haas, and they all sat down.

Masuda looked at Haas with an eyebrow raised. They'd been working together for a year, and this was the first time they were on opposite sides of a table.

Haas shrugged awkwardly and forced a smile. Obviously, this was hard for Masuda, but he hoped Masuda recognized how hard it was for him too. "Make yourself comfortable, Tom, won't you? Glass of water?" It was a scorching late summer day, and the chillers were struggling.

"Let's just get started," Masuda said, leaning forward and clasping his hands on the table.

Haas kicked the meeting off with a reminder of why they were gathered: WRA headquarters had temporarily suspended Masuda's leave clearance in order to take a closer look at certain intelligence information they'd received. He opened a folder on the table before him. "Mr. Masuda, will you please tell us the circumstances concerning your trial in Seattle for violation of the Registration Act?"

Did he really just call me "mister"? thought Masuda. The phrase sounded bizarre. Around the office he was always just "Tom," and Ted was just "Ted." Masuda should have expected it; this was a formal hearing. But he hadn't, and it threw him. "Umm," he replied, "I don't quite follow you, Mr. Haas." Two could play the formality game. "What do you mean by the 'circumstances' of my trial?"

"Well, Mr. Head received a confidential report which contains facts concerning your practice of law in Seattle, Washington, activities before the state legislature of Washington, and various other activities including your indictment before the federal grand jury. Just tell us how it happened and the circumstances underlying your practice of law and activities before the legislature, if any, and I think then other questions will arise." Haas was normally a model of precise expression, but he was finding it difficult to formulate his question. He noticed his mouth was dry.

Masuda leaned back in his chair. "The question you're asking is rather broad and far-reaching, so I think I'll try to discuss it in a cursory way—the main points—and anyone that has any questions can follow up. OK?"

Five men nodded in unison.

"I was first picked up by the FBI on the morning of December 8, under a charge that I was a member of an organization to overthrow the U.S. government by force and violence. That charge was dropped two months later. The charges I went to trial on were primarily my activities in the state legislature and three occasions of covering public meetings. The activities with the legislature were matters I handled as a practicing attorney in Seattle. I represented a number of organizations such as the Japanese Hotel Association, the Northwest Produce Association, and the Japanese Chamber of Commerce. Some of them paid me an annual retainer and others hired me for individual matters. The work I did for the Japanese Chamber of Commerce I did as a citizen— a resident of Seattle—and my services were always free."

Several of the men were taking notes, so Masuda paused to let them catch up.

"The trial covered a period of nearly two weeks, and it took into detail all of my activities. And as you undoubtedly know, I was acquitted of all of the charges." He stopped again, this time as punctuation, to let the fact sink in. "To go through everything would make this hearing far too long, but I will be happy to give one or two incidents for the record."

Haas suddenly sensed the eyes of the other men on him. He knew they were aware that he and Masuda were not just colleagues but friends. What did they expect of him? That he'd play it by the book? That he'd try to cut Masuda a break? He had no idea. "That'll be, uh, it'll be just fine, Mr. Masuda," he stammered, glancing at the others for signs of disapproval.

"Ninety-five percent of my practice was with Japanese people, so naturally I was interested in any legislation that stood to affect the Japanese business owners around Seattle. The Northwest Produce Association, for example, was an organization composed of wholesale merchants such as Safeway Stores, Associated Groceries, Pacific Fruit, and the like. I was a member of the directors of that association—the only Japanese member of the board, I might add."

Giles Zimmerman and Ernie Miller raised their eyebrows. That organization was a major player in the food industry. They didn't put just anyone on their board.

"As a member of the board, and also as an attorney, I had the duty to watch every session of the legislature, to check on all the bills that were introduced that might affect wholesale produce and agricultural interests in the state of Washington. When such bills came along, I would consult with my board and then work either to have the bill acted on favorably—or to have it killed. I still categorically maintain," he said, tapping the table with his index finger like a woodpecker pounding at bark, "that I was doing what any other attorney would do, whether he be Japanese or Irish or Norwegian."

Masuda realized his heart was pounding. *Not good*, he thought. *Stay calm*.

Easing back off the edge of his chair, he continued. "Now the other part of the case against me hinged on the fact that on three occasions the Japanese consul in Seattle asked me—as a favor—to cover three different meetings and give him a written report on what occurred. This was several years before the war. Two were in Seattle and one was in Tacoma. All were open to the public. The meetings concerned trade between the United States and Japan, at a time when an American boycott of Japanese products was being discussed due to the Sino-Japanese war. When I was arrested, I distinctly remember telling the FBI agent that I did not consider I had done anything wrong by covering these meetings—that it was in the interests of both this country and Japan to maintain good trade relations. I said nothing that would give away the secrets of this country. My report was almost identical to what anyone could read in the newspaper." Masuda let a beat pass. "And apparently a federal jury in Seattle agreed with me." He was not going to let them forget the acquittal.

Haas cut in. "Did you at any time register as an agent of Japan in connection with this work, Mr. Masuda?"

"I was very well acquainted with the act requiring registration of foreign agents, Mr. Haas. No, I did not. In fact, on behalf of the Japanese Chamber of Commerce in Seattle I had occasion to seek written opinions from the Japanese consulates in San Francisco, Los Angeles, and New York, and they were all of the opinion that the contacts between the Japanese chamber and the consulate—including my work covering these meetings—did not come within the terms of the American registration act and I did not need to register."

"And you were actually an officer of the Japanese Chamber of Commerce, Mr. Masuda, were you not?" *This is sounding like a cross-examination,* Haas thought as he heard his own words come out of his mouth. *Easy does it.*

Masuda allowed that he had in fact been the vice president.

"And would you explain the functions of the organization?"

"Briefly I would say that the work of that organization was similar to that of any chamber of commerce in any city—any *American* city. We held educational programs and blood drives, showed movies, raised money for the local community chest. Lots of money, actually; we always brought in more than our quota. We helped out with public functions in Seattle, like the Fourth of July parade, and made gift bags for soldiers at the local army base. One year we did two thousand of them, if memory serves."

Haas peered at his notes. "Is it not also true that this chamber of commerce distributed leaflets relating to the Sino-Japanese war, Mr. Masuda?" He clenched up inside as he said the words. *Cross-examination again,* he thought.

But Masuda took it in stride. "Yes, indeed we did, Mr. Haas, in I believe 1937 or 1938, until the practice was discontinued around 1940 because of local sentiment."

"Local sentiment?"

"It was obvious that the larger community was becoming increasingly uncomfortable with Japan's conduct of that war."

"And would it be correct to assume that the leaflets you distributed gave a favorable light to the Japanese side of the conflict?"

Masuda flared at the question. "To be frank with you, I don't know. I don't recall having read through any of them. I believe some were in question-and-answer form, like 'When was the war started?' and 'What was the war costing?' and things of that nature." He saw skeptical faces and recalibrated. "Were they favorable to Japan? It was the Japanese Chamber of Commerce issuing them, so yes, my guess would be that they were favorable to Japan. I doubt we would have issued leaflets favoring Japan's enemy."

The men around the table chuckled uncomfortably.

"And the other officers of the chamber, Mr. Masuda—were they engaged in activities sympathetic to the Japanese, aside from the distribution of pamphlets?"

"Mr. Haas, I have known those men in a business way for some time and I feel, personally, that none of the men were actively engaged in any subversive activities or any activities that would be detrimental to the United States."

Haas flipped the page of the document in his hand, scanning the text up and down. Several awkward seconds ticked by, until Giles Zimmerman leaned over and poked at a line on the page. "Ah," said Haas, glancing around anxiously, "yes, of course. Thank you, Giles. How about Japanese language schools, fencing schools, and other kinds of activities regarding the culture of Japan?"

"Are you asking if I was a member? Or are you asking me what I know about them?" Masuda was unsettled by the imprecision in Haas's questions. This was not like him.

"What is your connection with those associations? That is what I am asking."

"I am not acquainted with those details. As I explained to you before"—and here a hint of indignation crept into Masuda's voice—"my business was that of being an attorney and I focused on my clients. I did not know what my clients did, what they supported, what they offered, unless it was relevant to my legal work. So perhaps there were members of my client organizations who had dealings with language schools or fencing clubs, but I really couldn't say."

Sensing Masuda's testiness, and swimming in sweat, Haas looked around the table and suggested a brief break. Ralph Gelvin began to rise, but Masuda cut in.

"If it's all the same, Ted—uh, Mr. Haas—I'd like to keep going." He glanced at his watch. "I have some matters to attend to at the office that I'd like to get to before the close of business, if possible."

Gelvin, half-standing, looked at Haas, who shrugged and nodded him back into his chair.

"Certainly, Mr. Masuda," said Haas. "Whatever you prefer. Let's talk about money for a moment, shall we? You mentioned community chest contributions a moment ago. Did you ever have occasion to contribute money to fund drives supporting Japan or its military?"

Masuda tapped the table gently while looking off into the corner for the right words. "It depends how you mean that. There were occasions with the Japanese Chamber of Commerce where I was expected to make contributions for Japanese causes. Usually a community chest, the Red Cross, things of that nature. I would not choose the amount; the chamber would assess me a certain figure and I would pay it."

Haas eyeballed the paper in front of him, hesitating. Zimmerman again loomed in and stabbed a passage with his index finger. Haas sighed; the question seemed silly. But he asked it. "We have a statement here to the effect that you contributed twenty-five dollars to the Japanese War Chest in 1939. Do you recall such a contribution?"

Masuda flushed. Of course he had made little contributions here and there back in the 1930s—lots of people did—but he couldn't recall any one in particular. "I can neither dispute it nor affirm it," he said carefully. "If I made such a contribution, I really don't think it came as late as '39."

"And how about the activities of your clients insofar as the Sino-Japanese War was concerned, Mr. Masuda?"

The Nisei lawyer did not understand and waited a moment for clarification, but none came. "Look, Ted, I don't know just what kind of an answer you're fishing for here. As far as I know, none of my clients were engaged with things of that type."

"And were you aware of any, uh, irregular activities by any of your associates, business concerns, or individuals you represented?"

"Absolutely not. None whatsoever. That I can assure you."

"And just for the sake of the record, Mr. Masuda . . ." Haas paused to find an inoffensive way to phrase his question, but there wasn't one. "Were you ever paid by the Empire of Japan?"

"No, sir." Masuda straightened in his chair. "Never."

"And, um, espionage activities?" Haas mumbled, eyes down on the page in front of him.

"Did you say *espionage*?" Masuda's heart was racing.

Haas shrugged and pointed weakly at the paper, a pained expression on his face.

"None," spat Masuda. "Whatsoever."

"Well," said Haas hurriedly, "would you please tell us in detail about the relationship between you and the Japanese consul at Seattle?"

Masuda paused for a deep breath. "All my dealings with the consul were, well, like friends. He knew that I was well connected in the Japanese business community in Seattle, so he would call upon me for information about how the local businessmen were getting along, how they were being treated. These businessmen were Japanese nationals, of course, so it was the consul's job to stay in touch with them. And of course, he would also be very interested in finding out about any bills in the state legislature that could be bad for the Japanese."

"And did he ever retain you as a lawyer on a monetary basis?"

Masuda opened his mouth but then shut it. He sat silent for several beats and then said, cautiously, "I will answer that question no. I did receive certain gifts from time to time—I can recall a vase, cigarette cases, an ashtray, things of that type. He once gave me two hundred dollars, but of his own volition and not as any sort of fee we'd negotiated." Masuda noticed Ernie Miller's eyes go wide. "Perhaps I should have refused it, but it genuinely felt like a gift." He tugged at the cuff of his sleeve and shifted in his chair. "A token of appreciation. Nothing more."

Ted Haas placed the paper on the table in front of him. Zimmerman craned in to examine it, but Haas waved him back. It was time to end this awkward exercise. "Mr. Masuda, we have just one more area of concern. Did you ever have occasion to prepare reports for the Japanese consul regarding anti-American meetings or demonstrations?"

"Well, as I already mentioned, there were three occasions when I prepared reports on public meetings in Seattle and Tacoma where local politicians were arguing for embargoes, to punish Japan for its aggression against China. Those meetings were all thoroughly explored at my criminal trial." He paused for a moment, then added, "The one where I was acquitted, as you'll recall." He instantly regretted adding that; Gelvin and Zimmerman both rolled their eyes. He could see that he was laying it on too thick. "I'm sorry that I keep harping on that. It's just that—"

Haas cut him off. "Naturally you mention the acquittal often, Tom." He caught himself using Masuda's first name but realized that correcting himself would just make the situation even more uncomfortable, so he pressed on. "The acquittal is highly significant, particularly in the context in which it occurred, so soon after the start of the war." He watched his words bounce off the other men's blank faces. "Why, if I were in your shoes, I'd probably never stop mentioning it!"

For the first time, Masuda untensed a little, hearing Haas emphasize the unlikeliness of his acquittal.

Across the table, Haas briefly loosened as well. But shame now washed over him, so fast and so deep that he felt he might drown. He was mortified that he had allowed himself to become an instrument of Masuda's ordeal. He grabbed his papers and stuffed them back into their folder. "I think we have everything we need, Mr. Masuda—Tom." He looked quickly to his left and his right at the other men. "Unless any of you have any further questions."

Ralph Gelvin raised an index finger and took an audible breath, but Haas was already rising from his chair. "Thank you for your time, Tom, and for your cooperation. I'm sure a decision will be forthcoming soon."

One by one, Masuda thanked each of the men around the table. Back in Seattle on the day of his acquittal, he'd thought he was done with juries. Yet here was another, a new group of Caucasians with the power to define his future in a single judgment. He'd gotten lucky once; could he hope for a second break? He'd entered the hearing optimistic, knowing that Ted Haas was its chair. But Haas had seemed a different man until near the end—off-balance, jumbled, tentative. He just had no idea what to expect.

After the handshakes, the men stood uncomfortably around the table. It was a moment for small talk, but Masuda had no small words in him, so he turned and made quickly for the door.

"See you back at the office, Tom!" Haas shouted after him, but he was already gone.

Doctor's orders were to get plenty of rest, but Ted Haas could find none that night. He tossed in his bed until nearly three. The halting, imprecise questions he'd put to Tom Masuda kept surging up in his mind. He'd been flustered to find his tongue so tied; it was as if years of experience had suddenly fallen away and he was back in law school, floundering in a moot court competition. Now, deep in the night, the sense of it revealed itself: he couldn't find the words because he didn't want to. His head was trying to speak against his heart.

At three, Haas jumped out of bed, threw on a light jacket, and pushed through his apartment door for a walk. Perhaps the desert night air would help settle him. He didn't dare stray far from the staff residential area. Poston's snakes were night sleepers but not its scorpions or tarantulas. A few turns around the neighborhood would have to do.

Walking brought Haas no relief. The same words coursed through his mind. So did the image of Tom Masuda on the opposite side of the table, frightened, and combative, and alone, and . . . betrayed. Yes, that was the word Haas was looking for: *betrayed*. The scene looped in his brain—the awkward handshake, the stumbling questions, Tom's pinched and indignant replies. He wished he could run the film backward, rewrite the script. But of course he couldn't.

After a time Haas stopped and turned his eyes to the sky. Poston's starry nights were as rich and stirring as its days were dull and wilting. He often took comfort in these skies. Even with the bleaching glare of a three-quarter moon to the southeast he was able to make out the great summer square high overhead—four bright stars outlining the body of the winged horse Pegasus. Since learning to see the constellations as the Lakota people imagined them, he sometimes saw the square as not a horse but a turtle—Keya, the spirit of health and of healing. That is how the stars touched him tonight.

What was done was done. The hearing would play like a loop in his mind for a while. He couldn't stop it any more than he could stop so many other thoughts that plagued him. But he could fight to help Tom Masuda get out of Poston and move forward with his life. That was the one thing he could do.

By the glow of the moon, he walked a determined path back to his barrack and his typewriter.

COLORADO RIVER RELOCATION CENTER
Poston, Arizona

July 19, 1943

MEMORANDUM TO: Mr. W. Wade Head, Project Director
FROM: Theodore H. Haas, Chairman, Hearing Board
RE: Thomas Shinao Masuda

Thomas Shinao Masuda was born on July 15, 1905, at Seattle, Washington. He graduated from the University of Washington Law School in 1929, and was married on October 10, 1930. Since the summer of that year, he has continuously practiced law in Seattle, Washington. An active and ambitious practitioner with about 95% of his clients of Japanese ancestry, it was natural that he should be interested in legislation pending before the legislature of the state of Washington and should be an officer of Japanese trade associations. That many of his clients were Issei was understandable—Issei controlled most businesses and associations in Seattle.

Since coming to this Center on August 15, 1942, he has been employed as an attorney in the Project Attorney's Office. In this capacity, he has given unstintingly of his time and talents and cooperated wholeheartedly in assisting in the solution of center problems. During a period of several months, he ably and diligently headed the Project Attorney's Office during my absence.

Many members of the Poston staff and all of the members of the Hearing Board have had frequent occasions to meet and observe Mr. Masuda. I have worked closely with him during the past year and am also acquainted with his wife Kikuye. Prior to receiving the confidential information from the Federal Bureau of Investigation, I was well aware of the contents of that communication, for Mr. Masuda of his own volition had frankly discussed his indictment and trial. Most of the activities referred to occurred at Seattle several years prior to the declaration of war of the United States against Japan. Mr. Masuda states that the facts which were outlined to him before the hearing were covered during his two-week trial in the early part of 1942. Despite war hysteria and fears then prevailing on the Pacific Coast, he was acquitted by a jury.

The Hearing Board cannot, because of the absence of the witnesses in this Center, probe thoroughly those charges or determine their truth or falsity. However, we have no reason to doubt the veracity of Mr. Masuda's statements. In our relations with him, we have found him to be sincere and trustworthy and without a trace of bitterness despite his unpleasant experience. He has always manifested opinions favorable to our Government and its institutions.

Based on the hearing I chaired, and numerous impressions received during a period of almost a year, I unqualifiedly believe that Mr. Masuda is a loyal citizen of the United States and strongly recommend that he should be permitted to leave Poston upon complying with the appropriate requirements.

Theodore H. Haas,
Chairman

BOOK THREE

JAMES HENDRICK TERRY AT GILA RIVER IN ARIZONA

We, in our organization, are at present in a position
to do more than any other factor in developing . . . a
sense of loyalty to the United States which they have
never really had. Most of them have never learned the
meaning or principles of our government and have no
appreciation of the rights and obligations of their
citizenship . . . and have made no honest attempt to learn
about those rights and obligations and to date few in
our organization have made any attempt to put them
on the right track.

—Jim Terry, September 17, 1943

CHAPTER ELEVEN

DECEMBER 1942

GILA RIVER, ARIZONA

T he alarm clock woke Jim Terry at half past seven as he had instructed it to do. He lay in bed for a few moments, blinking away sleep and the grit of the south Arizona desert. Though he hadn't heard the wind during the night, he knew it had blown hard: sand everywhere, blasted in through the cracks in the walls and the gaps in the window frames. These staff barracks were supposed to be better built than the ones housing the evacuees, but they seemed pretty flimsy to him.

In the weak dawn light, the lawyer could see only outlines of the government-issued chair beside his bed and the dresser near the door. He hadn't yet adjusted to near darkness this late in the morning. Back in New York the sun would have been up by seven thirty, even now in December, with the solstice approaching. Of course, it would also be a hell of a lot colder back there, and wetter, and worse for his lungs. That was what had gotten him out here to the Gila River Relocation Center. Medical orders, more or less: "A few more New York winters might just do you in," his doctor had told him as he struggled to recover from yet another skirmish with pneumonia. The doctor had suggested someplace warm and dry.

Terry had gotten eight hours but felt tired. Yesterday had been a sixteen-hour workday, as the day before had been. Today probably would be too. In fact, most of his days had been long since he arrived at the end of November. They had warned him of the long hours during his orientation at the WRA's headquarters in Washington, D.C. They told him that being a project attorney would be like no job he'd ever had—that he'd soon find himself as an agency attorney and a city solicitor and a corporation counsel and a legal aid lawyer all rolled up into one, with maybe a dash of prosecutor for good measure. Jim Terry had scoffed. He'd worked long hours his whole career, on cases as simple as trespassing and as complex as reorganizing banks. What could this job possibly show him that he hadn't already seen?

A lot, as it was turning out. There were over 13,000 people at this center, Japanese aliens and Japanese American citizens whom the army had rounded up in the spring mostly because of the hollering of a lot of politicians and columnists, the whole crew that had wanted the Japanese out for decades. Pearl

Harbor had been a dream come true for those people. They'd pushed hard and gotten what they wanted: the Japanese gone and their property left behind, ripe for the grabbing. Shameful.

A few months ago, the Gila River center hadn't even existed, and now it was Arizona's fourth-largest city, or something trying to be a city under very unusual circumstances. Five thousand evacuees over in the Canal Unit, and about half again as many here in the Butte Unit, with about three empty miles between them. The old hands said it had been a lot of chaos and improvisation since July when the first evacuees arrived. But now he was here to help bring some order to the place—the guiding hand of the law. And if any lawyer could do it, James Hendrick Terry could do it.

He dressed as he did each day, jacket and tie. Things were more casual out here than back home in the city. A lot of the lower-ranking appointed personnel showed up looking like ragtag cowboys, in boots and bolo ties. He expected that from the men in charge of the motor pool or the food ware-house. But the senior administrators? Some of them walked around without jackets, and a couple never bothered with a tie. He could forgive this in the heat of an Arizona summer, but it wasn't getting up above seventy as win-ter arrived, and the desert mornings were downright chilly. Jim Terry was a graduate of Phillips Exeter Academy, Williams College, and Columbia Law School. He'd been a member of the New York bar since 1925. His attire would befit his pedigree and his profession. He would show the appointed personnel and the Japanese Americans alike that he was taking his work—and them—seriously.

He stepped out the door for the short walk to the administration building, giving wide berth to the corners of barracks where scorpions hid. People back east thought the little devils died off in the winter, but out here they said that was a myth, and Terry was taking no chances. He had almost stepped on one a few days after arriving as he left the staff mess hall on an unseasonably warm day. He had let out quite a yell and some evacuees hooted as they rolled by in the back of a farm truck. Terry thought he heard something about a lawyer finally meeting his match. Lawyer jokes.

As he walked over to the administration building, he noticed himself no-ticing the beauty of the morning. This was new. Back at the end of November when he pulled up after his drive across the country, he was convinced Gila River was the most desolate place on earth. A vast flat wasteland of creosote bush scrub and gangly cactuses. Flattened silhouettes of mountain ranges hugging the horizons far to the west and the south and the east. An absurd little uplift of dirty hills a stone's throw to the west, topping out a couple hun-dred feet above the center. The locals had a name for the formation, Sacaton

Butte, but buttes were stark red rock outcroppings in Gene Autry Westerns, and this was no butte. These were just big misshapen camel's humps on the desert floor.

This morning, though, something in Terry's vision had shifted. The sun was barely up. The camp was still mostly in shadow, but the sun lit the top of the butte with a crisp cream light you never saw back east. The sky was cloudless, on its way from gray to a crystal blue. Swallows darted around the barrack eaves and hummingbirds whizzed barely overhead. In the distance saguaros dotted the desert floor like sentries. There was an unfamiliar beauty to all this, and Jim Terry was pleased to be starting to see it.

Leroy Bennett was already at his desk and shouted a cheerful hello when Terry walked into the administration building. Bennett was Gila River's brand-new project director, the top WRA man at the center—the boss, really. Except he wasn't truly Terry's boss if you looked at the WRA's organizational chart. Terry's real boss was Phil Glick, the solicitor in Washington. Glick was six years Terry's junior, and Terry wondered whether he'd be able to hew to instructions from a younger, less experienced lawyer.

Terry returned Bennett's greeting and continued down the hallway toward his own makeshift office. Outside the door a young Japanese American man fidgeted on the edge of a wooden chair. The Nisei brightened when he saw Terry coming and opened his mouth to speak, but Terry silenced him with a gently raised hand and strode past him into the office. There is such a thing as an appointment, and as far as he knew that young man didn't have one.

Jim Terry had occupied some tony offices in his day. Back in the late 1920s and early '30s, as a young lawyer in the federal prosecutor's office in Manhattan, he worked out of the ornate City Hall Post Office and Courthouse across Broadway from the Woolworth Building. Then he moved five blocks south to the even more sumptuous chambers of the Wall Street law firm of Burlingame, Nourse & Pettit. His early career unfolded in a milieu of marble and polished brass.

At Gila River in December of 1942, Jim Terry found himself in a bare box: Four walls, a floor, a ceiling, and a window looking out on the unlandscaped dirt of block 70. A simple wooden office desk and chair for him and a little table and chair for Kimiko Yamamoto, the twenty-four-year-old Nisei secretary from Gardena who was handling the office's clerical work until Terry could manage to get the Caucasian secretary he wanted. This space was a temporary arrangement while a slightly larger office was being readied for him in the building, but he didn't have his hopes up. Already Jim Terry was outfitting the office with typewriters and office supplies out of his own pocket. Phil Glick wasn't happy that Terry was spending his own money on items the WRA should have been supplying, but Terry was there to work, not to sit around waiting for staplers that might never appear.

"Good morning, Mr. Terry," said the secretary, jumping to her feet as she still did every time Terry entered the room, even though they had been together for a couple of weeks and he had told her it wasn't necessary. Her notebook and pencil clattered to the floor.

"Good morning, Miss Yamamoto," he said as he placed his briefcase beside his desk. "So, what's up first this morning?" He reached for his appointment book.

"There's a Mr. Sato outside waiting to see you, sir."

Terry pulled the datebook closer, wondered if he had the wrong day, flipped to the next page, scoured it, then flipped back. "I don't see an appointment for a Mr. Sato."

"He says it's urgent, sir. Something that came up this morning. He doesn't have an appointment."

The lawyer settled into his chair. He pulled a legal pad out, put away a pen and several binder clips, took out and sharpened a pencil, and looked up at her. "I'll let you know when I'm available, Miss Yamamoto. Shouldn't be too long."

"He seems quite distressed, sir? Mr. Sato, outside?"

"The one without an appointment."

"Yes, sir."

"Well, as I said, I'll let you know when I'm available."

The secretary bowed almost imperceptibly and returned to her table.

Terry pulled an accordion file marked "Tada beating" from his briefcase and spread the papers on the desk before him. He had just arrived at Gila River when Takeo Tada was bludgeoned, and it was one hell of a welcome for the lawyer. A gang of evacuees had chased the Nisei down in the Canal Unit and opened up his scalp with an ironwood stick. Back in New York, a case like this would've been a snap: nab one of the thugs, get him to turn state's evidence, bring in the rest, and charge the whole gang with assault with a deadly weapon. Easy.

Here at Gila River? Not so easy. It was crazy: a man was violently attacked, and the community lined up with the attackers. Tada had been some sort of muck-a-muck at the Turlock Assembly Center in California's Central Valley and somehow made himself persona non grata there with the Issei and the Kibei. Rumors of favoritism, doling out goodies to friends. Terry didn't understand the dynamics too well, but he could tell there was big tension between the older and younger people here, and between the American-oriented ones and the Japanese-oriented ones. And the Tada beating was somehow wrapped up in all that. So even though it had been a group job, one Issei man stepped forward to say he'd done it—alone—and was proud of it. Tada had it coming, he said, and the community seemed to agree. Hordes showed up to support the attacker at his hearings in what passed for Gila River's community "court," and rumors of a general strike circulated.

Fortunately, Terry was new enough as all of this unfolded that he managed to avoid a big role in the drama. But he had to report on the mess to the solicitor in Washington. Terry took out a pencil and outlined the points he wanted to make. For one, the community's "hearings" were a joke and an embarrassment to the WRA. Hardly a word of testimony that would be admitted in a court of law. For another, the WRA had to face the fact that it was up against some dangerous and subversive organizations in these camps. The only way to ferret them out was through careful investigations by people who weren't rank amateurs. And then came the issue of what to do with those groups. Terry was for a firm hand: round up and segregate every member of every lawless anti-American or pro-Japanese cabal they could uncover. Would the higher-ups in Washington be ready to hear this message? Terry didn't much care.

As his outline spilled onto a second sheet of paper, he realized that putting all of this into a report was going to take time. And the incessantly tapping foot of young-man-without-an-appointment out in the hallway was starting to get on his nerves. He pushed the Tada paperwork aside and cleared his throat to get his secretary's attention. "I suppose I'll see our visitor now, Miss Yamamoto," he said. "Please send him in."

"Sending him in" meant walking a few paces to the door and beckoning to the twenty-seven-year-old just outside. Terry could have done this himself—in fact, he could have told Sato to come in without getting up from his desk and the man would surely have heard it—but that wasn't how Jim Terry did things. Lawyers have secretaries, and secretaries send clients in.

Terry wondered what Henry Sato's business might be. It could be almost anything. That's what he was coming to like about his job. At his orientation in Washington, they'd told him the project attorneys were expected to play three roles: advising the project director, advising evacuee organizations, and helping individual evacuees with legal programs. But Terry was learning quickly that those three categories didn't really begin to capture what he really had to do. He was just a few weeks in and already he'd been consulted on divorces, assaults, conflicts with Arizona officials, accidental deaths and injuries, elections, suicides, family squabbles over estates, and a whole lot more. There was just no telling what might be on Sato's mind.

"What can I do for you, Henry?"

Sato hesitated, looking around the office. He turned slightly, pointing to an empty chair, shoulders slightly raised.

"Certainly, of course. Pull up a chair. Have a seat." Whatever this was, it was going to take a while.

"It's about my mother," Sato started. "Kei Sato, apartment 27-5-C."

Terry tried to picture where that was. Block 27, building 5, unit C. He was still getting used to the numbering system, and it didn't help that every block looked exactly like every other block, with a mess hall, rec building, latrine, and fourteen identical barrack buildings, each with white fiberboard walls and red double roofs. Looking down a street at Gila River was like looking at one of those mirror-facing-mirror setups that made whatever was between them replicate itself infinitely to the horizon. Block 27. Could be any of them.

"And where exactly is block 27, Henry? Can you remind me?"

"In the southwest corner, sir, not far from the high school. Over in Canal."

Ah, so this young man had come all the way over from the Canal Unit to see him, first thing in the morning, and without an appointment. Maybe this actually *was* something serious. Terry asked what he could do for Sato's mother.

"She fell into a big hole this morning. My ma—she had a huge fall! She was out for her morning walk—she walks every morning early, around six thirty, it's a habit from back home—and she fell into this great big pit, right there in the middle of our block."

Terry remembered the dim light in his room that morning when he awoke, and that was at half past seven. An early-morning constitutional in December was risky business. Terry could imagine how a person might lose her footing and take a tumble.

"She's banged up pretty bad, Mr. Terry."

"I'm so sorry to hear that, Henry, very unfortunate," Terry said. "But can I ask why you are here, at a law office, instead of the hospital?"

"She's already there, Mr. Terry. The ambulance came. They had a time getting her out, but they managed. When I left to come over here, they were getting ready to do an X-ray, but the doctor already said he'd be surprised if her hip wasn't broken."

Terry grimaced. It sounded like a serious injury for anyone, let alone an older person.

"Awful situation, Henry. I'm sure she'll get the best of care in the hospital, and I wish her a speedy recovery." Terry paused and looked at the anxious young man across the desk, who showed no signs of getting up.

"We don't know what to do, Mr. Terry. Ma and Dad were only just starting to adjust to being out here. Really disoriented, you know?"

Terry nodded sympathetically.

"They've been worried sick about the farm back home, the rhubarb," he continued. "Dad's been worse off than Ma since we got to camp, not getting out much, you know? And now she'll be in no shape to look after him. And he's definitely in no shape to look after her."

The lawyer was getting accustomed to this, evacuees coming to him with stories of everyday worries and challenges that had nothing to do with the law. They came because they knew he was in the administration and assumed he'd be able to do something to help. Usually all that was needed was to point them in the right direction, toward the right office—and that is what Terry did here, suggesting an appointment with someone in the Community Welfare Division.

"No, that's not it, Mr. Terry." Sato gestured at a row of law books lined up on the floor under the window. "We want to know our rights."

Ah. So that's where this was headed.

Terry had worried about a scenario like this since the day he arrived. On the one hand, his job was to help these poor people. On the other hand, his job was to advance the interests of the WRA, which paid his salary. Until now he'd managed to avoid a conflict between the two. No more. *Job one, meet job two*, Terry thought acidly. The right thing to do was probably to end the conversation. Give him the names of a couple of Arizona lawyers fielding referrals and then send him on his way. But Terry didn't trust those outside lawyers, yokels from third-rate law schools who were out for a fee, with no understanding of the difficulties these people were up against.

What would Phil Glick say? Terry wondered. He'd probably say that when push came to shove, a WRA project attorney worked for the WRA, not for an evacuee. Glick would want Terry to end the interview. But Phil Glick was in Washington, and Henry Sato was right here in front of him.

"Why don't you tell me a little more about what happened, Henry?"

Sato explained that his mother went for a walk every morning at six fifteen and would be back to go to the mess hall for breakfast by six forty-five, that when she wasn't back home this morning by seven his father went out looking for her with a little flashlight, that his father couldn't see her anywhere but heard someone moaning, that he followed the sound and came upon an open hole in the ground, like a grave, probably eight feet across and six feet deep, that he dimly saw his wife at the bottom and figured that if he jumped in to help her, he'd get stuck down there too. So he ran for help.

Terry recalled that an outside contractor had recently been burying fuel tanks around the center grounds; he himself had drafted the purchase and in-stallation agreements. "But surely there must have been a safety light, Henry. And signs? That's standard practice at a dig like this. I'm not trying to cast blame on your mother, but how could she have missed those?"

There were no lights, no signs, Sato explained. Just a big gaping unguarded hole in the middle of a dark field where people lived. He leaned forward, agitated. "This is going to set us back something awful, Mr. Terry."

"Of course it will," the lawyer replied. "This would be a huge challenge for any family, even in the best of circumstances."

"Well, what should we do? We need some advice here. Can we sue someone? The company that dug the hole? Someone else? Should someone go out there and take a picture? Of the hole? As proof? Or measure how deep it is? Or something?"

Terry took a breath but said nothing because he didn't know what to say.

"Somebody's got to be responsible for this!" cried Sato. "Not my ma. She was just out minding her own business, you know? This wasn't her fault." Tears welled in his eyes. "She's in bad shape, Mr. Terry."

What could Terry say? If the young man was right, this was some damn serious negligence. The contractor's negligence first and foremost, of course— but maybe the WRA's too.

Behind Sato, Terry noticed his secretary hanging on every word of their conversation. Their eyes met and she made a show of refilling a stapler.

"Henry, these are important questions, but the most important thing right now is for your mother to recover. Help her. Help your father. These legal matters—all of them can wait." Terry explained that the law gave a person two years to take legal action. "I know things seem urgent to you as we sit here this morning," he continued, "but in reality, they're not. At least not the legal aspect of things. What's urgent is your mother's health. I will let the contractor know about the accident and have someone from Internal Security go out to take pictures of the site."

The lawyer rose and walked around the desk, putting his hand on Sato's shoulder. "Help your parents right now, Henry. Focus on your family. You've got two full years to take legal action against . . ." His voice trailed off. How should he put this? "Against, well, anyone that might be responsible." That came as close as Terry felt he could risk to suggesting the WRA itself might share responsibility for Mrs. Sato's fall.

He shook Sato's hand and walked him to the door, wishing him luck as he departed. After he was gone, Terry turned to Yamamoto. "Sad case," he mumbled.

"Yes, it is, Mr. Terry."

"Never in my life have I heard of such incompetence," Terry said.

The secretary nodded.

For a moment they were both lost in thought. Then Terry brightened and squared his shoulders. "Well, I guess this case shows what we do in this office, right, Miss Yamamoto? What we're here for?"

"Sir?"

"This case. It shows what we do," said Terry through a little grin.

"I'm not following you, sir?"

"I mean helping the evacuees out of the hole they find themselves in!" Terry looked pleased with himself.

"Yes, Mr. Terry," Yamamoto said, smiling tightly and returning to her stapler.

The lawyer walked to the window and looked out across the yard. The mid-morning light flattened the texture out of Sacaton Butte. A golden eagle rode a breeze up its northern slope. Terry felt good. Tricky situation, a delicate line, and he'd walked it pretty well, if he had to say so himself.

One of these days, though, he was going to have to decide who his client really was.

CHAPTER TWELVE

LATE JANUARY 1943

GILA RIVER, ARIZONA

There was something soothing about the drive from Gila River to Phoenix in the wintertime, something meditative. Open space to the horizon in every direction. Today the sky was gray and it took a little concentration to find the line where desert ended and sky began. It was mostly dirt and scrub, but every now and then tall cactuses loomed up and whooshed by. From a distance Jim Terry sometimes mistook them for hitchhikers. Once you got up on them, though, there was no confusion. These were cactuses— the kind you see in the comics. Never in his life had Jim Terry imagined himself in such a landscape. The playing fields of Williams College, the concrete corridors of the Financial District, the aqua views of the Hamptons—yes, all of that was Jim Terry, or "Hendrick," as intimates like Tom Dewey, the newly elected governor of New York, called him. How he ended up on the operetta set of *The Desert Song* still sometimes mystified him.

Terry wasn't setting the best example by doing the drive in his '41 Packard Clipper, the one he'd driven cross-country when he relocated from back east a few months earlier. This was official travel, and WRA rules said clearly that he should have reserved a motor pool car for the trip. But all they had on hand were a couple of scuffed-up '37 Ford Slantbacks with balding tires and disc brakes and seats that did your back no favors. Terry's Clipper had hydraulics and tires with some tread. And wool seats and carpets and a radio. He understood that things could get complicated, legally speaking, if he had an accident on official business in his personal vehicle. But if he was going to go on a rescue mission for the WRA, he was going to be comfortable. He'd work out the details later if there was trouble.

Yes, a rescue mission. Some Nisei kid named Joe Nozuki had gotten himself arrested on his way back to the center from work leave at a farm in Colorado. Maybe "gotten himself arrested" wasn't quite fair; the WRA was to have sent an escort to meet him at the Phoenix bus depot, but the escort hadn't shown up. The poor kid didn't know what to do so he made his way to the FBI's office a few blocks away to ask their advice. They obliged by arresting him and charging him with violating the travel restrictions. The last thing the WRA needed was for this to hit the newspapers, so Terry was on his way to try to talk the U.S. attorney into dismissing the charge and releasing Nozuki to him.

The project attorney was taking advantage of the city excursion to pick up a few things for his barrack apartment and the office. Teddy and the boys were scheduled to arrive any day now, and he knew how unhappy she'd be if the apartment windows were bare. She'd found a curtain color she liked at a Montgomery Ward in New York and instructed Terry to measure the windows and pick up a length of fabric at the Phoenix store. As for the office, Terry and his staff had almost nothing—no manila folders, no index cards, no paper clips, only one desk, and only one typewriter.

The last of these was the most painful. Days of dictation were always piling up. Several girls could tap out upward of seventy words per minute, but not without keys to tap. Poston had typewriters constantly on requisition, but nothing was coming through. The army was snapping up every available machine, or so they were told. If someone had asked Jim Terry before Pearl Harbor what sorts of goods a war would place at a premium, office machines would have been far down his list. But when the War Production Board blocked most typewriter sales, the market dried up. Terry was intent on remedying the situation the WPB had created even if it meant shelling out his own money. Phil Glick in Washington kept squawking at him about not spending his own cash on office supplies, but Terry's years on Wall Street had left him comfortable enough not to have to worry about a few bucks for legal pads or the occasional chair.

Terry parked near the Montgomery Ward at Adams and First, within sight of the bus depot where Nozuki had arrived to find no escort. "First *Street*, First *Street*," he repeated to himself as he entered the store and looked for the curtain department. Terry wondered who the genius was who put a First Avenue and a First Street just two city blocks from each other, both running north–south. Must be hell for letter carriers. Then again, he'd spent years in lower Manhattan where narrow streets snaked in seemingly random paths and had never gotten lost. At least Phoenix was a grid.

Once he had the fabric in hand, Terry set off in search of typewriters. The leading place in town was Walsh Brothers, a block east and two blocks north, at Central and Van Buren. He stopped when he hit Van Buren to watch the pedestrians crossing the street with their shopping bags and satchels, unaware that they were crossing a crucial, invisible border. Van Buren was the edge of the army's exclusion zone. North of the lane line separating east–west traffic, Japanese Americans were free go about their business. South of the line, here on the Walsh Brothers side where Terry stood, Japanese Americans were forbidden and subject to arrest unless they were in a WRA center like Gila River. Up in California and Oregon and Washington, the exclusion line ran north–south and mostly through the countryside. Here in Phoenix the line ran smack dab through the city center. Right at this moment, northwest of the city, small numbers of Japanese Americans were working the fields and sleeping in their own beds, just as they'd done since before Pearl Harbor, while thousands of their race were confined at Gila River to the south. Pretty damn arbitrary, though he supposed any line would be if you looked at it closely.

Terry turned to the big Walsh Brothers display windows. Normally you'd expect to see an array of typewriters and adding machines at a store like this, but it was mostly chairs and filing cabinets and desks behind the glass. Obviously, the WPB's typewriter regulations were taking a bite out of the store's business. But he had some hope, because he'd read in the papers that the WPB had decided to release thousands of Remington Envoy portables for sale to the public. The Envoys were flimsy contraptions with herky-jerky action, better suited to college essays than leases and construction contracts typed in triplicate. Any machine was better than no machine, though. Maybe he'd be able to sweet-talk the salesman into a better model if he flashed his government credentials.

Next to an array of portables, Terry spotted a spiffy Smith Corona Super Speed desktop model—a true office machine like his secretary back in New York used. A model like that would be a godsend for the Project Attorney's Office if he could get his hands on it, so he walked in to inquire. From the back emerged an aproned kid who looked like he could have just finished typing a college essay. The lawyer told him he was interested in the Smith Corona in the front window and took out his wallet to signal that he was serious. The kid shook his head. "That's just a display, sir. We're not allowed to sell those to the general public. Unless we want to risk trouble with the WPB."

"I'm an attorney, young man," Terry said. "I know all about the WPB regulations. I believe there's an exception for federal government sales. Are you aware of that?"

The young salesclerk's eyes brightened. "Oh, you're with the federal government? Well that's a different story. Let me check with my manager." He walked briskly to the back, whistling quietly. After a few moments he was back. "What branch are you with, sir? The manager says he needs to know before we can go ahead with a sale. What are you? Army? Navy? Agriculture?"

"WRA."

"WRA?" The salesclerk raised an eyebrow and shook his head slightly at a set of letters he didn't recognize.

"War Relocation Authority. I need this machine for official government business."

The kid's face showed no sign of recognition. "WRA. That's a new one," he said. "Let me go back and check with the manager."

He disappeared into the back room. Terry wandered through rows of office chairs, idly turning over price tags while he waited. After several minutes, a middle-aged man in a grease-stained work smock emerged from the back and approached him, his young salesman trailing behind.

"Sir? Can I help you? Tommy tells me you're interested in the Smith Corona Super Speed. That one's not available, unfortunately. We did just get in a shipment of these Envoys." He gestured a blackened hand toward a table of portables. "Nice machines—well made. Surprisingly tough for a portable."

"This is federal government business," Terry snapped. "As I told young Tommy here."

The youngster flushed and bent down to gather some paper clips that had fallen off one of the display desks.

"Now who are you with again? Which branch?" The manager cocked his left elbow and slowly rubbed a hand on his smock.

"WRA. War Relocation Authority."

"We haven't dealt with your agency before. WRA, you say? That's the Jap camp down on the reservation, isn't it?"

"It's the *relocation center* for *Japanese Americans*, yes."

"We hear you're treating those Japs real nice," the manager said. "In fact, better than how they're treating our boys over there." He glared at Terry. "Or so they say."

Was it worth the effort to explain the difference between the Japanese in Japan and the U.S. citizens and resident aliens at the center? Hardly, Terry decided. He identified himself as the project attorney at the center and, to make the deal more attractive, said he was prepared to pay cash on the spot rather than making the store grind through the tedious government procurement process.

The manager looked at Terry for a long moment and then shook his head. "I'd love to help you, mister, but that particular machine's not for sale."

Terry stiffened, a fight rising in him. Who did this flunky think he was, picking and choosing which part of the federal government he'd do business with? He had half a mind to keep arguing the point, and a quarter of a mind just to clock the guy, but the remaining quarter prevailed and he disengaged, storming out with an idle threat to file a complaint with the WPB.

Back on the sidewalk, Terry turned west along Van Buren toward the federal building for his appointment with the U.S. attorney but realized after a few paces he was in no frame of mind for it. Too irritated. And, he realized, too hungry. He took a left on First—*First Street*, he thought, quietly cursing whoever had laid out this cockamamie grid—and walked a block south to the fountain at Sun Drug for a Coke and a sandwich. While he ate, he tried to visualize the downtown area in his mind—the Montgomery Ward where he'd left his car, the bus depot, the two ridiculous Firsts, Van Buren, the federal building. He pictured Joe Nozuki standing alone at the bus station and then scampering up to Van Buren to the federal building for help.

The snack was helping him settle down, but as he pictured the young Nisei's northward path to the FBI's office, something clicked, and his irritation mounted. Shaking his head, he put three quarters on the counter and headed back up First Street to Van Buren and the federal building to pick up Nozuki and give the U.S. attorney a piece of his mind.

The federal courthouse at Van Buren and First Avenue looked nothing like the post office and courthouse in Manhattan where Jim Terry had spent his years as an assistant U.S. attorney in the late 1920s and early '30s. That building at Broadway and Park Row—mercifully demolished in 1939—was a monstrosity, with four ornate granite stories of columns and arch-top windows, that looked as though it had been modeled on a wedding cake. This courthouse in Phoenix was function over form, a rectangular box in light stone. Its only concessions to design were several arch-top windows on the top floor, a flagpole angling upward from a mooring on the second floor, and a sloping red tiled roof that hinted at Spanish colonial. And the palm trees out front. That was certainly different. No palms along Broadway.

"Mr. Flynn? James Hendrick Terry," he said with outstretched hand as he walked into the office of Arizona's U.S. attorney. Frank Flynn was about ten years Terry's senior, a Minnesotan who'd relocated to Arizona to practice law and then made enough of a name for himself to win an appointment as the federal prosecutor back in the mid-1930s. His gray hair and gentle features offset the powerful frame of an athlete. His handshake was firm.

At this point in his career, Jim Terry was accustomed to walking into engagements with the upper hand. Every Columbia Law School graduate—and the white-shoe firms of Wall Street had lots of them—would know him as the son of the late Professor Charles Thaddeus Terry, notorious for his terrorizing Socratic interrogations on the law of contracts. He and Teddy were regulars on the New York social circuit; Teddy, a direct descendant of a crew member on the *Mayflower*, could match pedigrees with any American. None of this would mean anything to Frank Flynn, no doubt a graduate of some middling school somewhere in the Midwest.

Terry had always sensed an unspoken bond among federal prosecutors no matter where they were from, so that's how he opened, citing his years in the Manhattan trenches. But the gambit failed. Flynn did not seem impressed by the names of the mobsters he'd put away for liquor trafficking. Dropping the name of his law firm—Burlingame, Nourse & Pettit, one of the city's most prestigious—got him no further. Not even a flicker of recognition. So he gave up on the pleasantries and turned to the matter at hand: Joe Nozuki. He led with a mea culpa, explaining that the WRA had been derelict in not providing a chaperone to meet the Nisei.

Flynn waved off the apology. "Look," he said, "once we realized we had a young Japanese guy wandering around the city, we had no choice but to charge him and hold him. You know the law as well as anyone, Mr. Terry, probably better. It's a crime for any Japanese to be in the exclusion zone without an escort or a pass."

The exclusion zone. So, this was really how they were going to play this thing. Terry stepped to Flynn's office window, looking out across Van Buren toward the northern horizon. "Lovely view you've got from up here," said the project attorney.

Flynn turned his gaze to the window. "Don't know about lovely, but I'll admit it beats lower Manhattan," he said, shooting Terry the first smile of their meeting.

"Do you know what I see when I look out there?"

Flynn scoured the horizon. "Well, that up there's what we call North Mountain, just slightly off to the east, if that's what you're referring to."

"I see the end of the exclusion zone. Right along the line in the middle of the street in front of us." Terry paused to see whether this would draw a reaction. He saw only confusion in Flynn's eyes.

"The exclusion zone?" Flynn looked down as a truck loaded with vegetables rolled by. "Oh! Why yes, I suppose that's true, Mr. Terry. The boundary does run along Van Buren in this part of the city."

"And Joe Nozuki arrived at the bus depot on Jefferson Street."

"Yes, that's right."

"Three blocks south of here," Terry said, pointing toward the wall on the opposite side of Flynn's office.

Flynn nodded.

"Three blocks inside the exclusion zone."

Flynn stiffened. "Three blocks or thirty miles, Mr. Terry; it makes no difference. The law's the law."

Terry was not finished. "Now let's imagine the bus depot happened to be three blocks north of Van Buren, *north* of the zone. There would have been no violation to charge him with. Isn't that correct?"

Flynn raised his hand to cut off the questioning.

Terry talked past the hand. "In fact, Mr. Flynn, if the bus depot were in that used car lot right across the street from us, thirty paces north of the line, there would have been nothing—"

"All right, Mr. Terry, I see your point—"

Terry cut back in. "When Joe Nozuki walked north to your office from the depot because he had no escort and wanted to do the right thing, Mr. Flynn, one of your agents could have just escorted him right across the street to that greasy spoon over there. Could have bought the boy a Coke. Could have given us a ring, told us to get our asses up here to pick him up. And that would have been the end of it." He paused. "Isn't that right?"

"Look, Mr. Terry, you and I both know Van Buren's the exclusion boundary, but do you think those pedestrians out there know it?" Flynn gestured toward a woman crossing Van Buren with three children tagging along behind her. "Of course they don't. If they saw your kid sitting in a restaurant here in town, they wouldn't think about which side of Van Buren he was on. They would panic, and we'd have a problem on our hands."

The project attorney listened impassively.

"Correct that," Flynn said. "It'd be *your kid* who'd have a problem on *his* hands." He pointed at a man walking along Van Buren toting a hubcap. "I don't think that gentleman would take very kindly to a Japanese wandering around town on his own." He reached out and tapped Terry's lapel. "I'd say we did Nozuki a favor by holding him here, to tell you the truth."

"Can't disagree with you there, Mr. Flynn. Holding him? There you did him right."

Flynn smiled. "Then we're agreed. Let me send for him and get the two of you on your way."

"But *charging* him?" Terry asked, eyebrows raised. "With a crime?"

Flynn was quiet. Somewhere down the hall a typewriter clacked. He turned to the window, hand on chin, thinking. After a few moments he nodded slightly and walked to his desk.

"We'll dismiss the charge, Mr. Terry." He looked up. "Just make sure this kid doesn't make the same mistake again."

"I'd say he made no mistake in the first place, Mr. Flynn. That was on us. It wasn't his fault there was no escort to meet him at the bus depot. He did the right thing. He came here, to the FBI, for help." Terry noticed Flynn's eyes tighten, so he changed course. "Anyway. This is very kind of you to dismiss the charge. Very kind. Thank you."

Flynn picked up his phone and instructed someone to bring Joe Nozuki up from lockup. "With his suitcase," he added. He pulled over a legal pad and began writing. Terry walked to the window and looked toward the horizon in silence. This was not a moment to make small talk.

There was a knock at the door. Terry turned to see an agent in a suit and fedora with his hand on the elbow of a young Japanese American man, easily in his midtwenties. A suitcase dangled at his side. The young man's eyes darted back and forth from the U.S. attorney at his desk to Jim Terry at the window.

This was the "kid" Flynn kept referring to? Terry thought.

"Joe, do you know Mr. Terry? From your camp?"

Nozuki shook his head.

"He's the lawyer down there, Joe. You're in luck. He's here to rescue you."

The young man let out a breath and his shoulders eased. The agent let go of his elbow.

Terry cut in. "I'm taking you back to the center. We've worked things out. Mr. Flynn understands that this was all a mistake."

Flynn snapped toward Terry at the window.

"That this was just a mistake on *our* part, Joe," Terry corrected himself. "Mr. Flynn has very kindly agreed to dismiss the charge."

Nozuki looked flustered and said nothing.

"You should thank Mr. Flynn."

Nozuki quickly thanked the U.S. attorney.

Flynn stood up and extended his hand. "Don't let this happen again," he said as they shook hands, but as he issued the warning, he scowled over at the project attorney. "No more of these so-called mistakes."

"Absolutely not, sir," said the Nisei. "Never again."

Jim Terry and Joe Nozuki briskly walked the several blocks to Terry's Packard Clipper.

"Wow, Mr. Terry. What a beautiful car!"

"Thanks," said Terry tightly. He tossed the Montgomery Ward bag with Teddy's curtains in the back seat, unlocked the passenger side, and gestured to Nozuki to climb in.

When the car started moving, the young man seemed to unclench, and he began talking rapidly. He really didn't know how it all happened, he said. He thought he'd alerted the right office at the center of his return. He was almost certain he had. He just couldn't understand how the whole thing had happened.

Terry drove in silence. He steered the Clipper east, toward the town of Mesa. From there it would be a straight shot south on Arizona Avenue over the reservation border and on to the center. Nozuki kept talking, seemingly happy to have a sympathetic ear after what he'd been through. He told the lawyer how confused he'd been when he couldn't find a WRA person in the depot, how nervous he was in asking the clerk in the ticket office for directions to the federal building, how relieved he felt when he got to the FBI office safely.

Terry just listened.

He'd been surprised when they put him in the lockup, he gushed, but they said it was for his own safety. And then they told him they were charging him with violating the exclusion order, which he just couldn't believe, because it wasn't his fault to begin with and he had tried to do the right thing.

They had reached Arizona Avenue. Terry turned the car south.

"Joe?"

"Yes, Mr. Terry?"

Terry stopped at a traffic light. They sat in silence, motionless, until the light turned green. Only then did the lawyer speak.

"Do you have any idea how much trouble you've caused?" Terry kept his eyes on the road as he spoke, his tone flat.

Nozuki opened his mouth as if to speak but didn't know what to say.

"Do you realize what a disaster this would have been for us if this little escapade had hit the papers?"

Nozuki closed his mouth and slumped a bit in the seat.

"Don't you ever—*ever*—let anything like this happen again. Do you understand me, Joe?"

"Yes, Mr. Terry."

They drove the rest of the way to the center in silence. Nozuki stared blankly out the passenger window, watching the desert brush whip by.

Kimiko Yamamoto met Jim Terry at the threshold of the Project Attorney's Office, her eyes bright. "You're back!" she exclaimed, extending a hand for his topcoat.

"Well this is quite a welcome, Miss Yamamoto!" Terry handed her the coat and swept a chivalrous arm across the doorway, beckoning her in ahead of him.

"I saw you pull in," she said, hanging up his coat, "and I'm so curious about how things went in Phoenix."

"Just fine, just fine. I put everything right with the U.S. attorney. Young Mr. Nozuki is safely back at the center."

"And?" Yamamoto thrust out her hands, playfully wiggling her fingers as if tapping a keyboard.

Terry stared, perplexed. "And what, Miss Yamamoto?"

"Typewriter?" she asked, eyebrows raised in hope.

"Oh, so that's what this is all about—the meeting me at the door, the smile. And here I thought you were just happy to see me!" Terry winked.

"Always happy to see you, Mr. Terry. But I'd be even happier to see you *and* a new typewriter!"

"I hate to disappoint, but I'm back empty-handed. I saw some nice machines for government purchase, but they wouldn't sell me one."

Terry sat down at his desk and eyed the stack of files needing his attention. It was very tall. In a few short weeks, the WRA would be launching a process of evaluating the evacuees' loyalties—to Japan or to the United States— and there was much to do to prepare. Suddenly he recalled a letter he'd been meaning to write, a little forewarning he wanted to send to headquarters, and it seemed a perfect way to procrastinate. "Miss Yamamoto," he called out, "would you please take a quick letter for me? It's to Mr. Glick in Washington."

The secretary pulled a stenography notebook from a drawer and looked up expectantly.

"Dear Phil," Terry dictated. "A most unlikely story has recently made its way to me, and on the off chance it will make its way to you as well, I want to alert you to it myself, and to its falsehood. It seems that a local attorney heard over the radio—he believes Friday or Saturday, the twenty-ninth or thirtieth of January, at 7:00 A.M. (9:00 A.M. eastern wartime) from Station WABC, the Columbia Broadcasting Station in New York, a news commentator say that it was the opinion of James Hendrick Terry, the project attorney at Gila River Relocation Center, that all loyal Japanese Americans should be separated from imperialist-minded Japanese."

Kimiko Yamamoto glanced up wide-eyed at Terry, who signaled with a raised index finger that he wasn't finished dictating.

"This sounds like a joke on my part, but it isn't. Perhaps it is a joke on the local attorney's part, but he swears to me that it is true. I have heard no other report of this fantastic incident. I am completely mystified, but you should not be. If you hear such a story, it is untrue. Please rest assured that I have never issued any such opinion for publication."

Terry paused, decided that this was all that needed saying, and asked Yamamoto to get the letter out in the next day's mail.

He shook his head at the unlikeliness of the radio story. It wasn't that segregating out the disloyal from the loyal was bad policy. It was a fine idea, in fact—long overdue. Probably where the WRA should have started.

But he had never been so foolish as to say so publicly.

CHAPTER THIRTEEN

LATE FEBRUARY 1943

GILA RIVER, ARIZONA

At this time of a February night, on toward dawn but still so dark that you could walk right into a cactus, the residential area for the staff would normally be pretty quiet. A few coyote howls or the stutter of a screech owl might cut through on the breeze, and you'd hear rustling here and there from little rodents or a tarantula. But the songbird chorus would not yet have begun. Over where the evacuees lived, closer to the butte, you'd hear the isolated sounds of the early mess hall shift workers hitting the latrine. But those sounds didn't usually make it over here to the staff area.

Tonight, though, hacking coughs continually broke the silence. They seemed to come from all directions at once, as though each of the barrack buildings were a sick bay. The culprit was valley fever, a mysterious respiratory illness that plagued the open desert areas of Arizona. Scientists were beginning to crack its mysteries; the best theory was that it was from a fungus in the desert floor. It caused no trouble buried there but plenty in the air, where the construction crews scraping at the desert floor to build the center had inadvertently lofted it. Chills, skin rashes, fever, headache, and a convulsing cough were its calling cards. There wasn't much to be done about it but try to rest and take all the aspirin and cough syrup you could get into you.

Some of the loudest hacking came from the apartment of Jim and Teddy Terry. The bug had hit them both on the same day and had kept Teddy to her bed, but the Project Attorney's Office called to her husband louder than his cough. He had not slowed down even though he felt miserable. Tonight, they had taken turns waking each other up with their hacking and wheezing and tossing and turning. Now as dawn approached, they both lay awake in the darkness.

"You are not going to the office today, Hendrick."

Terry heaved a sigh and started to speak but his words quickly turned into a cacophony of coughs. She waited while he spat phlegm into a cup beside his bed and slowly regained his breath.

She repeated herself, with greater emphasis on the "not."

"Yes I am, Teddy. I am going in. I have to go in. This place is falling apart."

He couldn't make out her face, but he didn't need to. A neighbor spewed phlegm into the darkness. "I just can't not go in, Teddy. I am days behind on paperwork—weeks, probably. Tax season's coming, the evacuee property situation is a disaster, people back in California are robbing these poor folks blind, I've got to get a judicial commission up and running."

He paused, hoping the list would have an impact, but Teddy was silent, so he made his case clearer. "Somebody's got to straighten all this out or we'll have massive problems on our hands here. I mean massive."

"Let someone else do the straightening today, Hendrick. You are not going to the office. When the sun comes up you are going to the hospital."

Terry reminded his wife that they were not allowed to use the center's hospital. It was just for the evacuees, a regulation the WRA was in the process of changing, but in the meantime the appointed personnel had to seek care outside the center.

"What about Stephen's tonsils?" she asked. Their youngest son had had a tonsillectomy in the center's hospital a few weeks earlier. Not only had the hospital accommodated them, but they'd jumped little Stephen ahead in line over several Japanese evacuees waiting for procedures. "If they could work Stephen in," she said, "they can work you in too."

"That was an emergency, Teddy."

"This is an emergency, Hendrick."

Terry began to say it wasn't, but coughs again erupted. When he could speak, he tried to change the subject, but Teddy wouldn't budge.

"You do realize we came out here for your health, right? Because New York was too cold and too wet, and you needed someplace warm and dry?"

He didn't respond.

"Someplace healthy? Someplace you'd be able to breathe? And regain your strength?"

She waited for an answer, but her husband said nothing.

"Do you realize that you're just as sick as you ever were back at home and you're working harder and you're not making even a *tenth* of what you were making back at the firm?"

This brought him to the surface. "Now, you know it's not about the money, Teddy."

She kept going. "And you realize that we left all our friends for this? And that we're living in a hovel in the middle of the desert? And that we've brought our sons into this . . . this environment? Do you realize?"

Terry corrected her. It was just Stephen; their two older boys were safely tucked away at a boarding school in Phoenix.

"Ugghh!" she cried, probably loud enough for the evacuees to hear over by the butte, and she threw herself back down on her pillow.

Terry stayed sitting up, his eyes searching the glass of the window for the first rose hues of dawn on the barrack wall next door. Yes, he realized. It was a god-awful job. In a godforsaken place. But by God, he loved it. Every day was fascinating and varied and full of questions nobody had ever thought about before, let alone answered. It was the most fun he'd had in years, infinitely more enjoyable than the niggling and parrying and haggling he'd been doing back at the law firm for his corporate clients. He wouldn't trade this work for a million dollars.

At the administration building he hacked and sputtered his way down the corridor toward his office. Heads popped out of office doors as he approached, greeting him with looks straddling a line between concern and alarm. Teddy plainly wasn't the only one who thought he should be home in bed, but he was not deterred. As he entered the project attorney's suite, he wobbled a bit on his feet and grabbed the doorframe. Kimiko Yamamoto jumped up from her desk to offer a hand to steady him, but Terry withdrew from her reach, waving her off with an "I'm fine!" that sounded like gargling.

"Sounds like you could do with a cup of tea," she said, hands on hips, and she swept out into the hallway to get one.

Terry really liked this young woman. She was poised and professional, kept a spotless desk, and seemed much more comfortable in Japanese than the average Nisei, putting the Issei at ease when they came for appointments. In conversation she was cooperative, polite, courteous—a little reserved, perhaps, but she was always ready with an answer to anything he asked her. She was still single at twenty-five, which perplexed Terry because she was a pleasant-looking girl, always neat and put together. She had a trade school diploma and experience working with customers in a tailor's shop, and the seasoning showed. She struck him as a model citizen, Japanese on the outside but American on the inside. She was just the sort of young person the WRA wanted to showcase in its relocation program, although in truth Terry hoped she would stay at the center a good while longer. He didn't want to lose her.

"No interruptions for the next two hours, Miss Yamamoto," he said. "Paperwork."

She hesitated. "Not even for registration?"

Registration. This damned questionnaire. It was taking up almost all his time. Evacuees coming up with every inane question they could think of,

from every possible angle. Registration was the very reason he was so behind
on paperwork. He nodded solemnly. "Not even for registration."

She nodded and returned to her desk. "Let me know if you need anything,
Mr. Terry—like a truckload of handkerchiefs." They exchanged a smile.

At his desk, the lawyer set to work on some property cases. If there was anything in this job that stoked his rage, it was these. Every day seemed to bring
at least one new case where some banker or some landlord or, worst of all,
some crook of a lawyer in California was sticking it to a Japanese who wasn't
around to protect himself. Insurance policies were lapsing, and claims were
being ignored. Caretakers were pocketing rent payments instead of forward-
ing them along to Japanese owners. Storage facilities were being looted with
impunity. Requests to ship valuables and belongings to the center were going
unacknowledged. Terry was convinced there was a full-blown conspiracy of
lawyers, collection agents, business managers, trustees, and the like all tied
in with one another, trying to grab as much Japanese property as they could.

Today brought a case that seemed not so much grasping as malicious. A
Nisei by the name of Misao Fukuoka had been in and out of the hospital at
Gila River since arriving back in August. The doctors were now saying she
needed surgery they were not equipped to perform. That meant a trip to the
hospital in Phoenix, and that meant money. Fukuoka had some funds at
the Bank of America back home in Suisun, California, and she'd written to
the bank to withdraw the cash, but one Mr. W. C. Robbins Jr., the branch
manager, had decided to run her around the block. Terry had in his hand a
letter from Robbins—dated a full month after Fukuoka's request—explaining
to the sick young woman that he could not release her funds unless she first
explained the nature of her illness and the nature of the surgery and told him
the name of the doctor who would be performing it and his precise fee.

The case mystified the lawyer. What was in it for this bank manager? The
usual thievery and self-dealing he could understand, even if it incensed him.
This Robbins character wasn't taking the sick woman's money for himself; he
was just withholding it from her. Not avarice. Cruelty.

When Fukuoka had come in with Robbins's letter, Terry could see she was
desperate. He couldn't tell what her illness was, but she was frail and lethargic.
Blushing, she had said she would tell him her diagnosis if she had to, but Terry
had stopped her with the palm of his hand and told her that what ailed her
was none of his business and it certainly wasn't any of the banker's business
either. He had told her that he would write Robbins a letter that would shake
the money loose in no time.

That was what he set about doing this morning.

GILA RIVER PROJECT

RIVERS, ARIZONA

Project Attorney

March 1, 1943

Bank of America
Suisun
California
Attention: W. C. Robbins Jr., Manager

Dear Sirs:

I refer to your letter of February 20, 1943, addressed to Miss
Misao Fukuoka, a resident of this center. I am at a loss to understand the legal basis for the position which your bank has
taken with respect to the withdrawal of funds by depositors and
I request that you advise me at your earliest convenience of the
statutory justification for requiring a depositor to state for what
purpose money is being withdrawn and how it is to be expended
before honoring a demand for withdrawal. I am interested in what
authority might require you to inquire into the personal affairs
of a depositor who is a citizen of the United States.

I am a citizen of the United States and have funds on deposit in
a number of banks throughout the country and I have never been
called upon to explain or justify the reasons for withdrawal of
my deposits to date. Is it your practice to require justification
for withdrawal of funds by all of your depositors without
discrimination?

You were informed that funds are to be withdrawn for the
purpose of a surgical operation. You then proceeded to inquire who
is to perform the operation and what the fees will be and what the
character of the operation is to be. I find it difficult to justify
your right to make such inquiry.

An undue length of time elapsed before any reply was made by you
to the first demand for withdrawal in this instance and while Miss
Fukuoka was entirely willing to go into detail with respect to the
projected operation, I have advised her that I wish to make this
inquiry before she does so, as I am concerned at the behavior of

your bank in this and other cases which have come to my attention.
The apparently unnecessary delays which have followed the demands
for withdrawals by depositors might well give rise to a belief
that there is intentional resistance by the bank to permitting
depositors to exercise their right to withdraw funds.

I am sending a copy of this letter to the Federal Reserve Bank
and I shall hope to receive an early reply from you.

> Very truly yours,
> JAMES H. TERRY
> Project Attorney
> cc: Federal Reserve Bank

Would the Federal Reserve Bank actually take the matter up if this bastard
Robbins persisted in harassing Fukuoka? Terry had his doubts but couldn't
think of a better way to try to scare him into releasing her money. It would be
different if he were in California: he would pay the branch a little visit, work
over this Robbins kid with a barrage of questions about banking regulations,
maybe let slip that the secretary of the Treasury would be troubled to hear
about the matter the next time Terry bumped into him at their Exeter Academy reunion. From here in the Arizona desert, copying the Federal Reserve
was the best he could do. He made a note in his calendar to follow up with the
bank in a week's time and set the file aside.

Terry next turned his attention to an accordion file marked "Community
Cooperative." He extracted two paper-clipped documents, one bearing the
title "Articles of Incorporation of the Gila River Cooperative Enterprises, Inc."
and the other the more cumbersome "Operating Agreement between Gila
River Cooperative Enterprises, Inc., and the War Relocation Authority." He
brushed some leftover eraser shavings off them with a touch of pride. The
documents represented several months of work to put Gila River's community
stores, hair salons, shoe repair shops, and other businesses on a stable footing,
one that would return some benefit to the evacuees who patronized them.
Terry was amazed every time he walked into one of these shops, dazzled and
even touched by the care and pride the evacuees put into them. Beautifully
painted signs announcing sales and specials dotted the walls; neatly attired
salesmen and saleswomen wandered the floor, pointing out a newly arrived
blouse here and a bolt of fabric there; eager clerks waited for customers at cash

registers. If it weren't for the bare wood walls and the dangling light bulbs and the open rafters, you might think you were in some small-town dry goods store, and a nice one at that.

At first many of the evacuees had been skeptical about the idea of converting the shops to a cooperative, even though they understood that this would return profits to the community through patronage dividends. Why couldn't the WRA just run the stores for them, they wanted to know, since the WRA was responsible for keeping them there in the first place? Why should the stores have to pay rent to the WRA and get insurance and bank accounts and all the rest?

These were not unreasonable questions, and it took plenty of meetings and conversations for Terry to persuade the community that they were better off with a cooperative that they themselves owned. There were tax reasons, liability reasons, insurance reasons, financial reasons, and he'd spent the winter going over and over and over them until he could recite them rote. What he hadn't mentioned was that the WRA thought it would be educational for the evacuees to be the owners of their own shops—a practical lesson in American enterprise.

Terry plunged into the documents, scouring them for unclear language and problems he hadn't yet managed to foresee. They were nearly ready to be signed but not quite. He had learned in New York that when you reached the point where you told yourself a document was finally ready, that meant it still wasn't ready. Something important always turned up on that extra read-through if you really concentrated.

Coughing jags were the only things to break Terry's focus for well over an hour, until a rapping on his door intruded. Without raising his eyes from his agreements he raised an index finger to keep the secretary from entering until he reached a stopping point in his scribbling. Looking up, though, he saw not Kimiko Yamamoto but an army uniform. Capt. Norman Thompson walked in and without asking plopped himself down across from Terry's desk. In the doorway Yamamoto gave a pained shrug to signal that she'd tried her best to hold him off outside. Terry could see from the tension in Thompson's eyes that he was not about to be delayed. He nodded understanding at Yamamoto, and she closed the office door.

Thompson was the man in charge of the little four-man team sent by the army to Gila River to run its piece of the registration program, the part directed at drumming up Nisei volunteers. They'd arrived in early February, set up shop in a couple of barrack buildings, and waited for young men to start pouring in. Terry had heard the soldiers debating how many of the 2,600 eligible Nisei men would volunteer. Would it be 400? 500? They seemed to agree that 600 was pie-in-the-sky, but when one of them guessed only 200, he was jeered. Terry had held his tongue; he hoped for a good showing but worried that a gang of troublemaking Kibei might use the moment to sow dissatisfaction.

By the end of the first day of registration, even the more cautious project attorney was in shock. The problem wasn't turnout; a total of 173 young men had shown up to fill out their registration forms. The problem was their answers. Well over half of them had answered no to question 27, the one that asked if they would be willing to serve on combat duty in the armed services if so ordered. Even worse, nearly a third of them had answered no to question 28, which asked if they were willing to swear unqualified allegiance to the United States. And not a single soul had volunteered to join the army. Not one.

Maybe it was his years of going after bootleggers and con men as a prosecutor, but Jim Terry knew foul play when he saw it. There was a disinformation campaign behind this—most likely Issei and Kibei intent on defeating registration and everything it stood for. Perhaps it went past disinformation; Terry didn't put physical threats past the worst of the bad eggs. He didn't have hard evidence against anyone, the kind that would stand up in court. But he had another option: Moab. The Moab Isolation Center, located in the middle of nowhere in the Utah desert, was a makeshift jail that Terry had helped the WRA establish in January. It was for situations just like this one—where a project director needed to banish a U.S. citizen evacuee from a center but lacked enough time and evidence to involve the courts.

On February 16, they pulled the Moab trigger. FBI agents and WRA internal security officers swept through the center and carted off more than two dozen evacuees. It was quick and efficient. No demonstrations, no protests. One day they were there. The next day they were gone.

With the worst of the rabble-rousers locked up elsewhere, the army recruiters and WRA staff heaved sighs of relief and resumed the registration process. Surely now the good people of Gila River would feel free to answer questions 27 and 28 favorably. Young men would step up and volunteer.

That was what they had thought two days ago. But the look on Captain Thompson's face across Jim Terry's desk told a different story.

"The new numbers are in, Mr. Terry," said the soldier. "They're still awful."

"What do you mean 'awful'?"

"I mean awful. The same as before. Nothing has changed. At least one no for every two yeses." Thompson reached across and laid a spreadsheet on the desk in front of Terry. "And no volunteers. Not a single solitary one." The captain explained that the evacuees were still confused and cautious. Despite all the informational meetings they'd run, all the leaflets, all the articles in the newspaper, people still didn't seem to understand just what they were committing themselves to if they answered yes to the questions. Nor could they seem to grasp the consequences of answering no.

Terry was incredulous. He opened his mouth to speak but his anger caught in his throat and a new seizure of coughs gripped him. It went on so long that the door cracked open to reveal Kimiko Yamamoto offering a handkerchief.

"Are you all right, Mr. Terry?" she asked.

He was unable to produce words but nodded. Yamamoto, looking sheepish for intruding, began to back out, but Terry gestured her back in toward the empty chair next to Thompson. She sat as the hacking subsided.

"Miss Yamamoto, I'd like you to take something down."

She jumped up to retrieve a pencil bag and steno pad from her desk in the reception room.

While she was out, Terry told Thompson it was time to clear up any lingering misconceptions in the evacuees' minds about the registration questions. He was going to say what they meant, and the newspaper would print what they meant, and that would put an end to the nonsense.

Yamamoto returned to her chair, balanced the steno pad on her knee, set her pencil to paper, and looked up expectantly.

"Here is what I want you to write down, Miss Yamamoto." He coughed once more, then continued. "There is nothing mysterious about questions 27 and 28. They are not trick questions. You may take my word for it that if you answer both questions yes you are saying no more than that you are loyal to the United States of America and that in your heart the United States comes first, ahead of any other country or government in the world, and that you are willing to obey the laws of the United States without reservation."

Terry paused to let Yamamoto to catch up.

"If you answer question 27 no, you are saying that you are not willing to obey the laws of the United States and are advertising the fact that you would disobey a law affecting you that you do not like, and that you are either disloyal to the United States or slackers. If you answer question 28 no, you are saying that you disown American citizenship, have no loyalty to the United States, and, on the other hand, have loyalty to an enemy of the United States and presumably would be willing to aid that enemy against the United States."

Terry again paused to allow the secretary to keep pace.

"Any attempt to read any other significance or meaning in the questions or to quibble about the effect of the answers is an indication of lack of good faith on your part as a registrant and a desire to look for loopholes to evade your expressions of loyalty and your responsibilities as a citizen."

Terry never looked away from Thompson as he dictated, enjoying the glow of authority he felt in his extemporizing and the wide-eyed mix of surprise and pleasure on the soldier's face. The captain had come to him for help, but Terry was sure he couldn't have expected a boost like this one.

"And one more thing, Miss Yamamoto. Please add this." He stopped and looked at the ceiling, reflecting, and then locked eyes again with Thompson. "Any citizen who answers no to question 28 without simultaneously asking to be repatriated to Japan is a traitor to the United States and as such is subject to the penalties provided for treasonous persons, which can include the death penalty."

The words reverberated in the small wooden room. Thompson cocked his head quizzically. "Forgive me, Mr. Terry, I mean no disrespect, but is that true? About treason? And the death penalty?"

The hint of doubt jarred Terry out of the rhythm of his performance. He realized his statement was not exactly a measured recitation of the law, particularly the bit about treason. While he'd never prosecuted a treason case back in New York, he remembered something from his law school days about a need for "overt acts" lending "aid and comfort" to the enemy. Would a refusal to swear allegiance meet that test? Suddenly he was doubtful. Only the federal statute books could answer the question for sure, and the nearest set was forty miles north in Phoenix. Terry shrugged off his doubts. He was trying to deal with an emergency here. Phil Glick might take a different view of the matter, but the solicitor wasn't here handling the crisis. Terry was.

"Yes, Captain Thompson. This could be characterized as treason."

The two men exchanged a grave look. "I'm sure this will turn some heads," said Thompson.

Terry turned toward his receptionist for the first time since beginning his dictation. "Did you get all of that, Miss Yamamoto?"

But Kimiko Yamamoto was frozen. She stared at the fabric of her skirt where it fell over her knees.

"Miss Yamamoto?"

When she again didn't respond, Terry craned toward her, scanning for even a flicker of movement. After a moment she raised her head and met his gaze. Her eyes were moist. She said nothing.

Captain Thompson shifted in his chair and looked away.

"I asked you if you got all of that down, Miss Yamamoto," Terry said flatly.

Her answer was a whisper. "Every word, Mr. Terry." Then she stood abruptly, tucking her steno pad under her arm, and bolted from the office. Her pencil bag remained on the floor beside her chair.

The lawyer and the soldier exchanged a baffled shrug.

"No clue what that was about," Terry said quickly. "Quite out of character."

Winter ends early in the southern Arizona desert. By mid-March the temperature was clearing ninety and the scorpions were wide awake. Butterflies billowed above the alfalfa fields in yellow rolling masses while dust devils spun across fields lying fallow. Those pint-sized dirt twisters were more dangerous than they appeared; they could stir up the spores that caused valley fever. Terry and Teddy finally had the worst of their illness behind them, and the last thing he wanted was a relapse.

Registration was drawing to a quiet close. Everyone noticed that things had grown more peaceful, but nobody was entirely sure why. Every staff member had his pet theory about what had quelled the resistance. Some thought the key moment was when the troublemakers got carted off to Moab. Others said it was just better marketing, the payoff from persistent efforts to calm the evacuees and help them understand the questions on the questionnaire. Terry liked to think that warning the community about treason had played a role, so he was irritated when Phil Glick wrote him—long after the fact, of course—that treason prosecutions were legally impossible. Glick said he knew Terry would have given better advice if he hadn't been under "pressure to shoot from the hip," as he put it. It was nice of the solicitor to temper the scolding, but it stung anyway. From his paneled office on Farragut Square a few blocks from the White House, what could Phil Glick possibly understand about the pressures they were under in the field?

That the registration process grew more peaceful in the latter part of February did not mean it grew more successful. The final results were far from stellar. Terry knew from the reports of the other project attorneys that registration hadn't lived up to the WRA's expectations at any of the centers, but the results at Gila River were closer to the bottom than the top of the list. Almost 13 percent answered no to the loyalty question at Gila. Ted Haas was reporting 5 percent at Poston, and in his latest letter Jerry Housel was bragging about 4 percent at Heart Mountain. Quite a difference.

Terry knew that the results at Gila weren't his fault, but when he sat down to write his biweekly report to the home office on the last day of the month he felt the need to explain them anyway. Some of it, he wrote, had to do with the leniency of the WRA administrators at Gila; they had generally spared the rod, so naturally the child had grown pretty spoiled. Some of it had to do with geography: unlike Heart Mountain and Poston, Gila was in the exclusion zone, so the evacuees felt more trapped. No shopping excursions into town to lighten the mood—indeed, no town nearby at all, and no shopping. But those were minor factors in the scheme of things. By this point, it was clear to Terry that much of the trouble rested with the evacuees themselves. There was only a small proportion of the population at Gila River that was loyal to a degree that anyone could count on. The largest percentage of the evacuees were just apathetic. They had no real sense of loyalty to anything except their own selfish interests. It wasn't that most of the people who answered no were pro-Japanese. It was that they were cowards and slackers. Maybe a bleeding heart such as Ted Haas over at Poston was telling Washington something different, but Terry could only write it as he saw it, and that was how he saw it.

Terry's walk home from the office that evening felt like a charge through volleys of bird shot. The sandstorms were back, seemingly fiercer and more violent than they had been before the short winter lull. These storms could be wicked. One minute the sky would be blue, and the next a billowing gray-brown wall of torn-up desert would be bearing down on the center like a line of squalls. Most people stayed in or took cover if the storm was a bad one, and if you had to go out, you'd cover your mouth and nose with whatever cloth you had handy and crook your elbow at your eyes and hurl yourself in the general direction you needed. That was what Jim Terry did to get home, advancing ten or twenty yards and then lurching into the lee of a building for a moment's respite and then striking back out for another advance. In his blindness he tripped over an exposed pipe, lost his balance, and instinctively opened the hand that was clutching the mess hall napkin over his mouth and nose. In an instant it was gone. The rest of the way home Terry stumbled, zombie-like, with both elbows across his face. By the time he hurled himself through his door, sand encrusted his nostrils and his teeth crunched grit.

By nine he was in bed.

By midnight he was up again, hacking up mucus and trembling with fever. A relapse, no doubt triggered by spores on the wind. He feebly protested when Teddy demanded they head to the hospital, but she would have none of it, so off they went. The sandstorm had passed and the night was quiet as they made their labored way out of the staff barrack block and across the street to the hospital complex.

It took their eyes a moment to adjust to the light of the reception area, but when the room came into focus it looked just as it had when they'd rushed Stephen in with his terrible tonsillitis. The space had a modern look about it, at least by comparison to the barracks and mess halls and even the administration building. Here the flooring was smooth and polished, unlike the gapping slatted floors elsewhere. Bright Celotex wallboard reflected the cool glow of overhead bulbs, creating an ambience of clinical cleanliness. The white bonnet of a nurse receptionist poked up on the far side of a small square reception window. Low benches of dark wood lined two walls, and folding chairs hugged a third.

Teddy guided her husband to one of the few empty seats and then stepped across to the reception window to register. Looking around, Terry realized they were in for a wait. Even at this late hour, now well after midnight, evacuees filled both benches and nearly all the folding chairs. Most of them looked to be feeling no better than he was, and some had the pall of truly serious illness. Many seemed to have fallen to the same valley fever that had Terry in its grips—the pale and sweaty faces, the caved-in slump of exhaustion, the sniffles and throaty coughs. Two young Nisei couples cast worried eyes on bundled-up, silent toddlers sitting listless in their laps. An elderly Issei man wearing only a thin jacket over a tattered nightshirt mumbled to himself in Japanese, tugging mindlessly at a fraying hem. A middle-aged man in a white mess hall uniform held a sloppily bandaged hand over his head, presumably stemming the flow of blood from the blade of a wayward knife. An emaciated young woman with a blanket over her shoulders curled uncomfortably at the end of one of the benches, twisting to shield her eyes from the light.

Teddy returned and sat down next to her husband. "I gave her your name," she said, casting a glance around the room and sizing up the crowd. "Looks like it might be a wait, though."

Terry grunted and slouched in his chair. The light was making his head pound, so he closed his eyes and twisted toward the wall, much like the young woman with the blanket. He would try to doze while they waited, at least between coughing jags. But the image of that young woman stuck in his mind's eye. Something about her nagged at him.

When it clicked into place, he rose and walked over to her. "Miss Fukuoka?" he said. It was the woman with the Bank of America problem. She had lost weight since her office visit, which was troubling because she had very little to spare. In the office she had clearly been sick, but she had been presentable. Not so tonight. Tonight her illness, whatever it was, hung heavy on her.

"Mr. Terry," she said softly, squinting at his silhouetted face. "Are you unwell?"

"Valley fever." He thought to return the query but recalled her discomfort over the bank's questions and decided against it. "Have you heard from the bank, by any chance?" He'd had no response in the couple of weeks since he sent his letter, but maybe it had set the manager straight and he'd just sent her the money she was so plainly due.

The young woman shook her head. No, she hadn't.

"Well, I sent them quite a letter on your behalf. Quite a letter. Hit them with my sternest stuff."

She smiled very weakly and nodded.

"I hope it will have its intended effect."

She nodded again.

"And that you feel better soon, Miss Fukuoka."

She thanked him and returned the wish, then twisted back toward the wall.

Terry pivoted back toward Teddy, aiming to sit and settle in for a long wait. Before he reached his chair, though, he heard their names. It was the nurse in the reception window. She was standing, leaning through the window and pointing toward the adjacent door that led back to the clinic.

"We're ready for you, Mr. and Mrs. Terry. Right this way."

He looked at Teddy. She raised her eyebrows and gave a slight shrug, then rose and reached out to hook a steadying arm around her husband's waist.

As they walked toward the door, the space fell silent. Had they been paying attention, the Terrys would have seen glances and scowls passing from patient to patient around the periphery of the room.

But they were just pleased to be seen so quickly, and vanished through the door.

CHAPTER FOURTEEN

MAY 1943

PHOENIX, ARIZONA

Another drive to Phoenix.

Jim Terry was really racking up the mileage on his Packard Clipper. Since mid-March, after the worst of his valley fever was behind him, it seemed he was in Phoenix at least twice a month. And the pace had been picking up as the mood toward the evacuees started to shift so badly to the negative. All these newspaper stories about the worse-than-expected results of the loyalty registration and the lurid "exposés" about the evacuees basking in the lap of luxury in the centers were really taking a toll on public opinion. The WRA's relocation program wasn't exactly being celebrated either. Perhaps it was incompetence in the communications division at WRA headquarters—Terry would never underestimate the WRA's incompetence— but people seemed to have the impression that the agency was preparing just to throw open the gates of the centers and let the evacuees move wherever they wished and buy up farmland once they got there. Which was ludicrous. But try telling that to an irate mayor or state legislator.

If Terry was honest, he had to admit that "irate" captured his own emotional state too. After six months of painstaking work to create it, the entire retail and service operation at Gila River was unraveling. Or being done in, to put it more accurately. Terry had done everything right in setting up Gila River Cooperative Enterprises, Inc. Back in January he had pressed for a legal opinion from the Arizona attorney general's office that the business could incorporate under the laws of the District of Columbia and still qualify for a business license to operate in Arizona. He'd gotten Amos Betts, the chairman of the state's powerful Corporation Commission, to issue the business license in April.

And now Betts was taking it all away with just a pen stroke, canceling the license. Terry had gotten word of it on the radio news, of all places. Betts hadn't even given Terry the courtesy of a phone call, let alone an opportunity to be heard. At least he'd managed to persuade Betts to convene the Corporation Commission for a hearing on the matter tomorrow. Hence the drive this afternoon up to Phoenix.

The situation was approaching crisis, so the hearing had to go well. The state was trying to choke off Japanese business activity completely; there was no other way to look at it. First the legislature had passed House Bill 187, which required anyone wanting to transact business with a Japanese American to jump through impossible hoops—three public notices in the newspaper, a notice with the secretary of state beforehand, and a monthly report to the secretary of state afterward. Tom Masuda over at Poston was sending Terry disgraceful stories of people using the law to treat the Japanese as if they had the plague—shop owners refusing to sell them anything, dentists refusing to extract their teeth, lawyers dropping them as clients. A linotype operator in Parker was refusing to typeset the Poston newspaper. Gas stations were refusing to pump gas. Some motivated storekeepers placed mimeographed copies of the law on tables in prominent spots and were putting them into the hands of anyone who'd take them.

Plunging the evacuees into economic isolation would have been enough to send them the message that they'd never be welcome on a single acre of Arizona farmland. But every two-bit politician wants his scene on the stage, and Amos Betts, who struck Terry as not even amounting to two full bits, wanted his own limelight moment. House Bill 187 made it all but impossible to do business with a Japanese person, but the cooperative at Gila River was a corporation. If Arizonans couldn't do business with the Japanese as individuals, Betts wasn't going to let them do business with 7,000 of them gathered together as a corporation. That's how Jim Terry handicapped the situation. Just a politician bullying a defenseless minority to impress the public and his patrons.

But if Amos Betts thought the evacuees were truly defenseless, he was in error. The evacuees weren't defenseless as long as Jim Terry was in town. Amos Betts and the bosses of agriculture might be accustomed to steamrolling the locals, but just let him try it with the lawyer who'd cleaned Dutch Handel and his gang out of Hell's Kitchen and prosecuted the father of the Prince of Monaco for bootlegging.

The WRA per diem would have forced Terry into a furnace of a room at some roadside tourist court, so he decided to splurge on a room at the Westward Ho downtown. On his own nickel, of course. There was no mistaking it for the Plaza Hotel or the Waldorf-Astoria. Some filigree stonework around the front door and a few blocky columns in the lobby aside, it was really just a tall cement box. But it was nice to feel what passed for luxury out in these parts—the brush of a high-thread-count sheet and a lobby bar that could mix a decent cocktail. Terry planned to spend the evening preparing for the hearing, but the commission wasn't making it easy. There was no agenda, no reports, no witness list—nothing to pore over but the revocation order and a stack of the cooperative's papers and financial ledgers he'd brought with him from camp. That didn't take him long, so he spent most of the evening at the bar. Tomorrow, Amos Betts. Tonight, Tom Collins.

He'd planned to hop in a taxi to the Capitol Annex on Monday morning, but when he stepped out onto Central Avenue, he found the air unseasonably cool, so he decided to walk. Between steps he flipped the pages of the morning edition of the *Arizona Republic*, scouring the headlines for mention of the day's hearing. Fortunately, nothing, just the latest war news—a bombing assault on Sicily, fighting in air and sea around the Solomon Islands, the destruction of U-boat bases in Bremen and Kiel. Maybe today's hearing wouldn't turn out to be as big a production as he feared. His nose was still in the paper when he got to the intersection with Van Buren, where a car's horn sent him scampering up onto the curb. When he was here a few months ago, fishing Joe Nozuki out of a federal holding cell, this street was important, the demarcation line between exclusion and freedom. Since then, the army had shifted the line south by sixty miles, so Van Buren was just a street like any other. So arbitrary, these lines. As he crossed over and continued westward toward the capitol, he shook his head, once again appalled by the way everyone, state and federal—everyone, he noted to himself, but the WRA—jerked the Japanese around.

Any hope of a low-key event evaporated when Terry entered the hearing room. Enough men in hats and bolo ties clustered in back-slapping and hand-shaking groups to fill every seat and then some. Two men with reporter's notebooks vaulted from their seats when they spotted him, but he waved them off as he made his way toward the front of the room. It was as bland a public space as he could recall. A small dais between the state and U.S. flags bore the seal of the Corporation Commission. Behind it sat Amos Betts—a silver-haired, square-jawed man of around seventy, who stopped winking and signaling to people in the audience in order to give Terry a barely perceptible nod as he approached—and to Betts's right, Bill Peterson, another commissioner. A photo portrait of Governor Sidney Preston Osborn hung on the wall between the flags. A clock ticked off seconds from the rear wall. A slightly-better-than-paint-by-numbers landscape of the Grand Canyon graced one of the two side walls. The other was bare. Terry took his seat, scooped his papers from his briefcase onto the table in front of him, slipped his newspaper into the briefcase as he placed it on the floor beside him, and waited for Amos Betts to open the curtain on his show.

As the hour hand on the rear wall clock hit ten, Betts called the hearing to order and the men in hats took their seats. "I have a brief statement to enter into the record," he said, peering over reading glasses at the sheaf of paper he held in his hand. "We are here this morning at the request of the War Relocation Authority to consider an order revoking the license and charter of the nonprofit cooperative they're running for the Japs down on the Gila River Indian land. Mr. Terry, Mr. James Hendrick Terry of New York City, is with us representing the cooperative." He looked up and nodded in Terry's direction and then adjusted his glasses to begin reading his statement, but Terry rose slightly out of his chair.

"Formerly of New York City, Mr. Betts. I moved to this great state going on a year ago now. Doctor's orders," he said, looking back toward the audience, "and the best orders a doctor ever gave me!" He beamed, expecting an appreciative chuckle, but the men in hats stayed silent. Betts opened his mouth to resume his opening statement, but Terry remained half-standing. "And I do not represent the Gila River Cooperative Enterprises, Mr. Betts. I am here for the War Relocation Authority."

Betts looked confused.

"The Arizona Corporation Commission failed to serve the cooperative with any sort of notice, either of the revocation of its license or of this hearing. The cooperative is not here today. I am here for the War Relocation Authority only."

The chairman peered at Terry over his reading glasses. "Now Mr. Terry, I'm sure an able New York attorney like yourself can handle the interests of both the WRA and the cooperative, which I assume are in close alignment, are they not?"

"Mr. Chairman, I am not here for the cooperative. The cooperative is not here today. It received no notice, to which it was every bit as entitled as is any other corporation under this commission's jurisdiction." Terry sat down but allowed himself another comment from his chair. "If I *were* the lawyer for the cooperative, I would advise its directors that fair notice is a fundamental principle of due process in our American system. And that they should expect nothing less."

Betts raised an eyebrow at Bill Peterson next to him, smoothed a crease out of the papers in his hands, and began reading. "The Gila River Cooperative Enterprises is a nonprofit corporation organized under the laws of the District of Columbia, with powers to buy, sell, own, and lease real and personal property. It is a membership organization, which means that rather than holding on to its profits, it returns a proportionate share to each of its members. It operates under a separate agreement with the War Relocation Authority, Mr. Terry's organization, but it is not a U.S. government entity. In fact, ladies and gentlemen, it's fair to say that it is not exactly an *American* entity. All eighteen of its incorporators are Japanese. All ten of its directors are Japanese. And all of its members are Japanese." Betts paused and scanned his audience. "All *seven thousand* of its members are Japanese."

A murmur rumbled through the audience.

"The cooperative filed with this commission as an out-of-state corporation intending to do business in Arizona and was granted a license on April 1 of this year. However, upon further review this commission determined late in May that the license may never have been properly granted and should be reconsidered. After careful study and mature consideration of just exactly who these incorporators are, just exactly what the corporation's goals and purposes are, and just exactly what the nature is of the rights and privileges this cooperative claims for itself, we"—and here he placed his hand on the shoulder of Bill Peterson, seated beside him—"were of the opinion that the cooperative could not legally qualify under the laws of the state of Arizona. That is why, on June 4, we issued an order canceling the license previously issued."

"Makes sense!" shouted a man in the audience.

Another: "Good call!"

Betts continued. "Before we begin calling witnesses, let me point out the aspect of this that's most concerning. This nonprofit corporation is set up to return moneys, a dividend of sorts, from the sale of ordinary commercial goods to the very members who are buying them. Now maybe that's how business is done in the District of Columbia or in other parts. But it's not how we do retail business here. The cooperative is not a concept our law recognizes. So the issue today is whether or not Japanese corporations shall be authorized to function in this state under more favorable conditions than are accorded to our own domestic corporations and individuals. Do these Japanese get better business terms than we make available to ourselves? Do we allow these Japanese to build—in our own fertile valleys—an empire founded on standards with which American growers and laborers cannot compete? An empire that is as foreign to us as the Japanese empire itself and quite possibly just as antagonistic and disloyal in spirit?"

"Heck no!" blurted a woman sitting in the first row, no more than two feet from Jim Terry.

Amos Betts scanned the room, gauging the impact of his words. "*That,*" he said, plunging his right index finger forward as if rapping a listener's lapel, "is the question before this commission today. And so we will call our first witness: Mr. M. O. Sharp of Phoenix."

A tall man of perhaps forty unfolded himself from a chair in the front row and strode to the witness box. Sharp was one of the leading vegetable growers in the Salt River Valley and the founder of the Central Arizona Vegetable Growers Association. With his pasty complexion, thin hair, and platter-sized round metal eyeglasses frames, he had the look of a man who spent more time with his hands in cash drawers than in seed bags. After swearing to tell the truth, the whole truth, and nothing but the truth, he settled himself into the witness chair with the ease of a man who was accustomed to addressing large groups of men and to having them listen carefully.

Terry had no idea why Betts was calling Sharp as a witness, let alone his first. Sharp had never visited Gila River and, so far as Terry was aware, didn't know the first thing about the cooperative, the corporation laws of the District of Columbia, or the WRA. But when Sharp explained he was there on behalf of the Arizona Farm Bureau Federation, all became clear. The Farm Bureau was a behemoth in Arizona politics. It spoke for the state's farmers—or at least its well-connected Caucasian ones—and had a storied history of telling legislators not just to jump but how long to stay in the air. These were the people behind House Bill 187, the people who'd never wanted a single Japanese farmer in the state and who, now that they were here, wanted them gone.

Betts moved out in front of the dais to question his witness. "Mr. Sharp, thank you for being with us this morning, and thanks also to the marvelous work the Farm Bureau does on behalf of the good farm people of this state. Would you happen to know how many Japanese we now have in this state, between the facilities over at Poston and the ones down on the Gila River land?"

"I do not know the precise number, Mr. Commissioner." Shifting in his seat to face the audience, he added, "All I know is that it's way too many."

"Would it surprise you to know that the number is over thirty thousand?"

"It wouldn't surprise me so much as terrify me."

"Why would it terrify you, Mr. Sharp?"

"Because even if you take away the old ones and the young ones, that's enough Japs right there to dominate our entire agricultural industry in this valley—in the whole state, really. If they're allowed out of those places and into our communities."

Betts put on reading glasses, opened a folder, and, with a flourish, took out a document. He looked it up and down, flipped to a second page, and then turned back to his witness. "What I have here in my hand, Mr. Sharp, is the articles of incorporation of the Gila River Cooperative Enterprises. I'd like to read you a couple of excerpts from the section that lists what the cooperative claims the power to do." Tracking the text with his index finger, he read aloud, "To engage in the manufacture, production, processing, distribution, marketing, storing, handling, sale, or trade of goods and commodities, at wholesale and retail." He looked up at the witness, who nodded in comprehension. Eyes back on the page, he continued, "To construct or acquire and operate establishments and facilities for supplying any kind of commodities to the general public, both at wholesale and retail." Another pause to make sure that Sharp had taken that in. "To acquire, own, hold, sell, lease, pledge, mortgage, or otherwise dispose of any property incident to its purposes and activities and affairs," intoned the commissioner, stressing the word "property." And then, adding a gap between each of the words for effect, he read, "And to engage in any activity in connection with any one or more of the foregoing purposes."

"Yes, sir," said the witness.

"Mr. Sharp, let me ask you something. If this Japanese cooperative can operate in our state, can it buy farmland?"

Terry rose from his chair. "I'll object to that, Mr. Betts. This man is not an expert on cooperative corporations and is in no position to offer an opinion about what the articles do and do not allow."

"This is not a courtroom, Mr. Terry," said Betts acidly. "Nobody is on trial. This is a commission hearing. Your rules of evidence do not apply here."

Terry sat heavily back in his chair, the contours of the day ahead coming painfully into focus.

"You may answer my question, Mr. Sharp. Do the articles of incorporation allow this cooperative to buy Arizona farmland?"

"That's sure how it sounds to me," said Sharp.

"And do these articles authorize this Japanese cooperative to cultivate crops?"

"So it would appear."

"And then market and sell them?"

Sharp nodded.

"To the general public?"

"Yes, sir."

Amos Betts dropped the paper to his side, shifted his reading glasses to his shirt pocket, and took a step closer to the audience. "And Mr. Sharp, if this Japanese cooperative were to do these things, what is your estimation of the impact it would have on the state of Arizona?"

"I have no doubt that the Japanese would very quickly come to dominate the agricultural industry of the state of Arizona. Drive the white farmer right out of business."

"And why is that, Mr. Sharp?"

"You have to understand something about how the Japs operate. They're not like us. The white farmer in this state is accustomed to a certain standard of living—is *entitled* to a certain standard of living. The Jap is accustomed to living very differently, is willing to get by at a level that frankly I think most of us would find shocking. This is why the legislature had the good sense to enact our alien land law going on two decades ago now, to keep them from buying up our farms. Now it looks as though they're going to get around that with this cooperative, by having *a corporation* be the one to buy the land. Different buyer, but same result: white farmers will simply not be able to compete with the Japs and uphold our standard of living."

Jim Terry could sense the rising anger in the crowd behind him without even turning around.

"One final question for you, Mr. Sharp," said Amos Betts. "How would you expect the typical Arizona farmer to respond to such a state of affairs?"

The witness rocked back slightly in his chair and let out a chortle. "There will be no such state of affairs. We are not going to let it happen."

Several men in the audience whooped; others applauded and stomped.

Betts returned to the dais. Before taking his seat, he asked Jim Terry whether he had any questions for the witness. The lawyer rose and strolled toward the side of the room, stopping and turning just beneath the painting of the Grand Canyon.

"Mr. Sharp, have you ever visited the relocation center at Gila River?"

The witness admitted he had not.

"And have you ever spoken with any of the officers or directors of the Gila River Cooperative Enterprises?"

Sharp again said no.

"And have you ever met any of the members of the cooperative?"

"I don't believe I have had the pleasure, Mr. Terry," said Sharp to titters from the audience.

Terry returned to his table and picked up the papers he'd placed there. "And are you familiar with the inventory of the store at the center, where the evacuees do much of their shopping?"

"I am not." Sharp shot a glance at the crowd. "Though I imagine there is rice?"

More titters from the crowd, this time louder.

Terry pressed on. "Are you aware, Mr. Sharp, that the cooperative does no business outside the confines of the center? That it has no plans to do business outside the confines of the center?"

"All I know, Mr. Terry, is what Commissioner Betts read to me a moment ago, and I don't recall any limits on where the cooperative can do business."

"Would you accept my representation that the cooperative has no such plans? And that the War Relocation Authority, which permits the cooperative to do business at the center and leases it space, would not allow it?"

"How am I to know what the cooperative plans for next month or next year? Or what the WRA will allow down the road?"

Jim Terry turned to the dais and exchanged a glance with Amos Betts. "Just one more question, Mr. Betts." The chairman nodded. "Mr. Sharp, are you aware that the WRA offered to have the cooperative amend its articles of incorporation to limit its powers to the confines of the relocation center? And that Mr. Betts did not accept that offer?"

The commissioner looked on impassively.

"I did not know that, Mr. Terry," said the witness.

"Thank you, Mr. Sharp. That is all." Terry reached for the back of his chair.

"But it doesn't surprise me, Mr. Terry." Sharp leaned forward to capture the lawyer's attention. "I myself don't make a habit of trusting the Japs. And you know what?" He swept his arm toward the dais. "I don't expect Amos Betts or Bill Peterson up here does either. One of 'em's more dangerous than a thousand rattlesnakes."

The crowd stomped their approval.

"Thank you, Mr. Sharp," said Betts, smiling broadly and rising from his seat. "The commission's next witness will be Mr. Arthur J. Barnes."

An enormous man under an enormous Stetson hat rose with difficulty from a chair along the back wall and lumbered forward. Six feet tall and easily 300 pounds, he clapped several onlookers on the back as he passed by, greeting them by name. Barnes was a large character in more ways than body: he was a member of the Arizona House of Representatives, representing a Maricopa County district, and was one of the state's leading milk producers. Late in the 1930s he had served as warden of the state penitentiary, where his size helped him intimidate the inmates. He could not, however, intimidate the prison's books into covering up the $40,000 in debts he ran up during his fifteen months at the helm, which got him fired.

Once Barnes was seated and sworn, Betts asked him whether it would be fair to describe him as an expert in law enforcement.

"Well, that's awfully kind of you, Amos." Barnes paused and corrected himself. "I mean, *Commissioner Betts*." These titans of Arizona agriculture and politics all knew one another well enough that titles came as afterthoughts. "I'm not sure I would call myself an expert, but yes, I've had years in law enforcement: the time running the penitentiary and years as a probation officer before that."

"And, Mr. Barnes, you heard the testimony or Mr. Sharp just now, did you not?"

"I did."

"Would you agree that the articles of incorporation of this Gila River Cooperative permit it to do business of any kind, anywhere in our state?"

"I heard nothing in the corporate documents that says otherwise."

"And how would you characterize the safety concerns that would arise as a result of that?"

Barnes paused and turned from the audience to the commissioner. "Do you mean the safety of the state? Or the safety of the Japs?"

Betts suggested he start with the state.

"Well, first off, there's our irrigation systems. Once the Japs are out and about, there's no telling what they'll get up to. Out on the coast the risk was to the ports and the bridges, but here in Arizona we need to be thinking about protecting irrigation. A few well-planted bombs could cripple the water supply, and then we might as well kiss our farms goodbye. In this climate the desert would overtake us long before the system could be repaired."

"So, you're talking about sabotage."

"Yes. Sabotage."

"Very good. And you also implied some sort of security risk to the Japanese themselves?"

"I wasn't finished describing the risks to the state," said Barnes.

Betts apologized and told him to continue.

"The danger to our irrigation systems is really the least of it. We could easily be looking at a mass crime directly against the health of the people of this state. A lethal attack."

"Tell us!" came a shout from the middle of the audience.

"Let's say the Japs get onto our farmland and start raising vegetables or nosing into my area, milk. Think about it: they would be producing *raw foods*. Raw foods can be 'fixed,' can be adulterated."

"Meaning what?"

"Meaning the Japs could put something into the food supply and practically annihilate the entire valley overnight if they set their minds to it. Mass murder on a colossal scale."

The hearing room erupted. Men jumped from their seats in a cacophony of shouts, gesturing to their neighbors and punching the air. Jim Terry was the only man to keep his seat. Slouched, elbows on the table and fingers on his temples, he tried to massage the edge off the headache that was pulsing up. The outcry continued for a few moments until Amos Betts called for order. When silence returned, Betts asked his witness to explain what he'd meant when he spoke of risks to the Japanese themselves.

"Well, it should be obvious, Mr. Betts. If a Japanese was caught committing a single act along these lines, it would trigger a crisis here that would be a discredit to the entire nation."

"Do you mean bloodshed, Mr. Barnes?"

"That's exactly what I mean."

"Damn right!" cried a member of the crowd.

Betts walked a slow looping path back to his seat on the dais, allowing the words of the threat to hang in the heated air. As he sat down, he looked at Jim Terry and raised an eyebrow. "Mr. Terry?"

Terry rose.

"Mr. Barnes, you spoke of a risk of annihilation of the good people of this valley by 'fixing' raw foods. What do you mean by 'fixing'?"

"I mean poison, sir. I mean infecting raw foods with toxic substances."

"Ah, I see." Terry put his arms behind his back and strolled a few steps toward the painting of the Grand Canyon. "And Mr. Barnes, would you be so kind as to explain to us the technique for concealing poison inside, say, a few tons of freshly picked cucumbers?"

"That is not my area of expertise, Mr. Terry. You'd have to ask your Japs down there at your camp."

Chuckles and whistles burst from the audience.

Terry continued. "And, Mr. Barnes, tell me if you would, do you have any information suggesting that anyone is actually contemplating such an attack? Or has ever discussed such an attack?"

"Fifth columnists don't usually put their plans on billboards, Mr. Terry."

"Would you answer the question, please? Do you have any information whatsoever that suggests the existence of any plan of the kind you've described?"

Before Barnes could answer, Amos Betts leaned forward. "And A.J., after you tell us that, can you tell us whether the Japs advertised their plans for Pearl Harbor?"

Laughter erupted from the rows of onlookers. It went on long enough that Terry realized he had nothing to gain from asking Barnes anything further. He returned to his seat, red in the face.

The rest of the morning went along in the same way. Betts called several more witnesses, all connected to the agricultural industry. From each of them he coaxed a slightly different version of the same story Sharp and Barnes told: the Japanese posed an existential threat to white farmers and the health and safety of the state. The WRA was pampering and coddling the evacuees, showering luxuries on them that ordinary Americans could not even imagine. The WRA could not control the Japanese, so the army should take over the camps and treat them as war prisoners.

Jim Terry seethed. He'd shown up for a hearing on the cooperative, but what Amos Betts was running was a trial of the WRA. Except it wasn't even a trial. Trials have rules. Evidence has to be relevant. Witnesses have to stick to things they know. This was no trial; it was rabble-rousing.

Jim Terry's turn to present the WRA's side of the matter came just after the lunch break. Laying out documents in a neat row on the table in front of him and scratching notes on a legal pad, he waited for the crowd to settle back into their seats. When the room finally stilled, he stood.

"Commissioner Betts, I would like to call you as my first witness."

The audience stirred and murmured. Betts turned to Bill Peterson on the dais with an upturned eyebrow, and they leaned together in whispered consultation for a few moments. Betts then rose, stepped down off the platform, and walked to the witness chair. "Bill," he said, "I guess you'll have to swear me in." Peterson pulled the Bible from the lectern and obliged. Betts took a seat, brushed a wave of gray hair from his eyes, and squared his shoulders.

Jim Terry plucked a piece of paper up off the table. He walked up to Betts, handed it to him, and asked him to read it.

"Do you recognize that letter, Mr. Betts?"

"I do."

"Who is the author of the letter?"

"Joe Conway."

"And who is Joe Conway?"

"He's the attorney general of the state of Arizona."

"And to whom is the letter addressed, Mr. Betts?"

"To me."

"And what's the date on the letter?"

"January 23, 1943."

"Just under five months ago?"

"Yes, Mr. Terry, just under five months ago."

The lawyer then asked Betts to read the letter aloud.

Betts pulled on his reading glasses and cleared his throat. "Reference is made to your letter inquiring whether a certain proposed corporation, as proposed in a draft of articles of incorporation and bylaws previously submitted to us by you, would be considered as a nonprofit corporation under the laws of Arizona, and if so, would this state extend to such corporation, if organized and qualified under the laws of the District of Columbia, the same qualification as given by the laws of the domicile."

Terry interrupted. "The letter refers to a 'certain proposed corporation.' Can you tell us which corporation that is?"

"It's the one we're talking about here today, Mr. Terry. The Gila River Cooperative."

"Very good, Mr. Betts. Please continue."

The commissioner peered back though his glasses. "It is our opinion that both queries should be answered in the affirmative. Respectfully, Joe Conway, Attorney General."

"So, Mr. Betts, let me be sure I understand this. You inquired of the attorney general—the highest legal authority in this state—whether the Gila River Cooperative meets the state's rules for a nonprofit corporation?"

Betts nodded.

"And you asked whether the State of Arizona would recognize that corporation as a lawful nonprofit if it were organized under the laws of the District of Columbia?"

Betts nodded again.

"And the highest legal authority in the state answered both of those questions in the affirmative?"

"Yes, Mr. Terry."

Terry took the letter from him and handed him another piece of paper. "Now, Mr. Betts—"

Betts cut in, dropping the paper to his lap, "Look, I'll spare you the questions. This is the license of the Gila River Cooperative Enterprises, Incorporated. Issued by the Arizona Corporation Commission. On April 1, 1943."

"That's your office?"

"Yes."

"Whose signature appears on that document?"

"Mine."

Terry took the documents back from Betts and placed them on the table. "So the attorney general said the cooperative was lawful, and you yourself said the cooperative was lawful, and now you're taking the position not only that the attorney general was wrong but that you yourself were wrong?"

"Lawyer double-talk!" came a shout from a person at the back of the room. "Technicalities!" yelled another.

Betts smiled and raised his arms, palms downward, to settle the audience. "Mr. Terry, dozens of these licenses cross my desk every week. If I stopped to scrutinize every one of them the corporate business of this state would grind to a halt. I paid this matter no mind—no mind at all—until it was brought to my attention just recently that the corporation's goals are inconsistent with the public good."

"Brought to your attention by whom, Mr. Betts? By the Farm Bureau? By the growers' associations?" Terry let a beat pass and then asked, more loudly, "By the people you handpicked to testify as witnesses at this hearing today?"

Betts lurched forward in the witness chair. "That's a lie, Mr. Terry! I handpicked no one!"

"So it's just a coincidence that every witness today comes from the agricultural sector? No one from any other field? Retail? The service industries? Transportation? Nobody from any industry that is profiting from the presence of the two WRA relocation centers in this state? Is that what we're supposed to believe?"

The metallic scrape of chair legs on floorboards cut in. Over near the Grand Canyon painting, M. O. Sharp was on his feet. "I am here of my own volition, Mr. Terry! Nobody picked me—by hand or anything else."

"Fair enough," said Terry. "We'll assume that it was just divine inspiration that brought you all here today." He wheeled back around to Betts, who was seated again. "You know, do you not, that the Gila River Cooperative was formed with one purpose only, which was to provide the evacuees with the essentials of daily living—clothing, toothpaste, cigarettes, and those types of items?"

"I know no such thing," said Betts.

"And you are aware that if the Gila River Cooperative loses its license to do business and has to shut down, many thousands of evacuees will go on needing those items just as before?"

"Stands to reason."

"And are you aware that in such a case the War Relocation Authority would have no choice but to consider a vast increase in the number of day passes we issue? To allow the evacuees to try to purchase the items they require in the shops of Arizona towns and cities?"

A hush fell over the crowd, which Terry found delicious. In all their haste and hatred they had obviously not stopped to realize that the WRA could open the gates and allow thousands of evacuees to descend upon them. This was not an idea Terry had ever raised, let alone cleared, with headquarters in Washington, and even as he said it, he realized that they probably wouldn't approve, and for good reason. It would only trigger a bigger political backlash—and, Terry supposed, put the evacuees in harm's way. Still, if the pin-drop silence in the hearing room was any indication, it was a smart strategic move.

The chairman's left heel bounced on the floor like a little jackhammer as he contemplated a response. "That would be very unwise," he finally muttered, shooting a sideways glance at Bill Peterson on the dais.

Terry decided to press his momentary advantage. "When we recently met in your office, Mr. Betts, you'll recall that I assured you that the cooperative had no designs on doing business outside the center. And I offered to make changes to the articles of incorporation of the cooperative to make that crystal clear." The lawyer wanted the audience to see that he had given Betts an out and that Betts hadn't taken it. "Did you believe I was lying when I said those things? As a representative of a federal government agency?"

"Probably *were* lying!" shouted a member of the audience, and that was enough to set the crowd grumbling again.

"My obligation is to protect the people of the state of Arizona, Mr. Terry. Not to sign on to some promise from the federal government that's obviously a bunch of bunk." Betts looked past Terry to the crowd. "This corporation of yours is nothing but a Trojan horse, a clever way to infiltrate this valley and cripple our standard of living. Just like the witnesses said."

Terry slapped his legal pad on the table. A pen skittered off the edge and dropped to the floor. "This talk of infiltration is ridiculous, and you know it! Every hateful word of it was bigotry and prejudice and nothing more!" The audience exploded in a tumult of boos and catcalls, but Terry shouted over them. "Last I checked, the Constitution of the United States still applies here in the state of Arizona! Your so-called witnesses would do well to read it!"

Betts was again on his feet, trying to hush the crowd but managing only to dampen the volume. "The Constitution?" he barked at Terry. "For the Japanese? Do not waltz in here from Wall Street and lecture the good people of Arizona about the Constitution, Mr. Terry. You know as well as I do that this country had no choice but to set aside the Constitution as to these people we know we can't trust!"

This did nothing but nourish the outrage in the hearing room, with calls of "Hear, hear!" and "You tell him, Amos!" punctuating the fracas.

Betts surveyed the scene for several moments, shooting Terry an occasional *see-what-you've-done?* glare. He looked theatrically at his watch and proclaimed a thirty-minute recess.

Terry wanted no part of the crowd, some of whom looked as though they might welcome the chance to give him big pieces of their minds—if not their fists—so he dashed out of the hearing room and escaped out onto the plaza. The pleasant morning air he'd enjoyed on his walk over from the Westward Ho had been baked off by the midday mid-June sun. Terry looked longingly across the vast lawn along Washington Street toward downtown. A whiskey would suit him nicely right about now, to settle him down and take the edge off his anger, but the nearest bar was at least a ten-minute walk. Too far to make it there and back. So he contented himself with pacing beside the groomed lawns and under the palm trees, turning over in his mind the options for how to handle the rest of the afternoon. He'd be damned if he was going to let these bigots dictate to the WRA what the evacuees could and couldn't do.

By the time a half hour was up, he'd made up his mind. He strode back into the building, past groups of men who stared daggers as he brushed by, and into the hearing room. Betts and Peterson were back up on the dais. He walked straight to his table, cleared his throat loudly, and said that he'd like to make a statement. Amos Betts motioned for the audience to take their seats, and when the room had settled down and the last stragglers were stepping gingerly through the door, he nodded for Terry to go ahead.

"Thank you, Chairman Betts. Today's hearing has degenerated into a trial of the War Relocation Authority and the administration of the Gila River center. Even so, with unlimited privilege to the witnesses to attack any phase of the administration by fair means or foul, by testimony however inadmissible, not a single word of competent evidence or fact was presented against the administration of the center. Not a subversive act was hinted at, because none could be. Not a single harm to Arizona or its people emanating from the Gila River center was specified, because there has been none."

Terry made a half turn toward the audience and continued. "The record amply shows the bigotry and prejudice of many of the witnesses, some of whom seem to believe that this country should abandon its principles of democracy, justice, and equality and adopt the tyranny and race prejudice of Nazi Germany." He paused for a moment, expecting an outcry, but the audience was still. "What was aired here today was in no sense public policy. It was personal and pressure group hatred. Nothing more."

He turned back to the dais. "It is and has been our wish to work with and have the confidence and respect of the people of this state. This is why we asked to confer with this commission and appeared at this proceeding on short notice. The action of this body in revoking the cooperative's license violates its powers and duties under the constitution and laws of Arizona. It is in direct conflict with the opinion of its legal counsel, the attorney general. And it is in flagrant disregard of the rights guaranteed by the Constitution of the United States."

Terry now walked across the front of the hearing room, stopping once again beneath the painting of the Grand Canyon. He turned and surveyed the entire room, making sure that all eyes were on him, and then fixed his gaze on Betts and Peterson on the dais. "Let me be clear, gentlemen. The WRA can safely ignore any order of this commission closing down the cooperative, because no court will enforce it. And I have absolute confidence that the members of this commission would be liable for any resulting damage to the corporation and to the government through the impairment of valid, existing contracts." Terry paused to let his words find their mark. "Personally liable," he added, to ensure they reached their destination.

Amos Betts opened his mouth to respond but had no words.

"What's more," Terry continued, "I am confident that a court would have no trouble finding that both this commission's order and this hearing today have contained statement upon statement that are libelous in character, upon both the corporation and others." The lawyer began pacing the front of the room, his voice slowly rising with each successive thought. "It was suggested earlier that the WRA is pampering the Japanese. That's a scandalous lie! Families as large as eight are living in single rooms, twenty feet by twenty feet, with nothing more than army cots and blankets provided by the government. They are using latrines and eating in common mess halls where the average cost of food per person is thirty-five cents per day—*half* of what's spent to feed a soldier. Meat is served at most twice a week, and it's of the lowest edible grade, full of gristle. There is no butter. There is milk only for young children and nursing mothers."

Terry stopped directly in front of the dais but turned his back to the commissioners to address the audience directly. "I have lived in and visited places all over the country and all over the world, including the remote and barren coast of Labrador, and I have never seen less luxurious living conditions that are consistent with health and decency. Never! In fact, war prisoners and enemy aliens in internment camps have better food and better conditions than these evacuees, most of whom are citizens of the United States against whom no charge has ever been made other than that they lived in California!"

The silence that followed jolted Terry into awareness that he was shouting. He strode back to his chair and turned back to Betts and Peterson on the dais. In a voice that was softer but still gripped with intensity, he wrapped up his presentation. "I suggest that we avoid litigation—litigation that would end badly for this commission, and expensively. I am prepared to deliver to you a formal surrender by the Gila River Cooperative of its license to do business in this state, which the commission could hold on to and make effective at the first moment the cooperative does business of any kind outside the boundaries of the relocation center. That moment, I can assure you, will never arrive."

Terry sat down solidly in his chair and folded his hands on the table in front of him. "I make this final appeal to your judgment, reason, and fairness," he said quietly, "to avert an unpleasant court dispute. Thank you for your attention."

"Well, he sure didn't leave anything out, did he?" said an unfamiliar voice. It was Bill Peterson from the dais, speaking for the first time all day. The audience tittered uncomfortably. Peterson, a stocky veteran of World War I with a wide face and a dimpled chin, had briefly served as state treasurer in the late 1930s but was better known as a chef and the author of a recipe column in the *Tucson Daily Citizen*. He was a man of few words as a commissioner, and as he spoke, he seemed to be measuring them with care. "Mr. Terry, as counsel for the War Relocation Authority, you've gone far afield in your remarks to attack the people of Arizona who appeared as witnesses before this commission. In fact, you've gone further and attacked the commission itself."

Terry rose to defend himself, but Peterson waved him back into his seat. "Now I want to say to you, Mr. Terry, that in my own family one boy has died in training in Missouri, one in Africa, one on USS *Houston*, one on the *Saratoga*, and one in Java. If you feel that we are doing something to the Japanese that we should not do, then you go ahead and bring those boys back to life, and then we can talk about your Japanese." The crowd began to applaud, but Peterson raised his voice and continued. "I say to you, Mr. Terry, to go back to that Japanese relocation center and represent them. I myself will stay on this Corporation Commission and represent the people of Arizona, and I am not a damn bit scared of your court action!"

The audience leapt to their feet, hooting and clapping. "We will take this matter under advisement," shouted Amos Betts. "We stand adjourned!"

Jim Terry quickly gathered his papers and began stuffing them into his briefcase. The mood in the room was not friendly and he did not want to stick around. But to his surprise, Betts hopped down off the dais and approached him, offering his hand. Terry shook it warily. "Let me walk you out of here," said the commissioner, "for your own safety." He smiled at the lawyer and winked, placing his hand on Terry's elbow and steering him through the crowd to the door in the rear. Out in the corridor Betts stopped Terry and once again reached out to shake his hand. "We'll be in touch, Mr. Terry," he said. "Don't go filing any lawsuits just yet. I'm sure we can work something out."

Ah, thought Terry, *so that was it*. Betts had staged the public spectacle he needed, and now he could get down to negotiations in private. "I see, Mr. Betts," said Terry, relieved. "Well, my offer to keep the cooperative from operating outside the center still stands."

They parted. Terry stepped out of the building into the late afternoon heat. *Not a chance I'm walking back*, he thought, and he looked for a pay phone to call a cab back to the Westward Ho, where a tall whiskey would be waiting for him in the lobby bar.

CHAPTER FIFTEEN

DECEMBER 1943

GILA RIVER, ARIZONA

J im and Teddy Terry saw *Algiers* at the Paramount Theatre in Times Square when the film was released back in 1938. She'd loved it; he didn't remember it. When Teddy suggested they go to the Butte Camp amphitheater for the Sunday evening showing of the movie, he didn't object. He wasn't in the mood to be around people, and the sound at the amphitheater was terrible, but he wasn't going to pass up the chance to spend a couple of hours looking at Hedy Lamarr. Along the way, high school students were out selling snacks from little tables to raise money for their annual dance. Teddy bought a candied apple for herself and peanut brittle for him. He stuffed it in the pocket of his windbreaker and kept walking.

"Oh, thank you so much for the peanut brittle, darling, you're an angel for thinking of me," said Teddy sarcastically.

"Sorry, sweetheart. I should have said thanks," said Terry without breaking his slow stride toward the amphitheater.

Teddy stopped short. "Hendrick."

Terry took another step or two before realizing he was walking alone. He stopped and turned back to her. "What?" He saw concern in her face. "What is it?" he asked.

"What's eating you? You've been a grump since you got home from the office."

"Nothing's eating me, Teddy."

"Now Hendrick, I know something's not right. What is it? Did something happen at the office today?"

"No," he lied.

She raised an eyebrow. "More problems with the property section?"

That wasn't a bad guess. The Los Angeles office had taken its incompetence to new levels recently, bungling even the simplest requests for investigation. Or maybe it wasn't incompetence. Sometimes it seemed that all of the WRA's property agents in California took pride in showing the rabid anti-evacuee feeling that pervaded the state. How was he supposed to protect a piece of property in Inglewood against a bank lien if he couldn't so much as get someone from the evacuee property office to go out and eyeball it? But no, that wasn't what was bothering him.

"It's Kimiko," he said.

"Kimiko? What's wrong with Kimiko? Is she sick? Is it valley fever?"

"No, she's not sick."

"Well, did she make some sort of mistake today? What could she have done to put you in the dumps like this?"

"It's nothing she did. It's what she's going to do."

"I don't understand."

"She's leaving," said Terry sullenly.

"But that's wonderful news!" Teddy had taken at least as much of a liking to the Nisei secretary as her husband and sometimes stopped by the office for no reason other than to visit with her. "You knew it was only a matter of time until she relocated. A talented young girl like Kimiko shouldn't be here; she should be out in the world, getting on with her life. Where is she going? A lot of young people seem to be having luck with Chicago recently. Is it Chicago?"

"It's Japan."

"Jim, *honestly*!" spat Teddy, exasperated. "Where is she relocating to?"

"I'm telling you. Japan. She's expatriating."

"Expatriating? Kimiko Yamamoto? *Our* Kimiko Yamamoto?"

"Our Kimiko Yamamoto."

Teddy was perfectly still, a statue holding a candied apple.

"You think you know someone," muttered Terry, "and then . . ." His voice trailed off. "I mean, if Kimiko Yamamoto isn't loyal, then none of these people are loyal!"

Evacuee families walking to the amphitheater parted to flow around the couple, giving their tense energy wide berth.

"Hendrick, you simply have to convince her what a grave mistake she's making."

"I tried. Believe me, I tried. I pulled out all the stops, told her that she was making a terrible choice, that Japan was sure to lose the war, that she'll have a terrible life over there. Told her that I would find her a better job here at the center, that I would find her a job in New York if I had to, that we would support her. Nothing. No impact."

"The girl is not in her right mind."

"I told her I simply can't believe she's one of the disloyal ones. Which I can't, Teddy, I just can't!" Terry was shouting, his voice raw with despair.

"Well, what did she say to all that, Hendrick? How did she respond?"

"She kept saying that it's not that simple, that it's not just a matter of loyal or disloyal. That it was a difficult decision and that she'd thought it through. That her mind was made up. She thanked me for trying to help, but she said she didn't want any special treatment."

"Oh, I'm heartbroken," Teddy whimpered, "just *heartbroken*."

They stood in silence. After a few moments, Teddy took her husband's hand and they continued toward the amphitheater, but in slower, heavier steps.

"You think you know someone . . ." Terry repeated under his breath. "And then they show you who they really are."

An Issei couple passed them by, deep in an impenetrable conversation in Japanese. "Hendrick," whispered Teddy, "how will she ever get by over there? How will she manage?"

"I have no idea. The only person she has over there is her fiancé."

Teddy stopped short again. "Fiancé?"

"Yes, that's what she told me. A Kibei. Never mentioned him before, in all this time. The guy got trapped over there when the war started, she said, and wants to stay."

Teddy gave her husband a hard, exasperated look. "Well," she said, "that puts things in a rather different light, wouldn't you say?"

Terry walked on. "You think you know someone . . ." he murmured yet again.

Terry didn't really understand why the center's schedule needed to shift an hour later just because it was early December and you could see your breath in the morning. The article in the *News-Courier* said project director LeRoy Bennett made the decision after hearing from the community council, which was concerned about schoolkids having to dash to and from breakfast in the early morning chill and farmworkers having to handle frost-covered vegetables. If Bennett had asked him, Terry would've told him that what these Californians really needed was a few days in the gray slush of a New York winter. People just shivered and slogged through it, and you didn't hear anyone complaining that nine thirty was too early for the opening bell at the stock exchange. But Bennett hadn't asked him, so Terry just let himself sleep in a little and went to open up the office at nine.

He'd left his desk clean yesterday evening, but now a folder sat square in front of his chair. Terry edged around the desk so that he could read the handwritten note clipped to the front. It was Bennett's handwriting: *Sorry, Jim— looks like we see this one differently.* Terry picked up the folder and glanced inside. It was a leave clearance file. His eye went immediately to the bottom of the face sheet, just above the project director's swirling signature: "It is recommended that this application for leave be approved." Son of a bitch. Bennett was overruling him. Letting someone out of the center whom Terry had recommended keeping in. This was a first.

Who was it? The name didn't ring a bell: Satoshi Kira, unit 11-B in block 32.

Kira ... Kira ... Terry turned the name over in his mind but couldn't conjure up a face, which was hardly surprising. It was the first of December and Terry had been running leave clearance hearings nonstop since summer's end—so many that they all blurred together. Nonetheless it nagged at Terry that he couldn't remember Satoshi Kira. Obviously, Bennett had spotted something distinctive in the file, something important enough to junk Terry's recommendation. A factor that significant should have made an impression. Terry sat down and flicked on the desk lamp so that he could scrutinize the file page by page. He was going to figure this out: Had he actually missed something big in this Kira case, or was Bennett just going soft?

One glance at a handwritten letter in the file brought the whole case rushing back: exquisite cursive script in perfect, crisp lines across unlined stationery paper. *Right*, thought Terry, *Satoshi Kira*. Went by Elmer. A wisp of a young man, early twenties, so slight he should be lashed down in a sandstorm. Delicate features. Every hair in place and exquisitely manicured nails. An artist from an artistic family, Terry recalled. The father was supposed to have been a big-deal photographer in Los Angeles before the war. Elmer had done artwork for the center's newspaper. And he'd answered no to question 28 on his registration form: he would not swear allegiance to the United States and forswear allegiance to the emperor.

That "no" answer was what the beautiful handwritten letter was about. He changed his mind back in August, a few months after submitting the form. Wanted to switch from no to yes. And as Terry reread the letter, he was reminded of how articulate the boy was, how careful in choosing his words.

Or maybe "cagey" was the word for it. "Months ago when the question was first asked," Kira wrote in the letter, "conditions prevailing—attitudes of the nation's press, people, and general treatment accorded us—forced me to cling to whatever ties I had with far-away Japan." His "no" answer had been "a protest to all those conditions thrust upon us since the outbreak of hostilities." But since answering question 28, Kira had sensed a change, or so he said. Newspapers had started printing positive stories about evacuees who were leaving the centers for the interior. The country seemed to be reacting well to publicity about the all-Nisei combat team the army was forming. Kira had friends who'd gone out and were reporting back on friendly receptions in places like Minneapolis and Chicago. All of these things, Kira wrote, made him feel the United States was, as he put it, "again the land of liberty and equality."

He would have been smart to stop right there, Terry thought as his eye tracked ahead to the next paragraph. Kira couldn't leave well enough alone. He had to wax poetic—and critical. "I will attempt with all my heart to forget our unconstitutional uprootment from our previous life and all the grief that accompanied it," he wrote. "Of finding ourselves in camps while Italians and Germans remain free. Of finding ourselves living in converted horse stables surrounded by a barb-wire fence. I am willing to give myself another chance as an American living in America." *As if it were his decision to make*, thought Terry.

And then there was the kicker, the letter's last sentence: "The greatness of a nation depends upon the ability to realize its mistakes and its willingness to correct them." Terry couldn't help but roll his eyes. It wasn't that Kira was wrong. Quite the opposite. This system of locking up a racial group was a betrayal of the nation's principles and a stain on its honor. Someday the men at the top of the WRA should be called to account for the existence of the whole unjust and confused situation. Of these things Jim Terry had no doubt.

But who the hell was Satoshi "Elmer" Kira to lecture anyone about this, after being given the chance to attest to his loyalty—and refusing?

Terry set the letter aside and turned his attention to the transcript of the leave clearance hearing he'd run for Kira back on the afternoon of September 14. Now that he remembered the kid, a vivid recollection of the hearing welled up. It had been a doozy. He came in loaded for bear—edgy, argumentative, trying to match wits but out of his depth. The heat didn't help either. It had to have been up well over 100 degrees that day. He recalled the sweat drenching Kira's white shirt and matting his black hair.

LEAVE CLEARANCE HEARING OF SATOSHI KIRA
Gila River Project, Rivers, Arizona

DATE: September 14, 1943
TIME: 3:15 P.M.

TERRY:

Q. What is your name?

A. Satoshi Kira.

Q. How old are you?

A. Twenty-one.

Q. What is the name of your father?

A. Hiromu Kira.

Q. What is the name of your mother?

A. Sadayo Kira.

Q. Your father is a citizen of Japan and your mother a citizen of the United States?

A. My dad is not technically a citizen of Japan as he was born in Hawaii and was taken to Japan at an early age.

Q. What has been your education?

A. I have gone to junior college almost two years in Los Angeles.

Q. You have never been outside the United States?

A. No, I haven't.

Q. Do you have any close relatives in Japan?

A. On my father's side, uncles and cousins, but I don't call them close.

Q. Do you know of any of them serving in the Japanese army or navy?

A. I think there was one uncle who might have served in the army.

Q. You are not married?

A. No, I am not.

Q. What is your employment record here in the center?

A. When I first came I worked in the administration building for a month, and then I went to the newspaper for a little while. Recently I've been waiting for the proper kind of job in art.

Q. What are your plans for the future?

A. I want to go to school to major in art, but I'll probably have to work first to pay for it.

Q. And your object and ambition is to be an artist?

A. Yes.

Q. Do you know anything about the attitude of the people on the West Coast?

A. Well, all I know is what I read in the newspapers and if the newspapers play up the disagreeable side, that is what I know.

Q. Have you any intention of visiting Japan in the future?

A. No. Not at present or in the future. The way I feel now, I have no desire to visit Japan.

Q. Have you been interested in sports, activities, and so on?

A. I have been interested in music, as a listener and also as a performer in the choir.

Q. Have you taken up any sports?

A. Not recently. In school I enjoyed swimming.

Q. Have you ever participated in any Japanese sport, such as judo or kendo?

A. No, no Japanese sport.

Q. Have you belonged to any Japanese organizations at any time, either here or before coming here?

A. No.

Q. What is your ability to speak and write Japanese?

A. I can speak a little bit and read a little bit. And write my name. That's it.

Q. Have you ever been arrested or questioned by the police?

A. No.

Q. When you first answered question 28 on the registration questionnaire, you answered that question in the negative?

A. Yes.

Q. Will you explain your reason for answering the question that way?

A. The main reason was because we were put in camp, while American citizens of German and Italian ancestry were not. That, and having to live in horse stables with no ventilation and lining up for hours at a time to eat in a mess hall at the assembly center last summer, before coming here.

Q. But the question also asked whether you were willing to forswear allegiance or obedience to the Japanese emperor. When you answered no, did you mean that you would be willing to swear allegiance to the emperor?

A. I don't know what you mean by that. We were placed in these camps, and the attitude of the press in this country made me feel that maybe Japan was where I would have my best opportunity for the future.

Q. So, at the time you answered this question you were inclined to feel that you might be willing to swear allegiance to Japan?

A. That is right.

Q. Since that time, have you expressed a wish to change your answer to question 28?

A. Yes, I have.

Q. Why did you wish to change your answer?

A. The attitude of the press had changed somewhat since we were first sent to camp and people seemed more willing to accept us as citizens and give us equal opportunities. Those prompted me to change my answer.

Q. Was your feeling of loyalty or lack of loyalty to the United States dependent entirely upon the attitude of the people and the press toward your racial minority group?

A. I would say yes.

Q. So if you discovered that the government had policies that affected your minority group unjustly, would you lose loyalty to the United States?

A. Well, that would depend on what happens to American citizens of German or Italian ancestry. If it affected them too, I wouldn't mind, but if they applied to only us, then I would not know. I might change my answer.

Q. Are we supposed to infer from your answer that your loyalty or lack of loyalty to the United States is entirely selfish in quality?

A. It could be interpreted as selfish, I suppose.

Q. I am asking you to interpret it for me. Are you saying that this is about what you feel is your own mistreatment? Or is that you feel democracy has failed as an institution and that you cannot be loyal to it?

A. Those two statements are slightly disconnected, aren't they?

Q. You will have to separate them and answer them. What I'm driving at is this: If you studied American history, you would know that there has always been oppression of one or another class or race. You probably also know that there is oppression in the south against Negroes, which doesn't exist for white people. Does the fact that the southern states oppress Negroes cause you to be disloyal to the United States? Or is it just when the oppression reaches you personally that your loyalty wavers?

A. I would say that if it affected me personally, I would change my answer. It would depend upon how I am treated personally.

Q. All I can say is this: Is the loyalty you now claim to have a loyalty to the fundamental principles of this country as you learned them in school and college? Loyalty to the Constitution, the Declaration of Independence, the Emancipation Proclamation, and all of the other documents that show our country's values? Or is it a loyalty that comes only from

how those values are administered when it comes to you
personally?

A. While the Constitution and the Declaration of Independence are
all fine documents, they are only documents. It would depend
entirely on how their administration is handled by the people.
Those documents can only stand as long as the people want to
carry out those principles.

Q. I assume from your initial "no" answer to question 28 that you
believe the constitutional provisions broke down and failed
insofar as your group was concerned.

A. I would not say that the documents broke down, but the
interpretation broke down.

Q. What test of the interpretation have you made, or what attempt
have you made to test the strength of those documents in
relation to your own situation?

A. Well, we've been promised that we could pursue happiness. I don't
think the pursuit of happiness is possible in the relocation
centers.

Q. I'm afraid again that you misunderstand the Constitution of
the United States, the fundamental law of the United States. You
are aware, are you not, that there are courts in this country,
courts where you can go with complaints about injustice?

A. Yes.

Q. And what efforts have you made to protect your rights through
the democratic channels of the United States?

A. I have not made any.

Q. Have you considered legal aid, which is free and available
through the bar association of most any community? Or have you
employed a lawyer? Have you taken that step?

A. No, I haven't.

Q. Have you ever been deprived of permission to communicate with
lawyers?

A. No.

Q. Have you ever, for instance, come to my office, to the office of
the project attorney here, and asked to obtain a lawyer?

A. No.

Q. There has been a lawyer right here. You haven't even attempted
to consult a lawyer, inside or outside. You have not raised a

finger to protect your rights. How can you blame a situation when you haven't done anything? I ask you. Don't you think you have neglected to even try to protect your own rights?

A. I guess I have.

Q. Do you think it's fair to condemn a system of government or to renounce your loyalty to a system of government without even giving it a chance to see whether it works or not?

A. I have been a schoolboy almost all of my life and led a sheltered life. I guess that's no excuse for me not doing anything about it.

Q. What I'm afraid of is that your original answer of no and now your new answer of yes are based exclusively on your own selfish interests, without any regard for your rights or obligations as a citizen. What can I conclude except that your loyalty depends on how the people of the United States deal with you personally?

A. I don't know what to say.

Q. Let's move on. Would you serve in the United States Army regardless of whether you were loyal to the United States?

A. If I were drafted, I would, yes.

Q. Give me a set of circumstances in which you would volunteer for service in the U.S. Army rather than waiting to be drafted.

A. Well, I would volunteer if the Japanese people in the camps were allowed to return home to the Pacific coast because the threat of invasion by Japan no longer exists.

Q. Would you, under those circumstances, volunteer for service in the Pacific?

A. Yes.

Q. You mean you would not object to fighting against your own people?

A. My people are Americans.

Q. You know what I mean.

A. I would not object.

BY MR. TERRY: That is all, Mr. Kira. You may go.

Terry flipped to the last page of the document, where his recommendation stood out in underlined letters:

He poses no security risk, but I cannot affirmatively recommend that he be given clearance to leave the center. He does not possess a real sense of loyalty.

Now that Terry had taken the chance to read over what Kira said—now that he could remember how the boy squirmed and sweated and tried to argue with him—he was more persuaded than ever that they had no business letting the boy go. He was too fickle, too edgy—he just seemed a little bit off the beam. And he was too focused on nursing his own sense of injury without seeing the bigger picture.

And yet the project director had overruled him. Ridiculous.

The Washington office hadn't yet made a final decision, so there was still time. Terry reshuffled the pages of the transcript into a neat stack, shoved them back in the folder, and stalked out to find LeRoy Bennett and talk some sense into him.

"You're late," said Bennett with a grin when he spotted Terry at his office door.

The lawyer instinctually looked at his watch but realized that he didn't have an appointment. "What do you mean, I'm late?" he replied, dropping into a seat across the project director's desk.

"It's almost ten o'clock, Jim. I expected you by nine thirty at the latest!"

Terry shrugged. "I have no idea what you are talking about, LeRoy. We had nothing on the calendar."

"I know, Jim. But you've just stormed in here with a file under your arm and you've plopped yourself down without even asking."

Terry blushed.

"You're here to tell me how utterly wrong I am about Elmer Kira."

Terry looked at the file under his arm and back at Bennett, stunned.

"When I left that file on your desk last night, I figured you'd be in here giving me hell by a quarter after nine. Nine thirty at the latest. What the hell took you so long?" Bennett winked at Terry. "You're slowing down, counselor."

"I don't understand what you're doing with this Kira case, LeRoy. You couldn't have read the file and decided to let this kid out. Impossible!" Terry threw up his hands. "Did you even read this hearing transcript?"

"Look, Jim, I'm sorry. I take no pleasure in this. I respect your views. I've pretty much always followed your advice. You know that. I just—"

A dull bang from outside stopped Bennett midsentence. He turned toward his window as an echo bounced off the butte and washed over the center.

"What was that?" Bennett asked.

"What was what?"

Bennett had forgotten that Terry's hearing was poor. "Never mind," he said. "Some truck must have backfired. Anyway, yes, of course I read the transcript. And I can see that Kira wasn't cooperative."

"*Wasn't cooperative?*" the lawyer exclaimed. "Cagey and combative is what I'd say! I couldn't get a straight answer out of the boy. All he wanted to do was give a Fourth of July speech about his rights. I didn't buy it for a moment."

Bennett drew in a breath to respond but another dull bang rattled the window. "What the hell?" he muttered, cocking his head to try to catch the echo more clearly. "Bad morning at the motor pool, I guess."

Terry pressed on. "Kira knows loyalty to one thing and one thing only, LeRoy: himself. He admitted it!" The lawyer flipped open the transcript, searched for a passage, and thrust the paper toward Bennett. "Look. Right here. He said he's 'selfish,' that his loyalty depends on how he feels he's being treated at any given moment."

"Yes, Jim, but these hearings are about safety more than loyalty, or at least they're supposed to be. Look at your recommendation." Bennett gestured toward the file. "You said it yourself—'no security risk.'"

A third bang made Bennett flinch. He jumped out of his chair and went to the window, craning from side to side to see the little bit of the center's landscape that wasn't concealed by the building opposite. Terry got up and joined him.

"That wasn't a truck, Jim. I think it might've been a gun."

"A gun?"

"Yes, a gun."

Bennett opened the window.

Ben Runyan, an assistant project director, leaned into Bennett's office, shoulder on the doorframe. "Did you guys hear that?"

"Sure did," said Bennett, wheeling around toward Runyan. "What did it sound like to you?"

"I'd say a gun, LeRoy," said Runyan.

"That's what I'm afraid of." Bennett closed the window and made for the hallway. "Let's go see if anyone knows what's up."

The men walked out into the corridor. Here and there quizzical heads poked out of office doorways. As they approached the front door, it burst open. Fred Graves, the head of Internal Security, skidded in, sweaty and out of breath.

"LeRoy!" he gasped at Bennett. "We've got a situation. An evacuee's been shot by an MP! Outside the gate!"

Bennett's face drained of color. "Is it serious? Please tell me he's not dead."

"No, he's not dead. Looks like the bullet just grazed a bone. He's up on his feet and they're walking him to the hospital."

"Do we know his name, Fred?"

"A young guy," said Graves. "Name of Kira. Satoshi Kira."

Bennett and Terry gasped. Terry flicked his hand at Bennett's arm and shot him a look that screamed "I told you so."

The project director waved the look off and turned to Runyan. "Ben, hold down the fort here, would you?" he said, and then brushed past Graves toward the door. "I'm heading to the hospital." Terry and Graves fell into step behind him.

The hospital waiting room looked just as it had the last time Terry had been there, the night of his valley fever relapse, except that more chairs were empty. An elderly couple instinctually rose and bowed when they noticed Terry's group included the project director. Two girls sandwiched their mother in mirror image on a bench, each leaning heavily on a shoulder with an open book in one hand and a pencil in the other. Two military policemen, one lanky and the other pudgy, sat bolt upright in the chairs nearest the clinic door. Terry scanned the room for a pair who might be Kira's mother and sister, but nobody fit the description.

"He's in surgery," said Bennett as he returned from the front desk and took a seat next to Terry and Graves. "I guess we wait." Bennett nodded at the MPs, but they looked back at the WRA men blankly. Even in the best of times relations between the WRA inside the center and the army at the perimeter were frosty, but one of their men had just shot an evacuee, so it was definitely not the best of times.

They sat in silence, avoiding further eye contact, until one of the MPs—the pudgy one—stirred and addressed the administrators. "It was by the book, you know," he said. "Strictly by the book."

"I guess we'll see about that, won't we?" said Terry. There would be an official inquiry, of course, but if Kira wasn't seriously hurt, he knew the army would protect its own. *Still*, he thought, *they should know the WRA wasn't taking the situation lightly.*

"Your kid's not in his right mind, you know," said the lanky MP. "Walked right past our man and through the gate as if he was late for an appointment out in the desert. Our man told him to stop but he said he didn't have to because he's the president of the United States."

This grabbed Bennett's attention. "What do you mean, 'the president of the United States'?"

"That's what he told the guard on duty. And then he kept on walking, right across the bridge over the irrigation ditch and out onto the road toward Chandler. Our guy followed protocol. Fired a warning shot in the air, but the kid just broke into a run. Our guy ordered him to stop again but he kept on running. So, he fired a second warning shot. That didn't stop him either. Our guy yelled one last time, just like he was supposed to—those are our orders, two clear warnings—and then when your kid didn't stop, he fired a shot in his direction."

"You mean he fired *at him*, don't you?" Terry interjected.

"He means *in his direction*, just like he said," the pudgy one replied. "That rifle's accurate out to sixty-five, maybe seventy yards. By the time he pulled the trigger your kid was a hundred fifty yards down the road, easy. It's basically an accident that the bullet hit him."

"Our guy just got lucky," said the lanky one, elbowing his partner in the ribs, and the two men guffawed.

"That's not funny," Bennett snapped. "This is not a laughing matter."

"Oh, come on, take it easy—the bullet barely grazed your kid. Knocked him down, but we didn't even need a stretcher to bring him in. He could walk OK with an arm around someone's shoulder."

"*My* shoulder," said the pudgy one, annoyed that he wasn't being given credit for his rescue efforts.

The clinic door opened and Herbert Hata leaned out into the waiting area in a white coat with bloodstains on the sleeve. Hata was one of the evacuee physicians at Gila River, a man in his early thirties, a graduate of a medical school in California, and well-liked by evacuees and staff alike. Terry, Bennett, and Graves jumped up from their seats to shake Hata's outstretched hand.

"Please come in, gentlemen," said the doctor, ushering them through the door into the clinic with a sweep of his arm. He tried to pull it closed behind him, but the lanky MP had jumped up and grabbed the knob to keep it from closing. Hata leaned back out and came face-to-face with the MP. "Can I help you?" he asked tightly.

"We need the slug."

"Excuse me?"

"The slug. The bullet. You took it out of him, right? We have orders to get it back."

Jim Terry's head now appeared from behind Hata in the doorway. He'd heard what the MPs wanted.

"I've removed it, yes, but—" stammered Hata.

"That slug's the property of the United States Army. We need it back."

Terry saw what they were up to. This bullet was evidence of a possible crime. There was no telling what the army would do with it if they got their hands on it. "Dr. Hata," he said, "you are under no obligation to turn over that bullet or anything else connected with this case."

Hata twisted back to make eye contact with Terry, whose arched eyebrows made clear that he really meant *no* obligation. The project director then stepped back into the doorway from inside. "Dr. Hata," he said, "I'd appreciate it if you would hold on to the bullet. The WRA will be undertaking our own investigation."

The MP stiffened. "I don't think you gentlemen understand. This isn't a request. It's an order."

"And I don't think *you* understand, Private," scoffed Terry. "The WRA doesn't take orders from the army." Terry gently touched Hata on the shoulder to signal that the conversation was over. Hata thanked the MPs for their concern and pulled the door closed on them.

"Sheesh," said Terry as the men made their way toward the surgical area. "Who the hell do they think they are?"

Hata pointed the men to a basin and asked them to wash their hands. After they'd done so, he steered them toward a curtained bay. Elmer Kira lay propped up on his left side, asleep, breathing slowly. His right arm hung forward across his chest, forced there by a mound on his left side that Terry assumed were bandages from the surgery. "Is he in pain?" Bennett whispered to the doctor.

"No," said Hata in full voice. "And you don't have to whisper. He's sedated."

"Because of the pain?" Terry asked, still automatically whispering.

Hata raised his eyebrows and his eyes widened. "Not exactly, no. That's a bit of a story. Let's step away from here and I'll fill you in."

The doctor led them to a room with several desks around the periphery and a table in the middle strewn with medical equipment—stethoscopes, clamps, bandages, a couple of X-ray films. They pulled up chairs.

"First, the physical issues. The bullet struck him on his right side, from behind, down toward the bottom of the rib cage—about here," Hata said, touching a spot on his side a couple of inches above his belt. We see a disruption of the cortical outlines of the ninth and tenth rib out toward the lateral aspect and a complete disruption of the ninth."

Terry, Bennett, and Graves looked at him blankly.

"Ah, sorry. What I am saying is that has a couple of broken ribs."

All three men nodded in unison.

"It's a minor thing," Hata continued. "In a young man like Kira, twenty-two years old, it should heal quickly as long as it's kept clean."

The men nodded again.

"But gentlemen, the broken ribs are the least of his problems."

Terry cut in. "The MPs told us something about him claiming he's the president. Is that what you're referring to?"

"Yes, Mr. Terry, but it runs deeper than that. He told me that he had a special device that would allow him to leave camp today. He heard someone yell at him to stop but he wasn't able to keep the device from magnetizing him to leave."

"Magnetizing?"

"Yes, that's what he said. 'Magnetizing.' He also told me that people have been insisting to him that he's the president of the United States. He says he's been receiving two thousand dollars a week for being president and that this makes him the richest man in the world."

Graves whistled softly.

"And that his IQ is around seven hundred fifty."

"Well now," said the project director.

"I *knew* there was something not right with that boy," Terry exclaimed, thumping the table with his fist.

Bennett ignored him and kept his eyes on the doctor. "What's your diagnosis, Dr. Hata?"

"Dementia praecox, Mr. Bennett, which translates to 'early madness.' We see this with patients right around this age—late teens, early twenties. Delusions, grandiosity, hallucinations, excitability."

"What are the parents like, Dr. Hata?" Graves inquired. "Do we know? Is this the kind of thing that runs in families?"

"We are hoping to sit down with the mother," Hata replied, "though as you can imagine, she is quite distraught. It will take a little time. But we are not sure what causes this condition. The literature references cases where there is a clear family tendency, but we also know of cases where the onset appears to follow some sort of traumatic episode."

"So what happens next?" asked Bennett.

"He won't need more than a few days to recover from surgery. He should be back on his feet as early as tomorrow, even. But he'll need psychiatric treatment that we are not in a position to provide here. He'll have to go to the state hospital."

"I can get the paperwork going on that right away," Terry offered.

"And then only time will tell. Some of these early-onset cases seem to resolve with treatment. Some don't."

The men sat silently for a moment. Bennett tapped the bell of a stethoscope gently on the table.

"It's a shame it came to this," said Terry, turning toward Bennett. "A real shame. But I told you this boy was off the beam. I knew that we had no business releasing him."

Bennett breathed in sharply and turned to Terry. "That's not what you said in your report, Jim. What you said in your report was that he didn't have a real sense of loyalty."

"Well, OK, fair enough, but I just had a bad feeling about this one. He was fragile and I didn't think he showed real loyalty to anyone but himself." Terry leaned forward again and shrugged. "In any case, he's clearly a security risk now."

"Agreed," said Bennett.

Hata rose and extended his hand. "We will keep you apprised of his condition, Mr. Bennett, and of what we learn from the mother."

The doctor accompanied the men to the waiting room door and shook their hands again as they walked out.

The MPs were still there, still waiting for their bullet.

Jim Terry braced himself for turmoil in the wake of the shooting, but none came. No one in the administration building seemed quite sure why the situation didn't turn into a repeat of the riot that had turned Manzanar upside down a year earlier. They heard about meetings and discussions, community council sessions running late into the night. After a few days the project director was asked to attend a council meeting, and he came back confident that there would be no big protest, no commotion. The community seemed to accept that Kira was not in his right mind and that the guard had issued warnings before shooting. Bennett said he'd made headway in getting the council to see that the WRA had no more love for the military police than the evacuees did, and that the feeling was mutual. He'd been presented with a formal resolution requesting that the MPs be more careful with their firearms, he said, and he'd happily embraced it. Nothing would make him happier, he'd told them, and that seemed to go a long way toward easing tension.

Kira was up and about within a few days, and on his way to the Arizona State Hospital in Phoenix for psychiatric care a few days after that. Life in the center seemed to pulse forward; Christmas was around the corner and the newspaper was full of announcements of plans for parties and pageants. Terry turned his attention back to property cases. The Christmas spirit didn't seem to touch Californians in their dealings with the Japanese. Every day seemed to bring a new outrage—a landlord selling off the property of an evacuee tenant, an insurer terminating an evacuee's policy for nonpayment, a state agency seizing supposedly "abandoned" farm equipment. Terry was firing off a testy response to a California lawyer about a lease agreement one afternoon when his desk telephone rang. LeRoy Bennett wanted to see him in his office. Terry marked the offending language in the lease with a paper clip on the margin so he could return directly to the source of his annoyance and then walked the thirty paces down the hall to Bennett.

"Sit down, Jim, sit down," said the project director, half rising from his desk chair.

Terry settled into his seat and looked across at Bennett inquiringly.

Bennett leaned back and joined his hands behind his neck. "Looks like we dodged a bullet on the whole Kira situation, wouldn't you say, Jim?"

Terry raised his eyebrows and cocked his head, unsure if Bennett realized how he'd phrased his question.

"Oh! Whoops! In a manner of speaking, of course."

The men chuckled.

Bennett's face darkened ever so slightly. "I'd like to tell you the rest of the story, Jim, if you have a few minutes."

"The rest of which story?"

"Of Elmer Kira's story. How he got to the point where he thought he was the president and a device was drawing him out of camp."

"There's more to the story?"

"Yes, there's more. Social Services interviewed the parents and the sister. Turns out he didn't just snap. It was a while in the making."

Terry glanced at his watch. He had a raft of letters still to bang out on property cases and, time permitting, a tax form to prepare for the cooperative. "Will this take a while, LeRoy?" he asked.

"Should be quick. But it's important. I need you to hear it."

Terry stretched his tall frame back in his chair, crossing knee over knee. "I'm all ears," he said.

"Walking out of camp a week or so ago wasn't the first erratic thing Kira did. He'd been falling apart for quite some time. Seems he's an introverted boy, sensitive, with a gift for drawing. Had only one friend here, another artistic type who relocated with his family a few months back. So he was pretty isolated."

Bennett leaned forward to glance at a document in an open file on his desk. "Now, of course you know that he answered 'no-no' on his registration form back in February. Turns out the rest of his family—his parents and a younger sister—all answered 'yes-yes.' His mother thinks that's one reason he wanted to change his answers—that he was afraid they would all relocate and abandon him here."

"Something he didn't see fit to mention at his hearing, I might note," interjected Terry.

"We'll get to the hearing, Jim. Hear me out. Kira's father relocated back at the beginning of November. Kira tried to sneak onto the bus with him but he had no pass, so he was pulled off. Soon after that he started telling his sister that people were trying to shoot him—guards and other evacuees—and at one point he asked her whether she'd heard the news that he'd been named project director."

Terry chuckled. "And here we all thought *you* were the project director, LeRoy!"

"There are days I'd happily give it up, believe me." Bennett ran a finger down the page on his desk and then leaned in to examine it more closely. "OK," he said, "that's where things stood in mid-November. Then they got worse. One day his sister came home and found Kira pulling all kinds of things out the front door—household items, letters, and a lot of food supplies. She tried to stop him but couldn't. He was especially upset about some bags of sugar. Told his sister that their mother had laced them with strychnine so as to kill him. She asked him where on earth their mother would have gotten strychnine from, and he told her she'd brought it with her to the center from Los Angeles. When she tried to bring the things back into their room, he started pounding on her. Blackened an eye. The mother came home and tried to break things up. Kira started smacking her around also and tried to choke her. They had to run away and take shelter at a friend's place in another block."

"Nobody called Internal Security at that point?" Terry asked.

"Seems not. Anyhow, that brings us to November 30, the day before the shooting. Kira's mother had an appointment with the leave office where she said in no uncertain terms that she could not leave without her son, but it seems Kira got wind of the meeting and became convinced that she was planning to leave with his sister any day. Early the next morning—the day of the shooting—Kira showed up at the beauty salon where the mother works as a cashier. He started screaming at her, so she left the salon to take him home. When they got there, Kira attacked her. Knocked her down, pulled her hair, tried to strangle her. She screamed for help and some neighbors came. Kira took off—just vanished for a little while. And then he showed up at the gate claiming he was the president."

Terry nodded slowly, looking off into the distance. "Sad case," he said, turning his gaze back to the project director. "So he started to unravel when his father left. Kind of a reverse Oedipal situation, huh?"

"No, that's not when he started to unravel. This is what I need you to understand." Bennett paused. "He started to unravel after the hearing."

"Which hearing?"

"Your hearing, Jim."

"*My* hearing?"

"The leave clearance hearing. Back in mid-September. That's what we learned. From a number of sources."

The lawyer could only blink and shake his head in confusion. Bennett pulled the hearing transcript from the file and pushed it across the desk.

"He went home from the hearing and went straight to bed, Jim. Told his family that he was exhausted, mentally and physically. Said that the hearing had gone on too long, that the questions had been too severe. Pretty much stayed in bed for days afterward. Started having bad dreams, night visions. Saying that there were people who were out to get him."

Terry stood up sharply. "Look, LeRoy, I find this very hard to believe. You read that hearing transcript yourself. Tell me you don't see a boy who's already off the beam. Who's not all there mentally."

The project director replied gently, "What I see in the transcript is a young man trying to hold his own against a very seasoned and suspicious attorney."

"Well, you weren't there to see him, LeRoy. I was. So was the stenographer. You can ask her too. The boy was nervous and fickle and shifty. It was very noticeable. We remarked on it after he left."

"Lots of the evacuees are nervous at their hearings, Jim."

"Well, we don't see others having mental breakdowns after their hearings, do we?"

Bennett rose and walked around his desk slowly, stopping to perch on its edge near where Terry was standing. "You're right, we don't. But we have heard that evacuees, especially the younger women, come out of your hearings and sob, Jim. We have heard that you have the reputation for using the bullying tactics of a criminal attorney. That the evacuees dread being assigned to a hearing that you are running."

"And you credit this, LeRoy? You believe these rumors?"

"I've read a lot of transcripts, Jim."

Terry inhaled sharply several times, each time as if to launch into a reply, but no words came. Bennett examined a scuff on his left shoe.

Finally Terry found words. "In my view it is necessary at these hearings to probe beneath the surface and uncover states of mind, character, and attitudes that the subject is often trying to conceal. That is what I did at this hearing. I suggest you send the transcript to the solicitor in Washington, LeRoy. Send it to Phil Glick. And if Glick says that I've done wrong, I will tell you with a huge sigh of relief that I am not competent or qualified to conduct the leave clearance hearings that are referred to me and step aside."

"Now, Jim—" said Bennett, reaching a hand toward Terry's shoulder, but the lawyer pulled away.

Muttering about "utter nonsense," Terry strode out of the project director's office and then out of the building. He needed to calm down.

It was a brisk late afternoon in the desert. The mid-December sun burned low and bronze in the west, backlighting the butte and a pair of golden eagles looping lazily above it. Plumes of smoke rose in neat rows from mess hall chimneys. Terry breathed deeply, settling himself. From a nearby recreation hall drifted the strains of an evacuee choir rehearsing "I'll Be Home for Christmas."

That boy was completely off the beam, Terry thought, kicking absentmindedly at an aloe leaf. *Completely and totally off the beam.*

And then he straightened and headed back toward the administration building. The workday was not quite over, and there were property battles to fight.

end the story of the WRA project attorneys here, in the short dying days of 1943. The camps featured in this account would not close for another two years—Heart Mountain and Gila River on November 10, 1945, and Poston on November 28. One of the WRA's ten camps, Tule Lake in northern California, would not close until March 1946, a full seven months after the end of the war with Japan. Lawyers continued to play key roles until the last of the prisoners departed and the camps became ghost towns. But it was the first generation of project attorneys—Jerry Housel, Ted Haas (and, when Haas was ill, Tom Masuda), Jim Terry, and seven others like them—who defined the role. They were the ones who charted the strange and twisting territory between the jailers and the jailed.

This is what became of them.

Alone among the couple of dozen lawyers who served as project attorneys during the years the camps were open, Jim Terry served nearly from start to finish. When he became unavailable a few weeks before the camp closed, the WRA sent Mima Pollitt, a lawyer from headquarters, to help wrap things up in November 1945. Practically speaking, though, Gila River was Jim Terry's camp. He had a larger hand in sculpting a camp's legal landscape than any other WRA attorney.

Even by Terry's own admission, it was rocky terrain. He had a unique capacity to irritate those around him with blunt opinions and cutting words. "I imagine that I exist in the minds of some as a prototype of a Lon Chaney or Boris Karloff," he wrote to his fellow WRA lawyers at the end of his tenure, and it's hard to imagine them disagreeing. Word once leaked back to him that WRA solicitor Phil Glick was finding him inefficient and his perspective less than reliable. Terry tore into his boss in his next biweekly report, a document that went in duplicate to every other lawyer on staff. If Glick would not tell him directly which of his "sour notes ha[d] brought on [his] concern," Terry would "fill all of my reports from now on with hearts and flowers and reiteration that all is well in the best of all possible worlds." It was his "habit and custom to be acidulous and hypercritical," a "perfectionist," and Glick would have to "put up with JHT as he is, for unlikely it is that he'll be changing his ways."

The most frequent target of Terry's tongue was the WRA division responsible for protecting the prisoners' property on the West Coast and the lawyer who oversaw its operations, Edgar Bernhard. No injustice inflicted on Japanese Americans rankled Terry as much as Californians' thefts and embezzlements, and Terry spent much of 1944 and 1945 working to protect prisoners' property rights and publicly sniping at Bernhard for falling down on the job. So harsh was Terry, and so openly, that the WRA solicitor was moved to scold him for it. Terry had to realize, the solicitor wrote, that his broadly circulated letters passed before the eyes of many Japanese Americans and that his allegations of incompetence couldn't help but demoralize them. Terry toned down his criticisms but never his passion for the property rights of the prisoners. It is not clear why, in a sea of deprivations tangible and intangible, the property losses were the ones that stood out most sharply for him. Perhaps these were just the easiest for a Wall Street lawyer and a man of means to appreciate.

It was not that Terry failed to see the wrongfulness in depriving Japanese Americans of their liberty, at least at the level of the group as a whole. As the 1943–44 school year drew to a close at the Gila River High School, Terry got himself in some hot water for anonymously sponsoring an essay contest, complete with cash prizes, that invited students to explore whether their detention could be squared with the protections of the Bill of Rights. A higher-ranking WRA lawyer clashed with Terry over the contest, fearing that it would "cause trouble and discussion of bitterness and resentments that were better left submerged." Terry did it anyway. Neither did he mince words in the comprehensive final report on Gila River's legal operations he filed as the camp closed late in 1945. The nation's entire program—locking up a minority group, without charges, on terms the majority would never countenance for itself—was a "betrayal of its principles" and "a stain on its honor."

Where Terry struggled was in seeing injustice in individual cases and his own role in the system. He followed orders to help establish Leupp, a desolate "isolation center" where the WRA could warehouse its "troublemakers," and then banished Gila River prisoners there on the flimsiest of evidence. One high-ranking WRA attorney called the gulag "an un-American institution . . . premised on Gestapo methods," and even Dillon Myer, the WRA's director, privately acknowledged its illegality. The agency eventually abolished it. But Jim Terry never showed the faintest compunction. In a postscript to his final report, he had no trouble acknowledging that Japanese Americans had been subjected to a "very unjust, confused and obscure situation." They were due a "full and open confession and explanation" of the "nearly inexplicable errors"

James Hendrick Terry (*center*), 1939.
(Courtesy of Stephen Terry.)

visited upon them. But it was the "high-ranking officials" of the WRA who owed them this. Not Jim Terry.

Terry intended to remain at Gila River until the final closing of its gates, but three weeks shy of that the Department of Justice urgently asked him to join a team of lawyers running hearings for Japanese aliens at the Tule Lake camp in California who had thought better of earlier demands for repatriation to Japan and were seeking to stay in the United States. While he was in California his license to practice law in Arizona came through, and when the Tule Lake hearings concluded he returned to Arizona to open a law practice. In 1949 he created the law firm of Terry & Wright. With five attorneys at its inception, it was one of the largest in the American Southwest. He practiced law in Tucson for the next thirty years, until he died there in December 1976. His eldest son recalls that Terry did not always have an easy time of the practice, at least in the early years; the old guard that dominated Arizona's bar and bench in that era did not always take kindly to the city slicker from New York. Perhaps their memories of Terry's incendiary, headline-grabbing confrontation with the Arizona Corporation Commission also took some time to recede.

Terry's son remembers his father as a workaholic who mellowed as he aged and spoke with pride of his work at Gila River. His obituary did not avoid mention of his work at the camp; it related that he "helped interned Japanese to relocate and to obtain compensation and return of their property." In a certain sense that was true, so far as it went. Terry and his wife received

Christmas cards every year, and even the occasional gift, from Japanese Americans they'd come to know at Gila River.

It is doubtful the Kira family was among the senders.

Elmer Kira's shattered psyche came back together quickly at the Arizona State Hospital after his shooting. By early January 1944, just a month after arriving, he was helping the staff with more seriously ill patients and playing the role of interpreter for older Japanese patients from Gila River and Poston. He was back with his family in camp by the end of January. At this point Elmer was promptly granted leave clearance—on the advice of doctors, who believed he would do better away from the scene of his mental break. The family left camp for New York at the end of April 1944.

After the war the family returned to Southern California, their home terrain before they had been removed in the spring of 1942. Elmer struggled with mental illness for the rest of his life. For much of it, the struggle was private; stigma and a cultural pressure to keep family problems within the family kept him from getting treatment until the 1970s, when he was in his midfifties. He never held a job and never married. He lived with his parents until they moved into a retirement home, and even then Elmer went with them, even though he was not of retirement age. His own health, physical and emotional, slowly deteriorated after his parents passed away. He himself died in 2011 at the age of eighty-nine.

Ted Haas came to Poston from the Office of Indian Affairs (OIA), and that is where he returned when his time at Poston ended. The transfer was not strictly of his choosing. From the start, administration at Poston was an awkward dance between two agencies: the WRA, which made the rules, and the OIA, which retained control of the camp and enforced the rules. The two agencies' visions never fully aligned. The WRA conceived of Poston as a temporary way station for loyal Japanese Americans, to be emptied—at least of its "loyal" population—as quickly as practicable. The OIA, under the influence of men such as Commissioner John Collier and Haas's friend and mentor Felix Cohen, couldn't help but conceive of the camp as something more like a reservation in the style of the Indian New Deal—a place to help Japanese Americans build an enduring, ultimately autonomous enclave. By the fall of 1943 the relationship was no longer sustainable. The Department of the Interior agreed to turn Poston over to the WRA entirely, effective January 1, 1944.

Unlike much of Poston's leadership, Haas had been on the WRA's payroll rather than the OIA's since arriving. If he wanted to stay on at Poston after the handoff to the WRA, his transition would be seamless, and Phil Glick quickly let him know that he was welcome to stay. "You are making an important and valuable contribution to the work at the center," the solicitor wrote Haas in early November, "and we should all of us like to see that continued." This was not an unattractive offer. After a year and a half of working with Glick and other WRA leaders he felt indebted to the agency for what he called the "poignant drama," the "profound, soul-searching experience," of serving as Poston's project attorney. At the same time, though, he'd made his first major professional mark before the war in the OIA in service of the Indian New Deal. The opportunity to resume that work, shoulder to shoulder with Felix Cohen, was also alluring.

In a mid-November reply to Glick, Haas presented himself as unable to decide. He took comfort that "whether asked to devote the remaining years of the war to one great minority, the Japanese, or to another, the Indians, [he would] continue to work for both," because "the problems of minorities are intertwined and closely related to each other and to world peace and democracy." But, he wrote to Glick, he felt "far too close to the [Poston] community and myself to gain a proper perspective of the effect here of my foibles and virtues."

In truth, though, Haas knew where his loyalties lay. In a letter to Collier on the same day, he placed the decision in the hands of the OIA. "If you feel that I should be more useful at Poston than in the Indian Service," he wrote, "I shall joyfully continue my work here." But if Collier thought the reverse was true, he needed only to "give the command . . . and I will be happy to undertake whatever you ask me to do."

Collier gave the command in December, offering Haas the job of chief counsel of the OIA, working out of the agency's Chicago headquarters. Thomas Masuda was in the office with Haas when he opened the offer letter and later remarked on the "strange expression of shock and surprise" on Haas's face as he read it. Chief counsel of the OIA was a position of far greater influence than he had expected, one that would allow him to rejoin Felix Cohen and carry forward the work of the Indian New Deal. He wrote Glick with the news of his impending departure on December 24, 1943. "The thought that my new work will be very much to my liking," he said, "prevents me from being unstrung by the realization that my official work with the WRA is drawing to a close."

"Station H.A.A.S., Poston, Arizona, signs off," he wrote to Glick and his fellow project attorneys in a final letter on February 17, 1944, just five days before departing for Chicago. "It will be hard for me to leave this drama which I have seen develop and in which I have played a role," Haas admitted. He was "looking forward eagerly to [his] new work with another great minority, the American Indian," but was "leav[ing] Poston with a heavy heart." "I would not have missed this experience; yet, I never would wish to repeat the first year." Never in his life, he said, apart from his teenage years, had he "felt so much mental anguish" as during that year. Handing off responsibilities to Poston's new project attorney, Drake University law professor Scott Rowley, Haas took comfort from knowing that Thomas Masuda would still be on hand to show him the ropes.

Haas brought energy and creativity to his work as the OIA's chief counsel. Some of it was conventional legal work: filing briefs in support of Indian voting rights, supporting tribes in the drafting and ratification of constitutions, fighting against the discriminatory treatment of Indians off their reservations. Some of what he did pushed at the boundaries of the lawyer's role. He spent the summer of 1946 in the company of Walter Goldschmidt, an anthropologist from the Department of Agriculture, traveling from one remote Alaskan village to another in an effort to document the land rights of the Tlingit and Haida peoples. The work they produced in 1947, *Haa Aaní, Our People: Tlingit and Haida Land Rights and Use*, combined ethnography, oral history, and legal analysis in a monumental study that remains an important resource in Native communities to the current day.

By 1947, much of the energy behind the Indian New Deal was ebbing. John Collier left the agency in 1945 as hints of change in the direction of Indian policy materialized under new president Harry Truman. Felix Cohen followed Collier out the door, leaving Haas among a vanishing and vulnerable group of Indian New Deal stalwarts. The enterprise of bolstering the distinctive sovereignty, language, and culture of Indian tribes faltered in the face of pressures on Indians to assimilate and on the government to get out of the business of supporting them. When the commissionership opened in the spring of 1948, the National Council of American Indians publicly endorsed Haas. They wanted a "militant commissioner to fight legislation intended to do away with the Indian Service and abolish reservations" and saw Haas as their champion. He didn't get the job, though; a succession of caretaker acting commissioners served instead as Indian policy continued to drift away from its New Deal orientation. It came as something of a balm that many of the nation's tribes continued to honor Haas for his commitment to their interests. In a 1949 ceremony in South Dakota, Chief Ben American Horse of the Oglala Lakota welcomed him as an honorary member with the official title of Loud Eagle and the name Wanblee-Ho-Tan-Tonka.

Haas must have been surprised, and might have been briefly cheered, when President Truman announced on March 23, 1950, that Dillon Myer would take over as commissioner of Indian Affairs. The men knew each other from their WRA days, when Myer was the agency's director. Haas quickly realized, though, that Myer's goal was not to praise the Indian New Deal but to bury it. Just as Myer came to see his WRA task as forcing the assimilation of Japanese Americans and emptying the camps, he brought the same understanding to American Indians and their reservations. Within a month of Truman's surprise announcement, Haas was brazenly condemning the new order in public. "Some important officials still mistakenly believe that they, as representatives of a 'superior race,' have broad, omnipresent powers as protectors of an 'inferior race,'" Haas said in an address that received nationwide newspaper coverage. "They do not believe in Indian self-government" and "are feared by the employees and the Indians of their jurisdiction." Myer himself, said Haas, had been appointed "in a miasma of secrecy and without consultation with Indians."

This is not the sort of public talk that endears an employee to a new boss, and within a month, Haas was out as chief counsel, fired by Myer. After six years helping to lead the agency, Haas now watched from the sidelines as Myer brought in other old hands from the WRA to dismantle what remained of the Indian New Deal. Felix Cohen, long gone from the agency and now in private practice, said that the moment Dillon Myer fired Ted Haas was the moment the Bureau of Indian Affairs lost its conscience.

Haas landed in the office of the solicitor of the Department of the Interior, heading the unit overseeing claims filed under the agency's agreements with private contractors. But this position was hardly enough to contain his energies or his passions, so he threw himself into all manner of extracurricular work as well. He served on the boards of editors of several publications on race relations and the rights of American Indians. He taught at Indian Service summer schools and at the New School for Social Research. He delivered lectures for national associations in psychology, anthropology, and sociology. He served on countless committees of the American Bar Association and chaired the Federal Bar Association's National Committee on Professional Ethics as well as its District of Columbia chapter.

The 1950s were not just years of activity for Haas, however. They were also years of struggle. Surviving family members note that he suffered from depression throughout his life. At times these episodes were quite severe—what at the time people called "nervous breakdowns" requiring hospitalization. The illness that took him from Poston to a Los Angeles hospital for weeks on end in 1943 was gastrointestinal, but his correspondence drops hints of a psychiatric component as well. Certainly, the frantic pace he maintained as project attorney, the eighteen-to-twenty-hour workdays, and the middle-of-the-night memoranda he banged out on his typewriter suggest more than a touch of mania, just as his startling confessions of deep mental anguish in his letters to WRA headquarters imply depression.

Theodore H. Haas, mid-1950s.
(Courtesy of Rosie Haas.)

Haas suffered a terrible blow in 1953 when Felix Cohen died suddenly of a heart attack at age forty-six. Since the late 1930s the two friends and collaborators had sketched the blueprint for radical change in the rights and status of American Indians and had begun to build the edifice; now Haas was left to witness its ongoing destruction alone. An especially severe episode of depression landed him at George Washington University Hospital on May 31, 1959. He underwent ten days of treatment in its psychiatric unit and was released midday on June 10. Several hours later, a motorist spotted him poised on the railing of the Calvert Street Bridge spanning Rock Creek Park. He jumped, plummeting to his death in a thicket 300 feet below. He was fifty-four years old. He left behind a wife but no children.

He was buried at the King David Memorial Gardens in Falls Church, Virginia, in a grave next to Felix Cohen's.

Thomas Masuda (*left*) in postwar Chicago with law associate Oscar M. Nudelman. (Courtesy of the Bancroft Library, University of California, Berkeley.)

With the support of Ted Haas and several other Poston administrators, Thomas Masuda finally was awarded leave clearance in late September 1943. He did not actually leave camp for good, though, until the late spring of 1944, because he had a hard time finding work on the outside. In May, Masuda left Poston on a zigzagging two-month road trip all the way to New York City, stopping in cities and towns to scope out relocation opportunities both for himself and for members of the community back in camp. When efforts to land a legal position in New York and a job in the WRA's Chicago relocation office came to naught, Masuda took up residence at the Chicago YMCA and hit the streets looking for work. In September 1944 he decided just to hang out his own shingle in a room on the twelfth floor of the Metropolitan Building on North La Salle Street. His wife Kay left Poston to join him in October 1944.

It was in Chicago that Masuda finally managed to step out fully from the shadow of suspicion that had unjustly followed him to Poston after his jury acquittal in Seattle in 1942. Slowly, persistently, Masuda built up a law practice, focusing at first on the needs of the burgeoning community of Japanese

Americans resettling in the Windy City after camp. He was a founding member and the second president of the Chicago Resettlement Committee, later called the Japanese American Service Committee, which lent a hand to refugees from the camps seeking to put down roots in Chicago. In time, as commercial relations grew between the United States and vanquished foe Japan, Masuda became a respected counselor to people and companies in international trade. He helped to found the Chicago-Tokyo Bank in 1964, which opened a path for Chicago banks to site branches overseas.

He also took on countless leadership positions in community organizations, including the Japanese American Citizens League and its credit union; the Japan-America Society; the board of the Chicago *Shimpo* newspaper; the Japanese Chamber of Commerce and Industry; the Uptown Chicago Commission; and the Robert McCormick Boys and Girls Club. He was president of the Chicago Japanese American Council in 1967 when it planted 1,000 cherry, crabapple, dogwood, and maple trees around the harbor to thank the city for welcoming Japanese Americans as they left the camps during and after the war.

Masuda developed his little office on La Salle Street into the law firm of Masuda, Funai, Eifert & Mitchell. Today it employs more than forty attorneys at offices in the Chicago area and in Los Angeles.

Thomas Masuda passed away in April 1986.

Kiyoichi Doi took advantage of Jerry Housel's departure by resetting his relationship with the Heart Mountain Project Attorney's Office. The Nisei lawyer warmly greeted Housel's interim replacement, Irvin Lechliter, and after a month or so asked Lechliter to hire him. Even though Housel had warned Lechliter to "watch his step" in dealing with Doi, the interim project attorney made plans to bring Doi onto the office's staff. "He's a pretty good lawyer," Lechliter wrote to Phil Glick, whose "good points outweigh the bad."

Lechliter left Heart Mountain in early September 1943 to make way for the camp's next permanent project attorney, a professor named John McGowen, who took leave from the University of Wyoming to take the job. Doi slipped into the office just ahead of McGowen, and the new project attorney saw no reason not to keep him on when he arrived, especially because Doi looked to be spending most of his time on judicial commission matters rather than with clients of the Project Attorney's Office. McGowen, however, did not last long in the job; he died suddenly of a brain tumor in February 1944 at the age of thirty-eight.

Having watched Housel, Lechliter, and McGowen come and go, Doi now welcomed yet another project attorney to Heart Mountain, a small-town Iowa lawyer named Byron Ver Ploeg. One of his first tasks was to take stock of the office he was inheriting. He found himself puzzled by the role played by Kiyoichi Doi. "It seems he is in theory connected with the Project Attorney's Office," Ver Ploeg reported to Washington on June 21, 1944, "but he does not work in this office or handle any of the routine of this office." Puzzlement quickly gave way to dismay, as the new project attorney soon learned that Doi had "created the general impression" that he was "using his office to further his own purposes" while "the administration [was] either entirely hoodwinked or conveniently 'looking the other way.'" For weeks, Ver Ploeg signed time cards for Doi under the impression that the pay was for his work on the judicial commission, but now he understood that Doi was actually "running a field extension of the Project Attorney's Office" out of his own space and was "handling correspondence of all types and legal matters for the residents" entirely outside Ver Ploeg's view. What was more, Doi was rumored to be "receiving quite a handsome renumeration [sic] for his services" from the people he assisted.

Ver Ploeg also learned that Doi was reputed to have "a heavy hand in the gambling rackets" that plagued the camp. This information alarmed WRA solicitor Phil Glick. He instructed Ver Ploeg to investigate the situation and, if he turned up anything concerning, to move Doi out of the office—even if the evidence didn't suffice to file formal charges against him for gambling. Ver Ploeg showed Doi the door in early August 1944. Six months later Doi—still sitting as chair of Heart Mountain's judicial commission—was one of eighteen men arrested for gambling in a raid of a barrack room reputed to house a wagering ring. There is no record of his having been prosecuted for the offense.

Doi and his wife left Heart Mountain in July 1945. They returned to Los Angeles, where Doi had practiced law before the war. In December of that year, they were living in a hotel in Little Tokyo. The hotel offered no kitchen facilities, so they were taking all of their meals in restaurants. Hoping to reestablish a law office, Doi managed to secure a loan to help him buy office equipment.

He must have been successful in reopening his office, because the records of the U.S. Supreme Court show him as a cosignatory on a "friend of the court" brief for the Japanese American Citizens League in a 1948 case challenging a California law that denied fishing licenses to aliens who were not eligible to become U.S. citizens. The challenge was successful.

Doi divorced in August 1948 at the age of fifty. In around 1953, he emigrated to Japan. Why he went there and what he did there are unknown. He died of cancer in Tokyo in July 1958.

By the time I first began to develop interest in the mass removal and imprisonment of Japanese Americans in 1997, Ted Haas and Kiyoichi Doi had been dead for some forty years, Thomas Masuda for more than ten, and Jim Terry for more than twenty. Only Jerry Housel was still alive.

From his stint at Heart Mountain, he had gone to Idaho for military training in August 1943, emerging in October with an officer's commission. He thought he would be sent into combat overseas, but due to his law degree the U.S. Navy assigned him to its base in Pensacola, Florida, where he prosecuted court-martial proceedings.

Returning to Cody and his wife Mary Elaine in 1946, he joined the law practice of Ernest "Gop" Goppert. After a few years Housel went out on his own, opening an office that came to be known for expertise in the law of insurance, farming, and ranching. Ranching was a special love of Housel's. In the 1950s he bought a property in Meeteetse, Wyoming, south of Cody, and began ranching cattle and sheep. He loved to hunt and fish. He was, in many ways, a typical man of the Mountain West.

In one way, though, he was not. Housel was a committed Democrat in some of the staunchest Republican terrain in the United States. He served as chairman of the Park County Democratic Central Committee, a member of the Democratic National Committee, and a Wyoming delegate to the Democratic National Convention. He was seriously considered for a seat on the U.S. Court of Appeals for the Tenth Circuit during the administration of President Lyndon Johnson. He was the Wyoming coordinator for the presidential campaign of Senator George McGovern in 1972. And he flirted with a run for the Democratic nomination for governor in 1974.

Housel was a leading figure in the practicing bar at state and national levels. He served on Wyoming's Board of Law Examiners for many years and in 1964 as president of the state's bar association. He was a member of the American Bar Association's House of Delegates for fifteen years and of its Board of Governors for four. Across his lifetime he also headed up countless community organizations in his beloved hometown of Cody.

According to his son, Jerry Housel never liked to talk to family and friends about his work as Heart Mountain's project attorney. He was terse about it when I interviewed him in Laramie in 1997. He volunteered that he'd always felt welcome when Japanese Americans invited him to social and athletic

Jerry Housel in his office circa 1955. (Courtesy of the Buffalo
Bill Center of the West, Cody, Wyoming; McCracken Research
Library; MS089- Jack Richard Collection; P.89.106.21007-28-N.)

events but didn't mention his opposition to Japanese sports and arts. He said
most of the people were "cooperative" despite some "troublemakers," but he
didn't mention his crusade against Kiyoichi Doi. He recalled helping the community set up a system of self-government and brokering a resolution to the
motor pool strike, but he didn't mention his fear of a violent uprising.

He did tell me that "this was the worst damned thing the country ever did."
But he didn't tell me it was the worst thing he ever did.

Now that you've read these lawyers' stories, you might be wondering how much of them is true. This is both an easy and a hard question.

I will answer the easy version first: everything of arguable historical significance actually happened.

In book 1, some examples among many: Jerry Housel really was the son-in-law of Powell's mayor; really did toil against Kiyoichi Doi; really did broker the motor pool strike; and really did exit his job with a letter calling for a much tougher WRA hand and the end of Japanese cultural activities. (The letter in this book is his letter, with only minor alterations.) Heart Mountain prisoners really did make a snow statue of Adolf Hitler under a gallows, and military police really did arrest a bunch of kids on a snowy day and take away their sleds.

In book 2, realities include these: Ted Haas really did pass around a petition against the Poston fence; really did argue that Japanese Americans should be running the place instead of white administrators; really did analyze and lament his time at Poston in the expansive, emotional document reproduced in the book; and really did interrogate Tom Masuda about his loyalty just as the transcript of that hearing—also real—narrates. Tom Masuda really was tried in Seattle for not registering as a Japanese agent, really was acquitted, really did serve as Poston's interim project attorney when Ted Haas was away sick, and really was blocked from joining the Military Intelligence Service due to the so-called intelligence information you read about here.

And in book 3, another small sampling of true events: Jim Terry really did counsel a young man whose Issei mother fell into an unmarked pit; really did help an innocent young Japanese American out of a federal holding tank in Phoenix after his groundless arrest; really did go toe-to-toe with the Arizona Corporation Commission at a headline-grabbing hearing about the prisoner-run stores at Gila River; really did try to talk a secretary out of expatriating to Japan; and really did pepper Elmer Kira with the blunt, argumentative questions that appear in the transcript in this book, which I edited only for length and context. According to Kira's family and friends, that hearing really was the trigger for the mental and emotional unraveling that really did get him shot.

The work stoppages and demonstrations in the book really happened. The strike at Heart Mountain really did force WRA staff out on tractors in the early morning to keep agricultural production going. The Poston demonstrations really featured bonfires, posters ridiculing inu, performances, and slightly altered Japanese flags.

The various assaults and instances of mischief—petty and serious—and the marital conflicts detailed in the book all really happened, though in most cases I changed the names of the Japanese Americans involved in them. (Certain events, such as the beating of Saburo Kido at Poston, are already prominent in historical literature on this period, as are the names of his assailants, so there was little point in changing those.)

What, though, about the truth of the book's depiction of the interior worlds of the historical actors that are its main subjects—Housel, Haas, and Terry—as revealed through the thoughts and conversations you read?

In a conventional work of historical nonfiction, a figure's interior world is off-limits, except for references to written evidence of their thoughts, feelings, and exchanges with others, which few leave behind. The historian William Cronon points out how constraining—and potentially warping—this choice can be. The information we lack, those pockets of archival silence, most particularly "stream-of-consciousness and informal conversation," Cronon notes, "are so fundamental to so much of life that it is a little hard to say which depiction of the past is more distorting: a history that says nothing about them, or a fiction that in the absence of authoritative evidence tries to represent them as responsibly as possible."

It is *not* hard to say which depiction is more distorting when the matter under study, as in this book, isn't a historical figure's actions but the subjectivity of their motivations—not so much "What did the lawyers do to help run the system of camps?" as "Why did they help run a system they disliked, and how did they manage the internal dissonance of doing it?" A narrative about such questions that pretends undocumented things do not exist will be more distorting than one that tries responsibly to imagine them, because it will—it must—be woefully incomplete.

The well-known Goldhagen-Browning debate about Holocaust perpetrators illustrates the point. Daniel Goldhagen looked at the German shooters of the mobile killing squads of Eastern Europe and saw men acting because they fervently embraced the genocidal antisemitism of the Nazi state. Christopher Browning, by contrast, saw men acting for many reasons of which but one was hatred: the men also felt strong social pressure to conform and the numbing effect of war's relentless degradation and brutality. Both of these rival ideas offer plausible accounts of *the squads*. But why did one shooter quit while another carried on? Why did the threat of peer mockery keep one man's hand on the trigger of his gun but not another's? Why, upon recognizing his targets as Jews from his own hometown did one shooter ask to be excused from that day's task, while another did not? The documentable outsides of things cannot suggest answers to these questions. They can be understood only be by looking to an interior that left no record.

I don't mean to suggest that a project attorney's work in the WRA camps was the same as shooting people into pits. The point of the analogy is only to illustrate that perpetrators do what they do and keep doing it until the work is done or they've had enough for an unknowable array of reasons, most of which their actions alone will not reveal. Jerry Housel and Ted Haas both confronted army plans to build security fences they thought unnecessary. Haas fought the Poston fence; Housel acceded to it at Heart Mountain. Why?

Neither man explained himself on the matter in the written record. Nor, of course, did he transcribe the back-and-forths he had with colleagues in the hallways. But that hardly turns their motivations on this issue—or any other—into "aspects of the past about which our documents are silent," as Cronon puts it. We have hundreds of single-spaced pages from these men, and from Jim Terry as well—pages in which they held forth about all sorts of other events, problems, interactions, conflicts, successes, failures, joys, and disappointments in their lives as project attorneys. Tones emerge, and differences in tones. Within the correspondence, language ranges from vivid to dry, irritated to solicitous, alarmed to arch, and technical to emotional. The record may lack the specifics of what the men said about any one particular thing, or how they said it, but it's full of what they said and thought about other things. That permits extrapolation, or as Cronon puts it, the creation of "fiction that in the absence of authoritative evidence tries to represent [thoughts and conversations] as responsibly as possible."

Naturally, responsible extrapolation has limits. For one, it must not present itself as something it is not. While the letters and transcripts excerpted in this book are historical documents, most of the conversation is invented, as are many specific settings. There is, for example, no record of Jerry Housel trying to build a relationship with Gop Goppert over lunch at the Irma Hotel (though his letters make clear he was in close and regular contact with members of the local bar), or of Jim Terry squabbling with a Phoenix store clerk over a typewriter (though his letters make clear he paid for office supplies out of his own pocket), or of Ted Haas sneaking out of Thanksgiving dinner with a pie for Tom Masuda (though his letters make clear he had warm and generous feelings for his Nisei associate). These are vignettes that, on the basis of the historical record, I've judged to be in character, but they are my own inventions.

Responsible extrapolation also must confine itself to the inner lives of those who left behind enough of a record to support it. This commitment weds the perspective of my narrative to a small number of men—chiefly Housel, Haas, Terry, and, to a smaller extent, Thomas Masuda. Women's perspectives are notably absent. At the camps in question during the period covered in this book, all of the project attorneys were men. Indeed, this was true of all but one of the project attorneys across the full three-plus years that the ten WRA camps operated. (One trailblazing woman, Mima Pollitt, served a total of about twelve weeks in interim stints at three camps in 1945—Gila River, Topaz in Utah, and Granada in Colorado—breaking the WRA's glass ceiling.) Women more consistently filled other WRA administrative positions, especially in the camps' Social Welfare Divisions. Their roles and complicity are the subject of Yoosun Park's excellent 2019 monograph, *Facilitating Injustice: The Complicity of Social Workers in the Forced Removal and Incarceration of Japanese Americans, 1941–1946*.

The historical record also limits my extrapolation to the minds of a particular breed of professional, the lawyer in the field. The WRA was a big agency, employing people in roles ranging from farmers to firefighters and food stewards. Its lawyers were its upper crust—better educated, more worldly, more progressive, and less in the grip of anti-Japanese racism than most. This book is an account of the complicity not of the WRA as a whole but of a small and elite segment.

Neither does the book serve as a reliable biography of the significant people the lawyers encountered in their work. It presents instead an account of how the lawyers *experienced* those people. To cite an important example, the book doesn't offer a biographical depiction of attorney Kiyoichi Doi at Heart Mountain but rather an account of how Jerry Housel experienced Kiyoichi Doi—and the record is clear that Housel perceived him mostly antagonistically.

Finally, responsible extrapolation has to take account of limits in the imaginative capacity of the extrapolator. This brings me to Nisei attorney Thomas Masuda at Poston, a character whose subjective experience this book depicts, though to a more modest extent than Housel's, Haas's, and Terry's. My decision to present segments of the narrative from Masuda's perspective was difficult for several reasons.

First, Masuda's paper trail is narrower. The Project Attorney's Office correspondence from Poston includes only thirteen Masuda-authored letters, a fraction of the number authored by the other three. The letters are shorter and more uniformly businesslike, which is not surprising given Masuda's vulnerability as a Japanese American holding down what was otherwise a white man's job and reporting to a white supervisor. Masuda could never have dared the candor or the personal tone of the other lawyers' letters to the home office even if he had been temperamentally inclined to write candidly and personally. While the record does contain a significant amount of additional information about Masuda, including, most important, the voluminous file from his trial and acquittal in Seattle, most of this additional information is *about* him rather than *from* him. So, whereas the archives project vivid pictures of the inner worlds of the three white lawyers, Masuda's inner world is more shadow than shape.

Just as significant, Masuda's position in the camps had only one thing in common with that of Housel, Haas, and Terry: their profession. The question the white lawyers had to ask themselves—or suppress—each day was whether to go on administering a system of which they disapproved. Masuda's question was whether to join those administrators in their work, a dilemma of collaboration rather than perpetration. It would be unjust to Masuda, and the very definition of irresponsible extrapolation, to turn the thin first-person evidence in the record into a detailed, imagined mental landscape on an issue as fraught as collaboration. It would also draw the book away from its focus on the phenomenon of the perpetrator. Masuda's position at the juncture of the prisoner and administrator communities at Poston would be a fascinating object of study, but in a different book from this one.

And probably by a different author. I had a third reason for caution in writing Masuda: he was Japanese American, and I am not. I trust myself to imagine the subjective experiences of Jerry Housel, Ted Haas, and Jim Terry. I've known people a lot like them. I went to law school with people like them. I worked closely with people like them in my career at a New York law firm, a federal government office, and a Wyoming law school. I've sat at Passover Seders and family gatherings with people like Ted Haas. These men's lives and careers feel familiar.

Thomas Masuda's do not. The gap between us is wide. Like Housel, Haas, and Terry, I have in common with Masuda only our profession. It is not just that Masuda grew up Japanese American in a time and place where that posed all kinds of identity-forging obstacles I've never faced or that the cultural norms of the prewar Japanese American community are not my own. It is also that his unjust removal and incarceration foisted on him a set of conflicts and pressures, both professional and personal, that I shudder to imagine. The camps could be dangerous places for Japanese Americans seen as too close to white administrators. Some, like Saburo Kido, for example, ended up on the wrong end of fists and metal pipes. There's no evidence that Thomas Masuda lived under a threat of violence, but his position must have been precarious—a tightrope buffeted by winds I can't imagine.

The result of all this is that I chose to confine my extrapolation of Masuda's inner life to the thoughts and reactions that almost any person in Masuda's position would be expected to have: distress over the persistence of the accusations of which he was acquitted, appreciation for the rarity of Haas's benevolent spirit among WRA administrators, disappointment over his rejection from a military in which he very much wanted to serve, betrayal at being interrogated by a man he considered a friend and advocate. The reader will likely encounter Masuda as a flatter, less fully sketched character than his white lawyer colleagues. This is a product not of disinterest on my part but of respect and a certain humility about the limits of my sources and my imagination.

When I said a few paragraphs back that the WRA lawyers feel familiar to me because I've known people like them, I omitted one such person: myself. The federal government office I mentioned earlier was in fact a prosecutor's office. Working there early in my career, I confronted dilemmas of conscience not wholly unlike theirs.

In my second year, a case landed on my desk that gave me pause—so much pause, in fact, that I wished the office could abandon it. It was the prosecution of an African American man for a rape on an army base. A first trial had produced a hung jury, but at a retrial a second jury found the defendant guilty, and my job was to defend that conviction in an appeals court.

The rape had taken place in the dead of night in a poorly lit bus shelter. The whole case turned on the confidence of the victim's identification of the rapist. Because she was white, the identification was cross-racial, and those are known to carry a significant risk of error. What's more, she first identified the defendant when she happened to see a "wanted" board in the police station that presented black-and-white photos and sketches of various people sought in connection with a number of crimes but featured two photos of the defendant at nearly four times the size of the others and in color, priming anyone glancing at it to attend to those. All of this had already failed once to convince a jury beyond a reasonable doubt that the defendant was guilty. For the first time, I didn't feel certain of the defendant's guilt myself.

Yet I said nothing. I wrote the brief and argued the case.

I don't recall why I kept my doubts to myself, but the reasons aren't hard to reconstruct. I was young, just three years out of law school. I lacked confidence in my instincts. I was new to the office, eager to establish myself as a member of the team. The prosecutor who had handled the trial was experienced, charismatic, and six years my senior. Voicing doubt about his case might have come off as maligning a respected senior colleague or even imputing racial insensitivity.

As it turns out, I lost: the court reversed the conviction. I imagine I told my colleagues I was disappointed. In truth I felt relieved.

But one other thing stands out. When I wrote the brief, I didn't do it with my usual prosecutorial zeal. I didn't argue that the "wanted" board's skewed layout posed no problem at all, as I imagined many of my colleagues might have done. Instead, I made concessions. I acknowledged that the two big photos of the defendant "stood out on the board." I allowed that in certain circumstances (though not the ones in this case), I "would be hard pressed to argue that the board was not suggestive." I remember holding my breath as I urged my supervisor to sign off on the brief with this unusual language and feeling relief when she assented.

I was telling myself, I suppose, that I was doing my best to temper a bad situation. I was doing more than others would have done.

No doubt that's how Housel, Haas, and Terry reassured themselves too.

ACKNOWLEDGMENTS

Though they may not know it and won't (I hope) be horrified to learn it, a fine group of scholars planted the seed for this book in the fall of 2017. It was at a Los Angeles meeting of the Densho Scholars Roundtable, a small gathering of people whose work focuses on the wartime removal and imprisonment of Japanese Americans. I talked for a while about the War Relocation Authority's project attorneys and their voluminous correspondence, but when the moment came to discuss our future projects, I said I could only envision the project attorneys' story as one small piece of a much larger history of the WRA that I hoped (and still hope) to write. The group—Connie Chiang, Tom Ikeda, Karen Inouye, Heidi Kim, Lon Kurashige, Brian Niiya, Greg Robinson, and Alice Yang—urged me to see that the project attorneys deserved a book of their own. I'm so very grateful to them. A book about these WRA lawyers wouldn't have come into being without their encouragement.

Early in the project I reached out to descendants of several WRA project attorneys in hopes of learning a bit more about them. A number spoke or corresponded with me: Annette Cohen, Florence Goldberg, Rosie Haas, John Housel, James Terry, Dr. Stephen Terry, Steve Terry, and Brenton Ver Ploeg. I am grateful for these generous and helpful conversations and exchanges. It will no doubt be jarring to see Ted Haas, Jerry Housel, and Jim Terry presented not as objects of scholarly examination but as thinking and talking "characters" in a story. I've tried to make clear that the book is my own imaginative extrapolation from the words they wrote, the actions they took, and what others said about them at the time, rather than a conventional academic analysis. I hope it's also clear I see the men not as caricatures but as complex people with a range of motivations, including good ones. Still, the descendants might find it challenging to see their forebears animated here by a stranger. I do hope they don't find my imaginings to be ungrounded or unfair.

For more than a decade I've had the privilege of involvement with the Fellowships at Auschwitz for the Study of Professional Ethics (FASPE), as a faculty member and as its academic director. FASPE is engaged in the deepest of inquiry and education about the phenomenon of the perpetrator, focusing on the German professionals in many fields whose energies were essential to the creation of the Nazi state. This book is suffused with ideas and energy I've drawn from my work with FASPE. I'm grateful to all the FASPE people I've worked and traveled with for helping me think more carefully about what leads ordinary people to contribute to injustice. My gratitude includes the many FASPE fellows I've taught (in particular the 2021 FASPE law cohort, who read and commented on excerpts of the manuscript) and the FASPE faculty and staff I've worked and traveled with—especially my coteachers Susan Carle and Jeff Ward and, in FASPE's "home office," David Goldman, Rebecca Scott, Thorin Tritter, and Thorsten Wagner.

I appreciate the support I've gotten from my home institution, the University of North Carolina at Chapel Hill. Several associate deans for faculty development at the School of Law offered kind support along the way: Carissa Hessick, Holning Lau, and Leigh Osofsky. I was fortunate to receive a William R. Kenan, Jr., Senior Faculty Research and Scholarly Leave in the spring semester of 2018 that allowed me the time to begin to conceptualize the project. My dean, Martin Brinkley, supported my application for that leave, and for that too I am grateful.

I've enjoyed a long and meaningful relationship with my publisher, the University of North Carolina Press, wearing several hats, but the most meaningful hat has always been that of author. The press greeted my manuscript with enthusiasm and showed that they "got it" from the very start. It takes a village to produce the book you're holding in your hands, and I'm thankful to everyone at the press with a hand in the project, but I'd like to say a special thank-you to the three anonymous readers whose comments on two drafts of the book improved it immensely and to several folks in the editorial department: Mark Simpson-Vos, Elaine Maisner, and especially my editor, Debbie Gershenowitz.

This is my fourth book and was the hardest to bring to life—not just to write but to manage self-doubt and maintain good spirit about. I came very close to giving up, and not just once. I don't have words to thank the small group of people who, alongside their many substantive contributions, just let me know again and again that they believed in me and in my vision of what the book should be. Joe Kennedy, Cary Levine, David Muller, Abby Muller, Nina Muller, and (most of all) Leslie Branden-Muller: You kept me going. I love you all.

NOTES

PREFACE

xiv **The lawyers in this book worked for the War Relocation Authority:** Lawyers
were not the only professionals to collaborate in the removal and imprisonment
of Japanese Americans; the scholarly literature has seen exploration of the roles
played by certain others as well. The most robust literature is on the roles of social
scientists. For this, see Orin Starn, "Engineering Internment: Anthropologists
and the War Relocation Authority," *American Ethnologist* 13, no. 4 (November
1986): 700–720; and the responses to Starn from two anthropologists who worked
in the camps: Morris Opler, "Comment on 'Engineering Internment,'" *American
Ethnologist* 14, no. 2 (May 1987): 383; and Rachel Sady, "Comment on 'Engineering Internment,'" *American Ethnologist* 14, no. 3 (August 1987): 385. Also useful
are Asael T. Hansen, "My Two Years at Heart Mountain: The Difficult Role of an
Applied Anthropologist," in *Japanese Americans: From Relocation to Redress*, ed.
Roger Daniels, Sandra C. Taylor, and Harry H. L. Kitano (Salt Lake City: Uni-
versity of Utah Press, 1986): 33–37; and the essays in Yuji Ichioka, ed., *Views from
Within: The Japanese American Evacuation and Resettlement Study* (Los Angeles:
UCLA Asian American Studies Center, 1989). More recently Yoosun Park gave an
incisive account of the roles played by social workers in *Facilitating Injustice: The
Complicity of Social Workers in the Forced Removal and Incarceration of Japanese
Americans, 1941–1946* (New York: Oxford University Press, 2020).

xv **biweekly letters:** The original reports and letters of all of the WRA project attorneys are in Record Group 210 at the National Archives and Records Administration in Washington, D.C. (hereafter cited throughout the notes as NARA
RG 210). Since 2018 they have also been available in electronic format among
the papers of the Japanese Evacuation and Resettlement Study (JERS) at the
Bancroft Library, University of California, Berkeley.

xvi **The project attorneys were also observed by others:** Alexander Leighton, director of the Bureau of Sociological Research at Poston, recorded vivid impressions
of Ted Haas. These are in the Japanese American relocation centers records,
1935–1953, collection 3830, at the Division of Rare and Manuscript Collections of
the Cornell University Library. At Gila River, Rosalie Hankey of the JERS took
notes about Jim Terry; these can be found in the online records of the JERS at
the Bancroft Library, University of California, Berkeley.

xviii **If this were a novel:** Two true novels shed light on the roles played by white people
in the imprisonment of Japanese Americans: Kermit Roosevelt, *Allegiance* (New
York: Regan Arts, 2015), a murder mystery set against the backdrop of the Supreme
Court's review of legal challenges to Japanese American incarceration; and Mar-
nie Mueller, *The Climate of the Country* (Willimantic, Conn.: Curbstone, 1999).

INTRODUCTION

1 **beset by worries:** Dillon S. Myer, interview by Amelia R. Fry, *Japanese-American
Relocation Reviewed*, vol. 2, *The Internment*, ed. Rosemary Levenson, Amelia

Fry, and Miriam Feingold Stein, *Earl Warren Oral History Project Series* (Berkeley: University of California, Bancroft Library, Regional Oral History Office, 1976), http://content.cdlib.org/view?docId=ft1290031s&brand=default &doc.view=entire_text.

1   **lost a year's sleep:** Milton S. Eisenhower, *The President Is Calling* (Garden City, N.Y.: Doubleday, 1974), 123.

2   **"a way of handling human beings":** *San Francisco Hearings before the House Select Comm. Investigating National Defense Migration,* 77th Cong. 11044 (1942) (statement of Francis Biddle, Attorney General of the United States).

2   **"an American citizen":** Greg Robinson, *By Order of the President: FDR and the Internment of Japanese Americans* (Cambridge, Mass.: Harvard University Press, 2001), 85–86.

2   **"inland concentration camps":** Peter Irons, *Justice at War: The Story of the Japanese American Internment Cases* (Berkeley: University of California Press, 1993), 38.

3   **"to the extent necessary":** Irons, *Justice at War,* 39.

3   **"such action will be taken":** John L. DeWitt, *Final Report, Japanese Evacuation from the West Coast, 1942* (Washington, D.C.: U.S. Government Printing Office, 1943), 34.

5   **self-government by the administered:** David E. Hamilton, "Building the Associative State: The Department of Agriculture and American State-Building," *Agricultural History* 64, no. 2 (Spring 1990): 207, 217.

5   **would run them:** War Relocation Authority, *WRA: A Story of Human Conservation* (Washington, D.C.: U.S. Government Printing Office, 1946), 28–29.

5   **gone when the war ended:** War Relocation Authority, *WRA,* 29. The Colorado and Utah representatives at the meeting were somewhat more receptive to the federal government's ideas than the representatives of their western neighbors.

5   **"horrible circumstances":** Eisenhower, *President Is Calling,* 119.

6   **system of "leaves":** War Relocation Authority, *WRA,* 34–35.

6   **celebrating Native identities:** Naturally, the OIA was pursuing these goals in the context of its time. Its agenda should not be mistaken for one we'd call progressive today. It was, however, a radical departure from what preceded it.

7   **"5,000 to 17,000 persons":** War Relocation Authority, *Legal and Constitutional Phases of the WRA Program* (Washington, D.C.: U.S. Government Printing Office, 1946), 53.

8   **more than Eisenhower could bear:** Dillon S. Myer, interview by Helen S. Pryor, July 7, 1970, transcript, Harry S. Truman Library and Museum, Independence, Missouri, https://www.trumanlibrary.gov/library/oral-histories/myerds3.

8   **"disposal of the evacuees":** "The Truth about the Japanese Relocation Program," *Los Angeles Times,* July 9, 1943.

8   **"slept soundly":** Myer, interview by Helen S. Pryor.

CHAPTER ONE

13   **it wasn't clear if this was a cost the WRA should absorb:** Housel raised the issue about financial responsibility for prisoners' stays at the state psychiatric hospital in a letter to the WRA solicitor; Housel to Philip M. Glick, October 17, 1942, NARA RG 210.

14 **A few months ago, he'd been one of them:** Housel's service in the Washington, D.C., headquarters of the WRA in the summer of 1942 is referenced in Housel to Glick, September 14, 1942, NARA RG 210.

14 **"The development of private enterprise":** The prohibition on private enterprise is in the WRA's administrative manual (1944) at section 50.5.2(E). The administrative manual can be found online in the HathiTrust Digital Library, www .hathitrust.org.

14 **Montgomery Ward recruited them:** Housel wrote about Montgomery Ward recruiting young women as "sales girls" and his sense that this would violate a WRA rule against private enterprise in the camp; Housel to Glick, September 23, 1942, NARA RG 210.

15 **deny them food in the mess halls if they didn't:** The idea of denying service in the mess halls to prisoners engaged in private employment who did not make subsistence payments to the WRA appears in Housel to Glick, October 17, 1942, NARA RG 210.

16 **Chris Rachford took every opportunity to insist the center needed its own project attorney:** The Heart Mountain project director's desire for a full-time project attorney stationed at the camp is discussed in Housel to Glick, October 24, 1942, NARA RG 210.

17 **"Ten Thousand Is a Lot of Japanese":** "Ten Thousand Is a Lot of Japanese," *Powell (Wyo.) Tribune*, May 28, 1942.

18 **Barber was a fish out of water:** Some information about Philip W. Barber's life appears in his obituary; *New York Times*, May 27, 1981, A22.

18 **he had signed up for a few Japanese lessons:** A biography of Housel that appeared in the *Heart Mountain (Wyo.) Sentinel* on April 3, 1943, noted his taking Japanese lessons.

18 **The county wanted reimbursement:** Park County officials' desire for reimbursement for additional burdens on county services is referenced in Housel to Glick, November 24, 1942, and January 14, 1943; and Housel to acting WRA solicitor Lewis A. Sigler, January 26, 1943, all in NARA RG 210.

18 **"I saw in the *Sentinel* that your office needs a stenographer?":** Sadie Tanabe is an invention, but Housel references Japanese American women working as secretaries in the Project Attorney's Office in Housel to Glick, January 14, 1943, NARA RG 210.

19 **the case the commission was trying:** The names Hada and Ito are aliases, but the case is real; Housel to Glick, October 24, 1942, NARA RG 210. The case was also covered in the *Heart Mountain Sentinel* on the same day.

20 **"Japanese stuff":** Housel voiced disapproval of Japanese cultural activities in camp in Housel to Glick, June 3, 1943, NARA RG 210.

20 **small groups clustered at the windows:** Housel related that prisoners would crowd the windows outside the courtroom when seating inside was full; Housel to Sigler, May 6, 1943, NARA RG 210.

20 **The room was impressive:** The description of Heart Mountain's courtroom comes from Housel to Glick, October 17, 1942, NARA RG 210.

21 **A middle-aged man of just-under-average height:** Details about Doi come from his evacuee case file—a collection of records about each prisoner that the WRA maintained—now in NARA RG 210.

21 **The session was chaotic:** Housel described the arguments in the Hada case in

Housel to Glick, October 24, 1942. He summarized other of Doi's courtroom be-haviors in letters to headquarters on February 19, 25, March 11, 18, April 1, 1943. All in NARA RG 210.

22 **"Now, if you'd seen me handling the Yamatoda case":** Details about the Yama-toda case can be found in "Yamatoda Relates Gaming Club Row," *Los Angeles Daily News*, May 26, 1943, 7.

22 **the power to dissolve California marriages:** We see Housel and Glick discuss-ing the issue of how Wyoming courts would handle California marriages in Housel to Glick, October 24, 1942; and Glick to Housel, November 24, 30, 1942, all in NARA RG 210.

22 **"what *I* need to do in order to appear in the local courts":** In a letter on Octo-ber 24, 1942, Housel informed Glick that he believed Doi thought he would be permitted to represent prisoners in the Wyoming courts. Glick referenced the rule against Japanese American lawyers appearing in local courts in a letter to Housel on November 24, 1942. Both in NARA RG 210.

23 **There would be only one law office at Heart Mountain:** Housel presented a plan to Glick for keeping Doi from doing legal work for prisoners in Housel to Glick, November 3, 1942. On November 17, 1942, Housel wrote to Glick that once the Project Attorney's Office was fully established, all legal work at Heart Mountain would run through that office and not through Doi. Both in NARA RG 210.

CHAPTER TWO

25 **Gop Goppert called out a hello:** Information on Goppert comes from the profile of him by Amber Peabody entitled "Ernest Goppert: Lawyer Dedicates Life to Philanthropy" in *Cody Country Legends*, Summer 2017, 24–27, https://www.scribd.com/document/364555222/Legends-Magazine-2017.

25 **showing himself to be more reasonable about things:** Housel's interim succes-sor at Heart Mountain, Irvin Lechliter, told Philip Glick that "Goppert is one of the few residents of Cody who is sympathetic to our program"; Lechliter to Glick, June 17, 1943, NARA RG 210.

25 **the partition he'd had installed:** Housel described the partition installed in the Project Attorney's Office in Housel to Glick, November 17, 1942, NARA RG 210.

25 **the help he was getting from a few evacuees:** The work of Japanese Americans experienced with business matters in the Project Attorney's Office was described in Housel to Glick, October 17, November 17, 1942, March 4, 1943, NARA RG 210.

25 **The issue was divorces:** The two divorce cases were described in Housel to Glick, November 17, 1942, NARA RG 210.

26 **"one hundred and fifty bucks a pop":** Housel reported the overcharging by local attorneys in Housel to Glick, November 17, 1942, NARA RG 210.

27 **"a few young able-bodied Japanese out and down to his ranch to work":** Carl Sackett's efforts to get cheap labor from Heart Mountain for his ranch were described in Housel to Glick, January 26, 1943; and John McGowen (Housel's successor) to Glick, November 27, 1943, both in NARA RG 210.

28 **an enormous bust of Hitler, that is, made entirely out of snow:** The Hitler snowman was the subject of a photo and caption in *Heart Mountain Sentinel*, November 21, 1942, 8.

29 **having just been elected chair of the Heart Mountain Charter Commission:** Doi's election to chair of the charter commission was reported on the front page of the *Heart Mountain Sentinel*, November 14, 1942.

29 **a knack for getting out ahead:** Housel told Glick that Doi had "a knack of talking to and influencing large numbers of the evacuees" and "might become a dangerous man" if pushed out of influence. He later reiterated that Doi "certainly has a knack for getting ahead among the evacuees." Housel to Glick, November 3, 17, 1942, NARA RG 210.

29 **"Protest Petition Sent":** The story entitled "Protest Petition Sent to WRA Director" was the front-page headline in the *Heart Mountain Sentinel*, November 21, 1942.

30 **They broke their own rules:** Housel informed Glick that military police were violating their own rules by patrolling the inner boundaries during the daytime; Housel to Glick, November 17, 1942, NARA RG 210.

30 **"May I read you a few words from the article?":** The *Heart Mountain Sentinel* published the text of the fence petition in its edition of November 21, 1942.

32 **"You are not prisoners. You are not internees":** Housel said this in a meeting of the Heart Mountain Charter Commission on November 14, 1942, a transcript of which is preserved among the papers of the Japanese Evacuation and Resettlement Study (JERS) at the Bancroft Library, University of California, Berkeley.

32 **"Without charge":** A later-serving project attorney, Byron Ver Ploeg, noted that Kiyoichi Doi had been running a private law office at Heart Mountain and was rumored to be receiving "quite a handsome renumeration [*sic*] for his services"; Ver Ploeg to Glick, August 10, 1944, NARA RG 210.

33 **they were now refusing to work:** Housel reported that the Japanese Americans hired to build the fence were not showing up to work; Housel to Glick, November 17, 1942, NARA RG 210.

33 **it wasn't really up to him:** Housel indicated his inclination to defer to either or both the project director and WRA headquarters on whether a fence should go up; Housel to Glick, November 17, 1942, NARA RG 210.

33 **"I mean the sleds":** Housel described the sled incident in Housel to Glick, November 17, 1942, NARA RG 210.

CHAPTER THREE

36 **The Issei were angry:** Housel spent much time in the late fall of 1942 trying to broker disagreements between Issei and Nisei over control of the community's governing structures that were triggered by the WRA's insistence that only U.S. citizens could hold elective office. Housel urged headquarters to allow the Issei a role, noting his sense that they would "die hard if no provision was made" for their representation; Housel to Philip M. Glick, December 16, 1942, NARA RG 210. Housel's work on community government structures is fully documented in Eric L. Muller, "Of Coercion and Accommodation: Looking at Japanese American Imprisonment through a Law Office Window," *Law and History Review* 35, no. 2 (May 2017): 277–319.

36 **who should run the community enterprises:** Trying and failing to get the community to agree on a corporate structure for the camp's commercial enterprises was a theme in Housel's letters to WRA headquarters from December 1942 through the spring of 1943. Housel's successors, first John McGowen and later Byron Ver Ploeg, had no more success than Housel. McGowen captured the disagreements in a letter, noting the "constant strife" around the issue and the suspicions of some prisoners that others were getting "a large rake-off and . . . good sized loots" from the operation of the stores. On August 4, 1944, Ver Ploeg

wrote to headquarters about the "tempest in the tea pot" that was "raging to new heights of fury." The conflicts remained intense as late as the end of 1944, when Ver Ploeg reported that men on the community council were looking to launch an investigation of the men running the community enterprises. McGowen to Glick, November 5, 1943; Ver Ploeg to Glick, August 4, 1944; and Ver Ploeg to acting WRA solicitor Edwin E. Ferguson, December 7, 1944, all in NARA RG 210.

36 **turned a profit of $50,000:** The annual net earnings of the various prisoner-run business enterprises at Heart Mountain appear in the final report of the Community Management Division, completed in 1945, NARA RG 210.

37 **Mary Elaine's brother decided Billings wasn't for him:** Housel referenced his brother-in-law's return to Cody and the resulting move to the Green Gables Inn in Housel to Glick, February 4, 1943, NARA RG 210.

37 **The menu in the Green Gables' little dining room:** The menu at the Green Gables Inn was the subject of a small news item, "Menu Written in Cowpuncher Style," *Casper (Wyo.) Star-Tribune*, September 6, 1938, 5.

38 **"Plans Mapped for Registration":** The article appeared in the *Heart Mountain (Wyo.) Sentinel*, February 13, 1943.

38 **the army insisted that you couldn't tell a loyal Japanese from a disloyal one:** Lt. Gen. John DeWitt, who ordered the mass removal of all people of Japanese ancestry from the West Coast in the spring of 1942, offered as a justification the view that "the Japanese race is an enemy race and while many second and third generation Japanese born on United States soil . . . have become 'Americanized,' the racial strains are undiluted." *Final Recommendation of the Commanding General, Western Defense Command and Fourth Army, Submitted to the Secretary of War*, February 14, 1942, reproduced in *Final Report: Japanese Evacuation from the West Coast 1942* (Washington, D.C.: U.S. Government Printing Office, 1943).

39 **"all-out relocation":** The "all-out relocation" approach is explained in the WRA's final report on its own program in War Relocation Authority, *WRA: A Story of Human Conservation* (Washington, D.C.: U.S. Government Printing Office, 1946), 41.

39 **a celebration of the anniversary of Pearl Harbor:** The story alleging that prisoners at Manzanar staged an uprising to celebrate the anniversary of the Pearl Harbor attack is in "Troops Called to End Riots at Manzanar; Violence Flares When Pro-Axis Japs Celebrate Bombing of Pearl Harbor," *Los Angeles Times*, December 7, 1942, 1.

39 **a sticky situation with the construction of the center's high school:** Housel recounted the dispute over wages for the Japanese American workers building the high school in Housel to Glick, January 14, 1943, NARA RG 210.

39 **whether the Community Services Division could sponsor Japanese language classes:** The permissibility of Japanese language classes and the complexities of applying from Wyoming for unemployment insurance in California were topics in Housel to Glick, February 4, 1943, NARA RG 210.

41 **no evacuee could hold elective office while also working in a WRA administrative office:** Housel reported that he had determined no members of the Project Attorney's Office could "be permitted to be members of the judicial commission or the community council"; Housel to Glick, November 17, 1942, NARA RG 210.

41 **it would be a terrible shame if a disruptive move by the administration blew up the process:** Housel reported that the chairman of the block managers and

the chairman of the community council were linking Doi's ability to continue doing legal aid work to the chances of success for the community's constitution; Housel to Glick, December 23, 1942, NARA RG 210.

41 **Housel backed down:** Housel wrote that he was permitting Doi to continue doing legal aid work for the time being; Housel to Glick, December 31, 1942, NARA RG 210.

41 **Housel's next move was to transfer the staff:** Housel summarized his continuing efforts to control Doi in a letter to Glick. And Housel inquired of acting WRA solicitor Lewis Sigler whether he could bar Doi from doing legal work for prisoners on a pro bono basis. Housel to Glick, January 14, 1943; and to Sigler, February 4, 1943, both in NARA RG 210.

41 **The room again fell silent:** The standoff between Kiyoichi Doi, speaking on behalf of his fellow judicial commissioners, and Jerry Housel is summarized in Housel to Glick, January 14, 1943, NARA RG 210.

44 **Dear Jerry:** Glick's letter is excerpted here verbatim, except for the paragraph that begins with "I continue to follow," which I've added for context.

45 **Housel wasn't surprised Lovell had reached out the first friendly hand:** Housel described the town of Lovell's warm relationship with Heart Mountain in Housel to Sigler, February 4, 1943, NARA RG 210.

46 **The teams were on the hardwood:** The basketball game between the Heart Mountain All-Stars and the Lovell Westwood Indians was the subject of articles in two issues of the *Heart Mountain Sentinel*, those of February 6 and 13, 1943.

46 **The Heart Mountain group occupied just a couple of rows:** While the newspaper accounts indicated that "on the Heart Mountain rooting section were found the school-teachers and administrative staff members who heartily cheered for the desperate All-Stars," they did not specify that Jerry and Mary Elaine Housel were among them.

48 **the mayor of the tiny neighboring hamlet of Byron:** The *Heart Mountain Sentinel* reported on February 13, 1943, that the town of Byron issued an invitation to the Heart Mountain All-Stars at the conclusion of the Heart Mountain–Lovell contest.

49 **"a joint resolution of the two towns":** The joint Powell-Cody resolution calling on the camp to stop permitting people to leave came in May of 1943; Housel mentioned it in Housel to Glick, May 13, 1943, NARA RG 210.

50 **The project director had tried to short-circuit problems:** The project director's statement about registration appeared in the *Sentinel Supplement* (Heart Mountain, Wyo.) on February 18, 1943.

50 **Around the table in a richly paneled conference room:** Housel described his meeting with the governor and county officials, and his subsequent private meeting with the governor, in Housel to Glick, January 26, 1943, NARA RG 210.

50 **pulled out the tally:** An accounting of Heart Mountain's payments to county and state appears as an attachment to Housel to Glick, January 26, 1943, NARA RG 210.

51 **"I need to know where they are":** Housel reported the governor's demand for the whereabouts of Japanese Americans released from Heart Mountain in Housel to Glick, January 26, 1943, NARA RG 210.

52 **"we're going to introduce a bill":** Housel reported that state legislators insisted they would pass restrictive laws on land ownership and voting by Japanese Americans even if they were unconstitutional, in order to "express themselves

. . . to discourage evacuees from becoming residents of Wyoming"; Housel to Glick, January 26, 1943, NARA RG 210.

54 **"there's the penal provisions of the Selective Service Act":** Housel embodied this advice about the selective service laws in an official written opinion, Opinion No. HM-4 (February 24, 1943), NARA RG 210. The advice turned out to be mistaken, and Housel had to withdraw the opinion.

CHAPTER FOUR

55 **they'd averted this kind of crisis with a couple named Tatsuno:** The family names in the Tatsuno/Yanari story have been changed. Housel discussed the case at considerable length in letters to WRA headquarters, March 4, 11, 18, 25, April 1, 9, 15, 29, May 6, 13, 1943, NARA RG 210.

55 **It had taken quite some doing:** Details of Housel's continuing efforts to outmaneuver Kiyoichi Doi appear in Housel to Philip M. Glick, January 9, 14, 1943, NARA RG 210.

56 **the couple now sitting in front of him:** Family names in the Fujii/Goto story have been changed. Housel described the matter in Housel to Glick, March 18, 1943, NARA RG 210.

57 **the bogus stories they liked to run:** The *Denver Post* ran particularly unflattering and erroneous reports about the supposed coddling of prisoners at Heart Mountain in the spring of 1943. An example is Jack Carberry, "Hostile Group Is Pampered at Wyoming Camp," *Denver Post*, April 24, 1943.

58 **it worked at Heart Mountain, and Housel was proud of it:** Housel's efforts to defend the unusual prisoner-centered judicial system at Heart Mountain are described fully in Eric L. Muller, "Of Coercion and Accommodation: Looking at Japanese American Imprisonment through a Law Office Window," *Law and History Review* 35, no. 2 (May 2017): 277–319.

58 **pilfering wallets out of the latrines:** Housel described the wallet-pilfering case and the sticky-fingered-roommate case in Housel to Glick, March 4, 25, 1943, NARA RG 210.

58 **Two hungry Los Angeles teenagers tried to score a second steak dinner:** The mess hall assault case figured in Housel to Glick, March 4, 11, 1943, NARA RG 210.

58 **the trial of Toshiharu Tago and Kanda Oharu:** Details of the Tago/Oharu case come from a story in the *Heart Mountain (Wyo.) Sentinel* on March 27, 1943; and Housel to Glick, March 18, 1943, NARA RG 210. The names of the perpetrators have been changed.

59 **Saturday night was date night for the Housels:** The story of Jerry and Mary Elaine Housel's date night is an invention, as are the Garveys.

60 **a kerfuffle over the evacuee swing band:** The details of the dispute over the musicality of George Igawa and his orchestra are true; they appeared in the *Heart Mountain Sentinel* on March 6, 13, and 20, 1943.

60 **"Did you hear about Bill Brady?":** News of the disappearance of Lt. William Brady circulated in Wyoming in "Report of Loss Unofficial," *Jackson's Hole Courier* (Jackson, Wyo.), March 11, 1943. The *Cody (Wyo.) Enterprise* reported on February 17, 1943, that Clifford Best had been killed in action.

62 **a little headline in the *Cody Enterprise*:** " Navy Recruiters to Visit: College Men Sought," *Cody Enterprise*, June 2, 1943.

64 **"The community's with Tatsuno":** Housel described the community's support for the assailants in Housel to Glick, March 11, 1943, NARA RG 210.

65 **Dear Philip:** This letter consists of verbatim quotations from Housel to Glick, March 25, April 1, 1943, NARA RG 210.

66 **Dear Jerry:** This letter consists of verbatim quotations from Glick to Housel, March 25, April 6, 1943, NARA RG 210.

67 **Dear Philip:** This letter consists of verbatim quotations from Housel to Glick, April 9, May 6, 13, 1943, NARA RG 210.

CHAPTER FIVE

68 **He'd been out driving since shortly after five:** The work of War Relocation Authority administrators on the early-morning farm shift was reported in "Volunteer Farm Workers Listed to Meet Manpower Needs," *Heart Mountain (Wyo.) Sentinel*, June 5, 1943, and mentioned in Irvin Lechliter to Philip M. Glick, June 24, 1943, NARA RG 210.

69 **The labor trouble had begun five days earlier:** Housel provided a fulsome report of the strife and resulting strike in the motor pool; Housel to Glick, April 29, 1943, NARA RG 210.

70 **Rankin did nothing to hide his dislike:** The characterization of Meyer Rankin and his views toward Heart Mountain comes from Lechliter to Glick, June 17, 1943, NARA RG 210.

70 **"Food Is Hoarded":** Jack Carberry, "Food Is Hoarded for Japs in U.S. While Americans in Nippon Are Tortured. Openly Disloyal Japs Pampered," *Denver Post*, April 23, 1943.

72 **"tonight at the special council meeting":** The joint meeting of the councils from the towns of Powell and Cody is referenced in "Would Curtail Visits by Japs," *Casper (Wyo.) Star-Tribune*, May 5, 1943; and "Restrict Japs in Park County," *Casper Star-Tribune*, May 17, 1943.

73 **"The motor pool boys":** Housel narrated his efforts to bring the motor pool strike to a peaceful end at great length; Housel to acting WRA solicitor Lewis Sigler, May 6, 1943, NARA RG 210.

76 **The motor pool workers introduced themselves:** The members of the motor pool committee were listed in "Motor Pool Probe Nears Conclusion," *Heart Mountain Sentinel*, May 8, 1943.

81 **She unfolded the paper and read aloud:** The text of the joint Cody-Powell resolution was published in the *Heart Mountain Sentinel* on May 8, 1943.

81 **"So basically, they're telling us only to let the evacuees out to work for them":** Housel's summary of the purpose of the joint Cody-Powell resolution comes from Housel to Glick, May 27, 1943, NARA RG 210.

82 **"I think it's time, honey":** Housel told me that he enlisted in the navy in part in order to get out of Heart Mountain; Jerry Housel, interview by the author, Laramie, Wyoming, fall 1997.

83 **Dear Philip:** Housel's letter consists of verbatim excerpts from two letters he wrote as his tenure at Heart Mountain ended; Housel to Glick, May 18, June 10, 1943, NARA RG 210.

88 **When he looked up, he saw Kiyoichi Doi approaching:** The final conversation between Doi and Housel is invented. However, correspondence from subsequent project attorneys at Heart Mountain makes clear that Doi carried on with private representation of prisoners for pay after Housel left.

CHAPTER SIX

93 **the Poston Art Club's sketch pads:** The art club at Poston went on excursions for painting and sketching in the surrounding areas. For example, an announcement in the *Poston (Ariz.) Press Bulletin* on August 29, 1942, informed the camp that class would be held "in the southeast woods," where members would "sketch in water colors and study the plant life." Images of the kind described here are among the works of celebrated watercolor artist Tokotaru "Kakunen" Tsuruoka that he painted while incarcerated at Poston.

93 **His boss from Washington, Phil Glick, was due to swing through Poston:** Glick's visit to Poston was noted on the front page of the *Poston Press Bulletin*, September 1, 1942; and in Haas to William Brophy, September 2, 1942, NARA RG 210.

95 **a young man had gone missing:** The disappearance and death of Mike Oita were chronicled in the *Poston Press Bulletin* on September 1 and 2, 1943.

96 **Haas's side of the desk was a mound of papers:** Psychiatrist Alexander Leighton, the head of a sociological study of incarcerated Japanese Americans at Poston, wrote of Haas's desk that it was always "with a mass of papers and folders strewn" across it. Japanese American relocation centers records, 1935–1953, collection 3830, Division of Rare and Manuscript Collections of the Cornell University Library.

97 **"Suicide?":** That suicide would be on Haas's mind comes from a conversation I had with Annette Cohen, Haas's niece, who told me that when Haas gave tours of Washington, D.C., to out-of-town visitors, he would note on the Calvert Street Bridge that "this is where people commit suicide." Haas would later die by suicide there.

98 **"A most valued member of my staff here, a very capable attorney":** Haas wrote to the WRA regional director about his belief that the Japanese American lawyers at Poston deserved trust and respect from, and recognition by, white administrators; Haas to Edwin Ferguson, October 13, 1943, NARA RG 210.

98 **"Do you think this is a fitting space for the office of this center's legal department?":** Haas's anger over what he saw as insufficient office space appeared in Haas to Nell Findley [of Poston's Community Services Division], September 4, 1942; notes from staff meetings, September 16, 17, 1942; Haas to Poston's director of community activities, memorandum, September 17, 1942; and Haas to Ferguson, October 13, 1942, all in NARA RG 210.

99 **"Just as it should be":** In a long list of reform proposals provided on December 19, 1942, Haas suggested "the gradual but immediate reduction of Caucasian personnel" so that "only key positions would be held by Caucasians," as "in many cases" the jobs occupied by white people "may be filled equally as well by residents; in some cases, better." He made the case for reduction in white staff and greater reliance on Japanese Americans in a document he drafted on November 28, 1942, entitled "Program for Immediate Action in Poston." Both in NARA RG 210.

CHAPTER SEVEN

102 **The Dow Hotel in Lone Pine amused Ted Haas:** Haas described a trip to Manzanar and mentioned the presence in the hotel lobby of the cast of the Republic

Pictures film; Haas to Philip M. Glick, January 10, 1943, NARA RG 210. I have taken the liberty of shifting these details to Haas's earlier trip to Manzanar in November 1942.

102 **Haas had spent most of the prior day**: Haas described this trip to Manzanar and back in Haas to WRA regional attorney Edwin Ferguson, November 25, 1942, NARA RG 210.

105 **And then there was the boundary fence**: Haas noted the demoralizing effect of the fence and later linked the construction of the fence with the general strike that ensued; Haas to Ferguson, November 14, 25, 1942, NARA RG 210.

105 **what he liked to call "Little Caucasia"**: "Little Caucasia"—Ted Haas's nickname for the residential block housing Poston's white administrators—appears in Haas to Glick, December 26, 1942, NARA RG 210.

105 *Looks like a general strike*: Many details in this chapter about the strike at Poston are drawn from Alexander Leighton, *The Governing of Men* (Princeton, N.J.: Princeton University Press, 1945); Ted Haas, "Poston Disturbance," memorandum prepared for Philip Glick, December 29, 1942, NARA RG 210; Ted Haas, "The Struggle for Power at Poston," November 28, 1942, NARA RG 210; Norris E. James, comp., "Chronology of Events in Disturbances at Colorado River War Relocation Project, Poston, November 14–November 24, 1942," n.d., prepared for the Japanese Evacuation and Resettlement Study, Bancroft Library, University of California, Berkeley; and Tamie Tsuchiyama, "Chronological Account of the Poston Strike," n.d., prepared by for the Japanese Evacuation and Resettlement Study, Bancroft Library, University of California, Berkeley.

106 **"no interest in prosecuting Uchida-san"**: The disinterest of federal law enforcement authorities in prosecuting Uchida is confirmed in Haas to Glick, December 22, 1942, NARA RG 210.

106 **"I will try to help him have it"**: Masuda's commitment to a fair trial for Uchida is reflected in Tsuchiyama, "Chronological Account."

107 **"It goes back to California before the war"**: The characterizations of Nishimura's prewar life come from Tsuchiyama, "Chronological Account."

108 **evacuees who cheered when newsreels showed the bombing of Buckingham Palace**: Tsuchiyama mentioned the cheers in reaction to German bombings of London and invasion of Norway in her "Chronological Account."

109 **"They started building bonfires"**: Descriptions of the bonfires, banners, and flags can be found in Tsuchiyama, "Chronological Account."

112 **two burning logs blocking their path**: Tsuchiyama, "Chronological Account," mentions the burning logs.

114 **"They let the air out of my tires!"**: The tire prank is related in Tsuchiyama, "Chronological Account."

115 **"Nothing could keep me away"**: The "Roastin' Toastin' Poston" sobriquet appears several times in Haas's writings, including in Haas, "Struggle for Power."

117 **"I'm sure I would have quit too"**: In "Struggle for Power," Haas reported that he told the project director confidentially that "if [he] were a resident of Poston, [he] probably would have been in the ranks" of those protesting.

117 **"It's how revolution works"**: Haas used the political theory of revolutions as his template for explaining the strike at Poston and its resolution; Haas, "Struggle for Power."

117 **"an idea that Tom Masuda came up with"**: Here I attribute to Masuda an idea that was actually generated by a different Nisei attorney at Poston, John Maeno.

118 "They want you, Ted": James, "Chronology of Events," specifies that Haas was the person the prisoners' committees deemed acceptable as an intermediary to the project director.

118 members of minority groups could quickly discern: "Members of minority races are quick to learn those who regard them with a superior attitude and those who will work with them"; Haas to Ferguson, October 13, 1942, NARA RG 210.

CHAPTER EIGHT

119 Haas had been feeling poorly: Haas described himself as a "slightly sick person" suffering from "loss of blood from an internal condition"; Haas to Philip M. Glick, March 22, 1943, NARA RG 210. He was minimizing his condition, because within days he was hospitalized in Los Angeles and gone from Poston for many weeks.

119 His usual flood of words: Psychiatrist Alexander Leighton, the head of a sociological study of incarcerated Japanese Americans at Poston, wrote that "Ted [Haas] speaks in a continuous flow whenever permitted to," is "physically active constantly," and is often found in the Project Attorney's Office with "his arms wav[ing]" and "mov[ing] back and forth behind his desk, never lounging or leaning and always planted firmly on both feet." Japanese American relocation centers records, 1935–1953, collection 3830, Division of Rare and Manuscript Collections of the Cornell University Library.

120 people who were doing their best to stir everyone up: Masuda referred to "groups . . . maliciously and intentionally spreading rumors around the camp for the purpose of keeping the residents constantly stirred up and nervous"; Masuda to Glick, May 22, 1943, NARA RG 210.

120 an evening Student Relocation Council meeting: Kay Masuda played a prominent role in Poston's chapter of the national Student Relocation Council. Student Relocation Council Poston chapter records, folder J2.304, papers of the Japanese Evacuation and Resettlement Study (JERS), Bancroft Library, University of California, Berkeley; Thomas Masuda Evacuee Case File, NARA RG 210.

121 Masuda's own registration form: The registration form reproduced here is a copy of the original in Thomas Masuda Evacuee Case File, NARA RG 210.

126 He thought back to May: The details of Masuda's prosecution for, and acquittal of, serving as an unregistered agent of Japan can be found in Thomas Masuda Evacuee Case File, NARA RG 210; and in FBI records obtained through the Freedom of Information Act.

127 Throughout January his health had slipped: The cause of Haas's illness and hospitalization that appears in the historical record is fistulas that required surgery and lengthy recuperation. Haas's niece confirmed that Haas suffered from lifelong bouts of severe depression, some requiring hospitalization; Annette Cohen, telephonic interview by the author, May 2016.

128 an imposing figure: The characterization of Ernie Miller comes from "Miller to Head Police Department," *Poston (Ariz.) Press Bulletin*, October 3, 1942.

128 evening seminars on proper police procedure: Haas noted that he was delivering a series of fourteen lectures on criminal law and police procedures to Poston's police academy in Haas to Glick, December 14, 26, 1942, NARA RG 210.

129 This wasn't the first time Kido was coming in for a bruising: Details about the beatings of Saburo Kido and the interrogation and prosecution of the perpetrators come from the following sources: Haas to Glick, January 30, 1943, NARA

RG 210; Poston project director Wade Head to WRA director Dillon Myer, drafted by Haas, February 11, 1943, NARA RG 210; Tamie Tsuchiyama, "The Beating of Saburo Kido," February 3, 1943, written for JERS, folder J6.19; and records from Poston's Internal Security Division, folder J2.52, JERS, Bancroft Library, University of California, Berkeley.

133 **"They want you to go down to Yuma with them":** Haas noted that Kido's assailants, mirabile dictu, asked him to defend them in the Yuma County Superior Court; Haas to Glick, February 13, 1943, NARA RG 210.

134 **"That's why Mr. Haas needs you":** Haas noted Masuda's role as interpreter for the perpetrators of the Kido beating in the courtroom in Yuma, Arizona, in Haas to Glick, February 17, 1943, NARA RG 210.

135 **In Yuma, Tom Masuda accompanied the suspects:** Haas and Masuda did take the trip to Yuma in connection with the prosecution of Kido's assailants, and they did the work described here. The hotel scene is invented, but it was common for restaurants, hotels, and other places of public accommodation to refuse service to Japanese Americans.

137 **"The court will be happy to pay you twenty-five dollars":** The payment to Masuda appears in *Yuma (Ariz.) Weekly Sun*, May 21, 1943.

137 **"prepare brief reports":** Haas referenced Masuda's report to the court on the Kido assailants in Haas to Glick, February 17, 1943, NARA RG 210.

CHAPTER NINE

138 **Dear Sir:** This is the text of an original letter, with minor adjustments, from Thomas Masuda Evacuee Case File, NARA RG 210.

139 **His spoken Japanese was far from perfect:** On his registration form, Masuda listed his Japanese speaking ability only as "fair."

139 **the community council had appointed him:** Masuda's appointment as city attorney was noted in *Poston (Ariz.) Chronicle*, June 5, 1943.

140 **Masuda's salary stayed at nineteen dollars per month:** A job application in Thomas Masuda Evacuee Case File reveals that he was paid nineteen dollars per month for his work in the Project Attorney's Office. In a list of proposals for improving administration at Poston that Haas prepared on December 19, 1942, he noted that "many . . . residents perform more important services for their $19 . . . or $16 per month than do many of the much higher paid Caucasians." And in a letter to Glick, Haas complained about the WRA's inability "to secure proper salary adjustments for those [Japanese Americans] holding responsible positions"; Haas to Glick, August 7, 1943. All in NARA RG 210.

140 **Haas had really stood up to her:** Haas described his confrontation with Community Services over cohabitation by unmarried couples in Haas to Glick, August 28, 1943, NARA RG 210.

140 **Haas believed deeply:** Haas described himself as "an obstinate and ancient proponent of an increase in evacuees holding responsible positions" in Haas to Glick, August 7, 1943, NARA RG 210. A number of his earlier letters bear this out. One particularly lengthy and fervent example is in the December 19, 1942, list of proposals, the very first of which was for "the gradual but immediate reduction of Caucasian personnel." Haas made his case for this over more than two single-spaced pages.

140 **needing to "Americanize" people who were already Americans:** In his correspondence, Haas frequently referred to the "Americanizing" mission of the

WRA. An example is his suggestion, in the December 19 list mentioned above, that the staff "should show by example and precept the democratic way of life and administration."

140 **The burglary wasn't the real story; a breakup was:** A letter from Masuda presented the story of the marital breakup when Haas was hospitalized in Los Angeles and Masuda was Poston's acting project attorney; Masuda to Glick, March 27, 1943, NARA RG 210.

141 **IMPRESSIONS OF POSTON:** This is a nearly verbatim reproduction of the original document Haas wrote in June 1943 while hospitalized in Los Angeles. Some passages have been omitted.

147 **"I'm sorry to let you know":** Masuda's rejection by the army and his offer to travel to Minnesota at his own expense are noted in Wade Head (Poston project director) to Harry L. Stafford (project director at the Minidoka Relocation Center in Idaho), August 20, 1943, NARA RG 210.

CHAPTER TEN

149 **No more nineteen-hour days:** Haas wrote frequently about the very late nights and very early mornings he worked. In one letter he banged out on his typewriter, he specifically noted that he was drafting the letter at 4:00 A.M.; Haas to Nell Findley (of Poston's Community Services Division), September 4, 1942, NARA RG 210.

149 **The dance unfolding before him:** Haas described the Obon festival—including the late rainstorm—in Haas to Philip M. Glick, August 21, 1943, NARA RG 210.

152 **Federal Bureau of Investigation:** This is a slightly edited reproduction of the FBI intelligence report that appears in Thomas Masuda Evacuee Case File, NARA RG 210.

156 **"Mr. Masuda, will you please tell us the circumstances":** The interrogation consists of mostly verbatim excerpts from the transcript of Masuda's hearing found in Thomas Masuda Evacuee Case File, NARA RG 210.

163 **MEMORANDUM TO: Mr. W. Wade Head:** The memorandum is a slightly edited version of the one in Thomas Masuda Evacuee Case File, NARA RG 210.

CHAPTER ELEVEN

167 **Medical orders, more or less:** Information about Jim Terry's prewar health troubles and their influence on his decision to relocate to Arizona come from his son; Dr. Stephen Terry, telephonic interview by the author, May 11, 2016.

168 **He dressed as he did each day:** Terry's business attire is reflected in a photograph of the staff of the Project Attorney's Office located in NARA RG 210.

169 **the twenty-four-year-old Nisei secretary:** Terry had a Nisei secretary whose work he came to value greatly and whom he eventually tried to dissuade from renouncing her citizenship and expatriating to Japan. Her name is unknown; I have given her the name Kimiko Yamamoto.

170 **an accordion file marked "Tada beating":** Terry narrated the story of the beating of Takeo Tada at length in Terry to Philip M. Glick, December 5, 1942, NARA RG 210. The case was the subject of a memorandum entitled "Tada Case" prepared on December 14, 1942, by Joseph Omachi, an attorney at Gila River; it is preserved in the records of the Japanese Evacuation and Resettlement Study, Bancroft Library, University of California, Berkeley.

171 **Terry was for a firm hand:** Terry laid out his harsh prescription for action in the wake of the Tada beating in Terry to Glick, December 5, 1942, NARA RG 210.

172 **"She fell into a big hole this morning":** The Sato personal injury matter is noted in Terry to Glick, December 18, 1942. Glick replied with advice on the case in Glick to Terry, January 8, 1943. Both in NARA RG 210.

CHAPTER TWELVE

176 **Yes, a rescue mission:** Jim Terry wrote to Philip M. Glick about a trip to Phoenix to retrieve a man who had been arrested after arriving by bus with no WRA representative to greet him and going to the FBI for assistance; Terry to Glick, December 19, 1942, NARA RG 210. The identity of the man is not disclosed in the record; Joe Nozuki is an invention.

177 **Terry and his staff had almost nothing:** Terry noted the dearth of office supplies and equipment in Terry to Glick, January 2, 1943, NARA RG 210.

177 **Phil Glick in Washington kept squawking at him about not spending his own cash:** On December 24, 1942, Glick wrote to Terry that he did "not relish the idea of [Terry] buying [his] own office supplies because of the difficulty of obtaining them through official channels." Terry responded on January 2, 1943, that it did not bother him "in the slightest" to be paying for official items with his own personal funds. Both in NARA RG 210.

182 **"We'll dismiss the charge":** Terry references the U.S. attorney's agreement to dismiss the charge in Terry to Glick, December 19, 1942, NARA RG 210.

185 **"A most unlikely story has recently made its way to me":** Terry mentioned the radio report in Terry to Glick, February 6, 1943, NARA RG 210. He denied that he had ever advocated "for publication" the separation of loyal from "imperialist-minded" Japanese.

185 **It was a fine idea, in fact:** In the final report on his activities that he prepared on October 26, 1945, Terry argued that the WRA should have segregated the "known pro-Japanese" from the "loyal or quiescent element" at the outset of the program. NARA RG 210.

CHAPTER THIRTEEN

186 **The bug had hit them both on the same day:** Jim Terry wrote about his and his wife's simultaneous cases of valley fever in Terry to Philip M. Glick, February 27, 1943, NARA RG 210.

187 **they were not allowed to use the center's hospital:** WRA regulation 50.2.20 stated that "appointed employees should utilize the services of physicians and hospitals in neighboring communities" rather than in the camps. In a JERS document entitled "Conciliation Begins at Gila," dated October 20, 1943, Japanese Evacuation and Resettlement Study researcher Rosalie Hankey reported that "when Terry's son required a tonsillotomy he was placed at the list ahead of a great many evacuee children although the operation was not urgent." The hospital also made an emergency run to Phoenix for ether to perform the operation on Terry's son after refusing to order more at the request of Japanese American doctors on the hospital staff.

188 **He wouldn't trade this work for a million dollars:** Terry wrote frequently of his enjoyment of the work at Gila River: "I am enjoying every minute of this, even if my working hours do measure sixteen or more hours every day as I expected

they would." "I cannot tell you how interesting I find the work here nor how much I am enjoying it." "The work here is constantly fascinating and infinitely varied and often novel. Some of my colleagues don't share my joy and enthusiasm but I assure you I wouldn't trade for a million dollars." Terry to Glick, December 5, 18, 1942, January 1, 1943, NARA RG 210.

189 **a full-blown conspiracy:** Terry alleged the existence of a conspiracy to steal Japanese American property on the West Coast in Terry to Glick, September 17, 1943, NARA RG 210.

189 **Bank of America:** The letter is a lightly edited version of Terry to W. C. Robbins Jr., April 1, 1943, NARA RG 210.

191 **an accordion file marked "Community Cooperative":** All of the project attorneys, including Jim Terry, devoted a great deal of their time to helping organize the retail and service businesses Japanese Americans ran in the camps. Terry first wrote to Glick about his work on the community enterprises on December 12, 1942, and problems relating to commercial life at Gila River appeared frequently throughout his correspondence (NARA RG 210).

192 **the registration program, the part directed at drumming up Nisei volunteers:** Details about registration at Gila River and Terry's attitudes about it come from "A History of Relocation at the Gila River Relocation Center," WRA document, December 21, 1945; and Terry to Glick, "confidential" letter, February 15, 1943, both in NARA RG 210.

193 **but lacked enough time and evidence:** Terry explicitly stated that he lacked sufficient evidence to support criminal charges against any of the men sent to Moab in Terry to Glick, February 15, 1943, NARA RG 210.

194 **"Here is what I want you to write down":** Terry's interpretation of the registration questions is reflected in Terry to Capt. Norman Thompson, memorandum, February 18, 1943, NARA RG 210.

195 **"which can include the death penalty":** Terry raised the specter of treason and the death penalty as noted in a short newspaper announcement, "Terry on No. 28," *Gila (Ariz.) News-Courier*, February 18, 1943.

196 **treason prosecutions were legally impossible:** Glick upbraided Terry for his mistaken advice about the death penalty in Glick to Terry, March 27, 1943, NARA RG 210.

197 **except their own selfish interests:** Terry asserted the absence of a sense of loyalty to anything but self-interest in Terry to Glick, September 24, 1943. He shared his opinion that many of those answering no were "cowards and slackers" in Terry to Glick, March 13, 1943. Both in NARA RG 210.

197 **It took their eyes a moment to adjust to the light:** The scene in the hospital waiting room is invented but is based on the report, cited earlier, that the Terrys jumped the line in getting a surgical procedure for their son in the camp hospital ahead of Japanese Americans in need.

CHAPTER FOURTEEN

200 **He'd gotten Amos Betts:** Jim Terry noted the issuance of a business license by the Arizona Corporation Commission in Terry to Philip M. Glick, June 5, 1943, NARA RG 210. "Betts on Stand in Jap Hearing," *Arizona Daily Star* (Tucson), June 16, 1943, confirmed that Betts himself had been involved in the review and issuance of the license.

200 **on the radio news, of all places:** In the June 5 letter to Glick, Terry reported that he had learned of the revocation of the license of the Gila River Cooperative in a radio report.

201 **disgraceful stories of people using the law to treat the Japanese as if they had the plague:** Terry related the stories of shop owners, dentists, lawyers, gas station employees, and typesetters refusing to do business with Japanese customers in Terry to Glick, May 15, 29, 1943, NARA RG 210.

201 **just let him try it:** Terry's bootlegging case was reported in "Society Drinkers to Go on Stand," *Daily News* (New York), August 8, 1929; the Dutch Handel case was reported in the same paper on October 12, 1928.

203 **"I am here for the War Relocation Authority only":** "Hearing Goes Deeply into Problem of Japs," *Arizona Republic* (Phoenix), June 15, 1943, reported that Terry appeared only on behalf of the WRA and not on behalf of Gila River Cooperative Enterprises, Inc. This led to considerable confusion in the hearing room, according to "Enough Japs in State to Rule Farm Industry," *Tucson (Ariz.) Daily Citizen*, June 14, 1943. "Betts on Stand in Jap Hearing," *Arizona Daily Star*, June 16, 1943, noted that the Corporation Commission did not serve the cooperative with notice of the cancellation of its license.

203 **smoothed a crease out of the papers in his hands, and began reading:** Betts's comments are drawn nearly verbatim from reporting on the hearing in "Enough Japs in State to Rule Farm Industry," *Tucson Daily Citizen*, June 14, 1943.

204 **"Mr. M. O. Sharp of Phoenix":** The witness's name was actually M. O. Best, but the name has been changed to Sharp here to avoid confusing the names Betts and Best.

205 **"to dominate our entire agricultural industry in this valley":** The testimony about the Japanese dominating the Arizona agricultural industry comes from "Hearing Goes Deeply into Problem of Japs," *Arizona Republic*, June 15, 1943.

208 **"are you aware that the WRA offered to have the cooperative amend its articles of incorporation":** The WRA's spurned offer to have the cooperative amend its charter to limit its operations to the center is noted in "Hearing Goes Deeply into Problem of Japs."

208 **"more dangerous than a thousand rattlesnakes":** Terry related the testimony about rattlesnakes in Terry to Glick, June 23, 1943, NARA RG 210.

208 **Once Barnes was seated and sworn:** Barnes's testimony about the dangers to Arizona farming is quoted from "Enough Japs in State to Rule Farm Industry," *Tucson Daily Citizen*, June 14, 1943.

209 **"Raw foods can be 'fixed,' can be adulterated":** "Enough Japs in State to Rule Farm Industry" is the source of Barnes's quoted words about the dangers to raw foods and his threat of a crisis that would discredit the nation.

211 **"Do you recognize that letter, Mr. Betts?":** Betts's acknowledgment that the cooperative obtained a favorable ruling on its license months before revocation appears in "Betts Admits License Ruling Was Obtained," *Arizona Republic*, June 16, 1943.

212 **"By the people you handpicked to testify as witnesses":** Terry's charge that Betts handpicked the witnesses for the hearing is reported in "Threats against State Group Made," *Tucson Daily Citizen*, June 21, 1943.

213 **"a vast increase in the number of day passes":** Terry's threat that the WRA would issue large numbers of day passes to Japanese Americans appears in "Threats against State Group Made."

214 **"no choice but to set aside the Constitution":** Betts's statement that it was necessary to set aside the Constitution in dealing with Japanese Americans appears in
"Threats against State Group Made."

215 **"Today's hearing has degenerated":** Terry's comments about the lack of ad-
missible evidence, the absence of harm to Arizona, bigotry, Nazi Germany, the
Constitution, and the personal liability of the Corporation Commissioners all
appear in "Threats against State Group Made."

216 **"I have never seen less luxurious living conditions":** Terry's characterization of
conditions at Gila River and his offer for the cooperative to conditionally surrender its license come from "Hearing Is Ended on Jap Co-operative," *Arizona
Republic*, June 17, 1943.

216 **It was Bill Peterson from the dais, speaking for the first time all day:** Peterson's
comments are reproduced from "Threats against State Group Made," *Tucson
Daily Citizen*, June 21, 1943.

CHAPTER FIFTEEN

218 **That wasn't a bad guess:** Complaints about the WRA's property division pervaded Terry's correspondence from late 1942 all the way through 1945. The opinion mentioned here—that the agents were infected by rabid animosity toward
Japanese Americans—appeared in Terry to Philip M. Glick, September 17, 1943,
NARA RG 210.

219 **"She's expatriating":** Terry alluded to his efforts to persuade a secretary from
his office not to expatriate to Japan in Terry to Glick, September 17, 1943, NARA
RG 210. Tamie Tsuchiyama of the Japanese Evacuation and Resettlement Study
(JERS) referenced these efforts as well in a report entitled "Administrative
Notes" in September 1943. JERS, Bancroft Library, University of California,
Berkeley.

220 **the center's schedule needed to shift an hour later:** The administrative decision
to shift the working hours at the center was noted in "Working Hours Shifted an
Hour by Cold Weather," *Gila (Ariz.) News-Courier*, November 30, 1943.

221 **One glance at a handwritten letter in the file:** Kira's handwritten letter is in Satoshi Kira Evacuee Case File, NARA RG 210. The quotations in the text are taken
verbatim from the letter.

222 **This system of locking up a racial group was a betrayal of the nation's principles:** Terry's blunt condemnation of the WRA's mission and leadership appears
clearly in the final report he wrote on October 26, 1942, and in a postscript he
added to the report two weeks later. NARA RG 210.

222 **LEAVE CLEARANCE HEARING OF SATOSHI KIRA:** The transcript of
Kira's hearing is a shortened and edited version of the original transcript in
Satoshi Kira Evacuee Case File, NARA RG 210.

222 **Hiromu Kira:** Kira's father was a celebrated photographer.

228 **A dull bang from outside stopped Bennett midsentence:** Details about the
shooting of Kira and about his medical and psychological condition come from
Satoshi Kira Evacuee Case File, NARA RG 210; and Rosalie Hankey, "Shooting of Satoshi Kira," December 17, 1943, JERS, Bancroft Library, University of
California, Berkeley. Terry's presence on the scene after the shooting and at the
hospital is an invention.

231 **"We need the slug"**: In "Shooting of Satoshi Kira," Hankey relates that two military policemen waited at the hospital to be given the bullet removed from Kira's body and that the request was refused.

236 **"He started to unravel after the hearing"**: The family's impression that Kira's mental unraveling began with Terry's interrogation is documented in Satoshi Kira Evacuee Case File, NARA RG 210, as are the details of Kira's actions between the hearing and the shooting.

237 **"a young man trying to hold his own against a very seasoned and suspicious attorney"**: In "Shooting of Satoshi Kira," Hankey reported hearing "many accounts of the bullying, criminal-lawyer methods which Mr. Terry employs in his hearings" and of prisoners "dreading" being assigned to a hearing with him. In a different JERS document, "Conciliation Begins at Gila," dated October 20, 1943, Hankey described Terry's "rudeness and briskness" and his "criminal attorney manner" that "made him very unpopular with young evacuees who appear before him." In a different document dated October 1943 and entitled "Comments on 'Tamie and "X" on Gila,'" Hankey reported that young people were "reputed to break into tears" upon hearing they are to be interrogated by Terry. A JERS document entitled "Legal Department" by Robert Spencer and Charles Kikuchi, dated April 19, 1943, referred to Terry's "particularly aggressive personality" and his "fondness for argument." All documents in JERS, Bancroft Library, University of California, Berkeley.

237 **"it is necessary at these hearings to probe beneath the surface"**: Terry's characterization of the hearings as venues to uncover attitudes a Japanese American was trying to conceal comes from Terry to Glick, October 25, 1943. In Terry to Glick, March 17, 1943, Terry threatened to withdraw from doing the hearings if Glick would not support his findings. Both in NARA RG 210.

EPILOGUE

239 **"Lon Chaney or Boris Karloff"**: Terry to Philip M. Glick, October 12, 1945, NARA RG 210.

240 **"changing his ways"**: Terry to Glick, March 17, 1944, NARA RG 210.

240 **demoralize them**: Edwin E. Ferguson to Terry, November 3, 1944, NARA RG 210.

240 **"better left submerged"**: Terry to Edgar Bernhard, June 26, 1944, NARA RG 210.

240 **"stain on its honor"**: James Hendrick Terry, Narrative Report of Project Attorney, October 26, 1945, 117, NARA RG 210.

240 **"Gestapo methods"**: Lewis Sigler to Glick, August 14, 1943, quoted in Richard Drinnon, *Keeper of the Concentration Camps: Dillon S. Myer and American Racism* (Berkeley: University of California Press, 1989), 106.

240 **acknowledged its illegality**: Myer quoted in Drinnon, *Keeper*, 117.

241 **returned to Arizona**: "James Hendrick Terry Will Open Law Office," *Tucson (Ariz.) Daily Citizen*, December 25, 1945.

241 **one of the largest**: "Five Tucsonians Open Law Firm," *Arizona Daily Star* (Tucson), November 18, 1949.

241 **city slicker from New York**: Dr. Stephen Terry, telephonic interview by the author, May 11, 2016.

241 **"helped interned Japanese"**: "Attorney J. H. Terry Dies at 77," *Arizona Daily Star*, December 10, 1976.

242 **back with his family:** Memorandum, April 10, 1944, Satoshi Kira Evacuee Case File, NARA RG 210.

242 **died in 2011:** Dr. Nana Sadamura, email message to author, June 11, 2018.

243 **"valuable contribution":** Glick to Haas, November 3, 1943, NARA RG 210.

243 **"foibles and virtues":** Haas to Glick, November 13, 1943, NARA RG 210.

243 **"give the command":** Haas to Collier, November 13, 1943, NARA RG 210.

243 **"drawing to a close":** Haas to Glick, December 24, 1943, NARA RG 210.

244 **"Station H.A.A.S. . . . mental anguish":** Haas to Glick, February 17, 1944, NARA RG 210.

244 **Tlingit and Haida peoples:** Dr. Walter Goldschmidt, telephonic interview by author, December 27, 2004.

244 **publicly endorsed Haas:** "Indians Are Seeking Friend's Appointment," *Holdredge (Neb.) Daily Citizen*, March 31, 1948.

244 **"militant commissioner":** "Indians Plan Big Pow-Wow," *Sheboygan (Wis.) Press*, March 31, 1948.

244 **honorary member:** "Sioux Make Haas Member of Tribe," *Rapid City (S.Dak.) Journal*, September 23, 1949.

245 **"Some important officials . . . without consultation with Indians":** "Indian Bureau Counsel Says Officials Oppose Self-Rule," *El Paso (Tex.) Times*, April 13, 1950.

245 **lost its conscience:** Felix S. Cohen, "The Erosion of Indian Rights, 1950–1953: A Case Study in Bureaucracy," *Yale Law Journal* 62, no. 3 (1953): 383.

246 **He jumped:** "Indian Law Expert Dies," *Arizona Republic* (Phoenix), June 12, 1959; Florence and Rosie Haas, telephonic interview by author, May 19, 2016; Annette Cohen, telephonic interview by author, May 4, 2016.

248 **it planted 1,000:** "Japanese Here Say Thank You with Flowers," *Chicago Tribune*, September 4, 1967, E12.

248 **Masuda passed away:** "Thomas Masuda: 1905–1986," *Pacific Citizen* (Los Angeles), May 2, 1986; "Thomas S. Masuda; Led City's Japanese Natives," *Chicago Tribune*, April 7, 1986.

248 **"outweigh the bad":** Lechliter to Glick, July 15, 1943, NARA RG 210.

248 **slipped into the office:** Lechliter to Glick, September 3, 1943, NARA RG 210.

248 **spending most of his time:** McGowen to Glick, September 24, 1943, NARA RG 210.

248 **died suddenly:** "University Professor Dies," *Casper (Wyo.) Star-Tribune*, March 3, 1944.

249 **"in theory connected":** Ver Ploeg to Glick, June 21, 1944, NARA, RG 210.

249 **"'looking the other way'":** Ver Ploeg to Glick, July 14, 1944, NARA RG 210.

249 **"handsome renumeration":** Ver Ploeg to Glick, August 10, 1944, NARA RG 210.

249 **move Doi out of the office:** Glick to Ver Ploeg, July 25, 1944, NARA RG 210.

249 **showed Doi the door:** Ver Ploeg to Glick, August 8, 1944, NARA RG 210.

249 **wagering ring:** Ver Ploeg to Edwin E. Ferguson, March 8, 1945, NARA RG 210; "Nine Will Face Gambling Count," *Heart Mountain (Wyo.) Sentinel*, March 10, 1945.

249 **buy office equipment:** Earl L. Kelley to S. W. Owen, December 5, 1945, Kiyoichi Doi Evacuee Case File, NARA RG 210.

249 **"friend of the court" brief:** Brief of the Japanese American Citizens League as Amicus Curiae, April 16, 1948, Takahashi v. Fish and Game Commission, 334 U.S. 410 (1948).

249 **challenge was successful:** *Takahashi*, 334 U.S. at 410.
250 **died of cancer:** "Ex–L.A. Lawyer Succumbs in Tokyo," *New Japanese American News* (Los Angeles), August 15, 1958, 1.
251 **court-martial proceedings:** John Housel, email message to author, October 25, 2019.
251 **known for expertise:** Housel email.
251 **seat on the U.S. Court of Appeals:** "Cody's Housel Urged for Judge," *Billings (Mont.) Gazette*, December 19, 1965.
251 **coordinator for the presidential campaign:** "Cody Lawyer Joins Campaign," *Billings Gazette*, September 1, 1972.
251 **flirted with a run:** "Cody Attorney Eyes Race," *Billings Gazette*, March 21, 1974.
251 **Board of Law Examiners:** "Jerry W. Housel," *Powell (Wyo.) Tribune*, May 14, 2001, https://www.powelltribune.com/stories/jerry-w-housel,10015.
251 **president of the state's bar association:** "Cody Man Heads Bar Association," *Casper Star-Tribune*, September 29, 1963, 18.
251 **House of Delegates:** "Jerry W. Housel," *Powell Tribune*, May 14, 2001, https://www.powelltribune.com/stories/jerry-w-housel,10015.